Cruise & Maritime
Voyages
Celebrating
the
first decade
2010-2019
Richard Kirkman

Published by:
Ferry Publications, PO Box 33, Ramsey, Isle of Man IM99 4LP
Tel: +44 (0) 1624 898445   Fax: +44 (0) 1624 898449
E-mail: ferrypubs@manx.net   Website: www.ferrypubs.co.uk

Contents

Foreword

by Nikolaos Tragakes

The past decade has been a quite remarkable journey since the Global Maritime Group joined forces with Cruise & Maritime Services to launch Cruise & Maritime Voyages to create a more traditional brand of cruising.

Under the CMV brand, we commenced operations with Marco Polo and Ocean Countess back in 2010 carrying just over 37,000 passengers.

We were Britain's newest independently owned cruise line. Unbelievably, ten years on, we enter a new decade with a fleet of six ships with two more being delivered in 2021.

We are now recognised as Britain and Australia's leading independent cruise line winning a growing number of prestigious industry and consumer awards and on course to carry a staggering 200,000 passengers in 2021 and now employing almost 4,000 worldwide seafaring and shoreside staff.

In the formative years, we soon realised that despite the economic downturn and challenging market conditions, the resilient and more mature segment of the British cruise market were, in the main, highly appreciative of the traditional value-based, cruise experience we had introduced. Adopting the historic London Cruise Terminal at Tilbury as our home UK port was welcomed by many and the introduction of more convenient regional departure ports, now up to 15 in the UK & Ireland, proved to be very popular.

This early validation was a source of great encouragement reinforcing our firm belief that there was a niche mainstream market opportunity waiting to be exploited.

The cruise market was becoming increasingly dominated by bigger ships expanding in size and innovation, essentially becoming floating mega resorts with climbing walls, ice-skating rinks and much more. A new style of more impersonal, mass market cruising was well and truly born!

We all believed that there had to be an alternative option. We wanted to deliver a more personal, friendlier, more authentic level of service and offer a richer more traditional maritime experience with a wider range of destinations and the simple pleasures of cruising aboard smaller to mid-sized ships.

2011 proved to be a pivotal year when the Global Maritime Group,

Cruise & Maritime Services and London Docklands based South Quay Travel & Leisure came together with other private British interests with the incorporation of Cruise & Maritime Voyages Ltd and a re-structured business based on growth and ambitious development.

Our stated aim was to build a truly independent cruise line and international brand to uniquely develop tailormade home market cruise products at a fair and more affordable price. Importantly, we also took the decision to invest in new international markets and our own network of sales offices in Australia, the United States, Germany, Mexico and now France too, all supported by a highly skilled ship management team based just north of Athens.

The introduction of *Magellan* in 2015 was a real game changer and the start of a special relationship with the Carnival Corporation, the World's largest cruise conglomerate. *Columbus* and *Vasco da Gama* followed with the recent announcement in November 2019 of two more ships, the *Pacific Dawn & Aria* (to be renamed) being delivered in 2021 taking the total number to five in as many years.

2015 also marked *Marco Polo*'s 50th Anniversary 36-night epic voyage to Canada & Greenland retracing part of her journey when she commenced operations back in 1965 on a transatlantic liner service to Montreal. She is indeed still a very special lady.

As classic ship lovers, we are also proud to be playing our part in extending the illustrious careers and being the custodians of six fine cruise ships in our fleet although always mindful that they must still deliver the commercial returns required within the competitive market we serve.

As we enter the Twenties, there will of course be new challenges ahead, but we believe that we have built the solid foundations of a unique and thriving international business whilst still retaining the important family ethos that pleasingly extends throughout the Group.

Our growth and successful development would not have been possible without the dedication, commitment and loyalty of many of our hard-working management team, shoreside staff, officers and crew who have been a true credit to our business. Many of them have been with us since the beginning and I hope that you enjoy reading the chapter about some of

Astor seen on 2nd April 2017 during her Northbound Voyage from Fremantle to London Tilbury. *(CMV Library)*

our key management team members.

This special tenth anniversary commemorative book charts in some detail the history and development of Cruise & Maritime Voyages filled with wonderful illustrations and a chapter devoted to all the voyages undertaken by the nine ships that have served in the CMV fleet over the past decade.

Since our inception we have carried almost 800,000 passengers and I am proud that close to 45% of our passengers' have cruised with us more than once with a growing number of Columbus Club members having now cruised over 500 nights and our two most cruised passengers surpassing 1,000 nights in 2019. Quite extraordinary and a testament to our traditional brand of cruising.

It was an honour and privilege to join so many of our Columbus Club Members onboard Columbus in Tilbury on Saturday 9th November 2019 for a special commemorative tenth anniversary overnight gala event. I was simply overwhelmed by the many accolades and glowing tributes received and I came away from the event with a real sense of pride in what has been achievement in a relatively short time frame.

On behalf of the CMV and Global management team, all our shore side staff, officers and crew, I would like to most sincerely thank our passengers for your custom and amazing support in helping us reach this first important tenth anniversary milestone.

As we enter a new decade, we look forward to welcoming back, our many loyal repeat passengers and first time cruisers alike, on our ships for many years to come.

Nikolaos Tragakes
Co-Founder
Global Maritime Group

Chapter one

The Formative Years

Marco Polo alongside the London International Cruise Terminal, London Tilbury in 2010. *(Port of Tilbury)*

"As the New Year of 2010 dawned, and the mists of a chilly winter's day began to clear, the familiar profile of the elegant Marco Polo *could be found berthed alongside the London International Cruise Terminal. This lovely ship was no stranger to London Tilbury, but keen observers noted that it was very rare for her to call in the UK so early in the year.* Marco Polo *was being prepared to sail on a new season of cruises from the port, and it was evident that the deck department team was unusually grappling with scaffolding towers to adjust a new funnel logo. Elsewhere, new house flags were being unfurled ready for hoisting.*

The scene was a hive of activity: stores and provisions were arriving and being loaded, new crew members were joining, and local officials and company staff streamed up and down the gangway to ensure that everything would be in place for her first sailing, a 30 night cruise to the West Indies.

Marco Polo *slipped her berth at 17:00 on Saturday 2nd January 2010 and, in so doing, her complement of 701 passengers became the very first to sail under the Cruise & Maritime Voyages (CMV) flag"*.

Top: An early publicity shot of Richard Bastow (left) and Chris Coates at Dartford on June 1996. *(John Carr)*

Above: Preparations for **Marco Polo**'s new funnel logo. *(CMV Library)*

This is the compelling story of how CMV gradually evolved from humble beginnings into the UK's largest independent cruise operator. All the key personnel could be found fulfilling a wide range of different functions at London Tilbury that day: they became the founding shareholders of 'Britain's Newest Cruise Line', a clever strapline devised by Commercial Director, Chris Coates, and used extensively in the first couple of years to market the cruise programmes.

Chris Coates and Richard Bastow started their fledgling company some 14 years earlier in June 1996, in a serviced office room in Dartford, Kent. They looked to represent shipowners and cruise operators seeking to enter the UK cruise market and adopted the name Cruise & Maritime Services (CMS), to describe their offering. The market in 1996 was small compared to today, just 416,000 passengers that year (source PSA Census) compared to over two million sailing from the UK in 2018 (source Cruise Lines International Association (CLIA)).

Three months later the intrepid pair were joined by Sharon Bastow, who brought her invaluable administrative and organisational expertise to the venture. The three had worked together at CTC Cruise Lines in London since 1983 and their experience as charterers and operators of Soviet (and later Ukrainian) cruise ships stood them in good stead for the new venture. However, as with most start-ups, it was a very lean operation – so lean in fact that the lads always liked to claim that on the first day of business, Monday 3rd June 1996, their only assets were just 'two pencil cases and a broken Amstrad'. In addition, whilst they were undertaking research and working the telephones through that summer, Sharon was moonlighting as the part-time receptionist for the office building in order to help make ends meet.

Above: **The CMS Cruise Staff line up in *Funchal*'s main lobby May 1997.** *(Sharon Bastow)*

Below right: **The first CMS produced brochure for the 1997 Classic International Cruises programme of *Princess Danae* and *Funchal*. (CMV Library)**

An introduction to George P. Potamianos of Lisbon's Arcalia Shipping Company led to CMS' first General Sales Agency in the UK. Arcalia had recently acquired the 600-passenger *Princess Danae* as a fleet-mate to *Funchal*. A UK brochure was hurriedly compiled under the Classic International Cruises brand, to feature the two ships and their sailings through to September 1997. This appointment was swiftly followed on 14th October 1996 by a second General Sales Agency this time for Transocean Tours of Bremen, operators of the 600-passenger *Astor*, the slightly smaller *Calypso*, and charterers of Cunard's *Sagafjord*, which they had renamed *Gripsholm*.

Significantly, in addition to finding passengers for the scheduled cruise programmes of its new principals, CMS became active as brokers of whole-ship charters for the Arcalia fleet. This was a lucrative business, as most charterers needed fully staffed cruise and entertainment teams, and a shore excursion programme for their passengers. Sharon Bastow had previously built and operated such teams in her CTC days and was now able to utilise her expertise, and her contacts book, for *Princess Danae* and *Funchal*. Roger Evans, another former CTC colleague, joined CMS in 1996 to prepare the tour programmes; his shore excursion expertise stretched back to 1973, when working in the Tours Offices aboard such ships as *Ithaca*, *QE2*, and *Cunard Countess*. The first CMS

negotiated charter was with *Funchal*, which sailed from Harwich on 24th May 1997 on a 12-night 'Midnight Sun' cruise for the tour operator Travelsphere. It was very much a 'hands-on' operation and both Sharon Bastow, as Cruise Administrator, and Roger Evans, as Tour Manager, sailed as part of the cruise staff, whilst Chris Coates and Richard Bastow handled the embarkation of passengers.

The young business was up and running and, ever optimistic, a bookkeeper was engaged to count the money. The fact that Georgina Self was part-time gave an indication that the scale of her task was not huge in those early days. Georgina went on to become one of the company's longest serving employees,

In 1998 CMS moved from the serviced office arrangement into their own premises, a converted former Baptist church in Sutton-at-Hone, just outside Dartford. More charter business was forthcoming and by 2001 a smooth operation had evolved, with an increasing number of ships, including *Aegean I*, *Arion* and *Van Gogh*, supplementing *Princess Danae* and *Funchal* in offering cruises from the UK for the CMS tour operator clients.

Close links were also being established with other cruise lines and operators including, significantly, Louis Cruise Lines in Cyprus and Club Cruise in Holland. Another notable introduction made around this time was to Simon Weeks and Stephen Moore of London-based tour operator, South Quay Travel & Leisure (SQT), which had developed an attractive programme of short city breaks and specialist tours to such destinations as Disneyland Paris.

2002 proved to be a pivotal year for CMS. The order book for charters for the 2003 season looked thin, due mainly to the advent of newly-built large ships being introduced by the big brands, such as Celebrity, Norwegian, and Princess Cruises. The latter's 3,100 passenger capacity *Star Princess*, for example, could easily accommodate the entire 600-passenger complement of a chartered cruise aboard *Princess Danae*, as a single group booking. Tour operators logically opted for group bookings over chartering whole ships.

CMS responded with a plan to sell their own cruises, by proposing to their main cruise line partner, Classic International Cruises, that the 300-

passenger *Arion* could be utilised for a programme of UK market cruises in summer 2003.

This concept required considerable expansion of the CMS operation to act as a reservations office in its General Sales Agent capacity, obtain trading licences, engage additional staff, acquire a computerised reservation system and devise effective marketing plans. It was clear that some elements would be best accomplished by working with an existing licensed tour operator, and discussions with South Quay Travel & Leisure were successfully concluded in July 2002 to that effect, enabling CMS to launch an inaugural series of 13 *Arion* departures between May and November 2003 under the Classic International Cruises brand.

Neither company could have foreseen that, nine years later, their relationship would be formalised and that the proprietors of their respective companies would become four of the initial shareholders of Cruise & Maritime Voyages.

Over the next few years, CMS worked with South Quay Travel & Leisure to represent a number of ships and cruise lines, trading under the brand name of its various principals. Brochures appeared on the UK market offering cruises through a Sutton-at-Hone-based General Sales Agent with ships such as *Athena* (Classic International Cruises) in 2005; *Calypso* (Louis Cruise Lines) in 2006; and *Arielle* (Transocean Tours) in 2007. However, the operation of older, smaller ships from unfamiliar companies in the face of competition from established brand names and their newly-built larger vessels required CMS to be very creative in its planning in order to fill the ships for the owners that it represented. The strategy became clear: if you could not always get the market to come to the ship, there might be better success if the ship was taken to the market. From that standpoint, occasional sailings from Belfast, Dundee, Greenock, Hull, Liverpool, Newcastle and Portsmouth all featured in 2004 and 2005. A lack of suitable ships was the only barrier to developing the concept further, but the experience gained from these tentative steps into bringing cruising to different regions of the UK was to prove invaluable.

During these formative years, both Richard Bastow and Chris Coates inspected many different vessels. It was during such visits that contact was first made with Global Entertainment, part of the Global Maritime Group of Piraeus, Greece. Global occasionally provided the entertainment product aboard some of the Louis Cruise Lines fleet, whose *Calypso* provided the main CMS cruise programme from London Tilbury for the 2006 season. As an indicator of the impact that the company's success was having on the UK market, Thomson Cruises, who were long-time charter-partners of Louis Cruise Lines, hurriedly arranged to charter *Calypso* for the 2007 season, leaving CMS without a main season ship for

Top: **Captain Dimitrios Daoutis on the bridge of *Ocean Countess* with (left to right) Lloyd Cross, Richard Bastow and Chris Coates London Tilbury on 19th March 2011.** *(CMV Library)*

Above: **Constantine Zalacosta of Majestic International Cruises with Coates and Bastow alongside *Ocean Countess* in Piraeus on 12th June 2009.** *(CMV Library)*

Arielle in Transocean Tours livery off Dubrovnik in October 2007. *(J. Neven)*

the following year.

But CMS had already initiated discussions about increasing cooperation with their colleagues in Transocean. By coincidence, the German company had chartered the 1,100-passenger *Aquamarine* from Louis Cruise Lines, which was to be renamed *Arielle* for her time with Transocean.

The British and German cruise markets have different peaks and troughs in demand, making it possible to 'share' vessels during the respective seasons. CMS agreed to sub-charter *Arielle* from Transocean for a short series of cruises in May and June 2007, with further sailings in September exclusively for the British market. This was a landmark decision for CMS. It was the first time that the senior management felt able to commit the resources to taking the full risk of chartering a ship, and a higher capacity vessel at that. The new operation also brought the company closer to Global Entertainment, and CMS Operations Manager Lloyd Cross worked closely with the *Arielle* entertainment team and its director, Anita Bistere, to produce consistently high levels of passenger satisfaction with the on-board product.

To everyone's delight and relief, the *Arielle* cruises were a resounding success, and the programme sold out very quickly. With the business flourishing, CMS were particularly keen to produce and market a 2008 programme. The team expanded to handle the enlarged operation and the Dartford premises were extended through purchase of the neighbouring building to accommodate 16 people. Whilst the CMS directors were contemplating a second season with *Arielle*, their Transocean counterparts were in fruitful negotiations with the Global Maritime Group (GMG) about a new acquisition that was to be available from the spring of 2008.

GMG was created by the husband and wife team of Nikolaos C. Tragakes and Anita Bistere, with an operational headquarters in Greece.

Transocean Tours

From left to right, Peter Waehnert of Transocean Tours, with Nikolaos Tragakes, Chris Coates, Richard Bastow and Captain Alexandr Golubyev, Master of *Marco Polo,* prior to her maiden voyage on 19th April 2008. *(CMV Library)*

The company had previously operated three cruise ships and was now actively seeking new tonnage. In summer 2007 the new GMG acquisition was revealed to be the Orient Line flagship *Marco Polo,* which was familiar to both the Transocean and CMV management from her previous life as *Alexandr Pushkin*. Orient Line had completed a high-quality rebuild of the former Soviet vessel in 1994 and, despite having traded successfully since then, she was now surplus to requirements for Norwegian Cruise Line, which had purchased Orient Line in 1998. This was to be a very significant purchase by GMG as, although unforeseen when the ship was delivered in Lisbon in March 2008, the transaction set a unique train of events in motion.

The outcome of this busy period of talks was that *Marco Polo* would be chartered on a long-term basis to Transocean, which in turn would sub-charter her to CMS for an agreed number of days each year. In 2008 there would be an exclusive 'British' period from London Tilbury between April and August, and a jointly marketed 2008–2009 winter season featuring the Caribbean, South America, and Antarctica. As with the previous season of *Arielle* cruises, the inaugural 2008 *Marco Polo* programme was operated through South Quay Travel & Leisure and marketed as Transocean Tours, which gave an important sense of continuity.

Marco Polo's maiden voyage from London Tilbury took place on Saturday 19th April, a typically grey drizzly and windswept afternoon, which saw a sizeable audience gather to watch the Transocean House Flag being officially presented to the Master by Nikolaos Tragakes of GMG. Also present were Peter Waehnert of Transocean Tours and Chris Coates and Richard Bastow from CMS.

The maiden season was successful for all concerned and itineraries featuring the Baltic, the Norwegian Fjords, Iceland, and the British Isles were again programmed for the 2009 season, which was to culminate in a 32-night West Indies cruise in October, prior to commencing another winter season in South America and Antarctica.

But circumstances conspired to disrupt the plans. There were early signals of an economic recession in Europe following the 2008 financial crisis and on 1st September 2009 the internationally-respected 55-year-old Transocean Tours was forced into provisional administration following a difficult trading period with its other vessels, *Astor* and *Astoria*. GMG was faced with a difficult situation. The company still had its own expenses on *Marco Polo* and the crew were on board, but there was still income available from future bookings until the end of the published German season on 10th November. GMG therefore decided to carry on operating the vessel at its own expense whilst searching for new business for the ship.

Urgent talks were held with CMS and South Quay Travel & Leisure, whose participation was vital, and eventually agreement was reached that the UK operation would take over the remaining period of the Transocean charter to commence from London Tilbury on 2nd January 2010.

The planned South American winter season was cancelled and the entire management and staff at CMS dealt with the challenge of devising and advertising an attractive cruise programme for *Marco Polo*, engaging

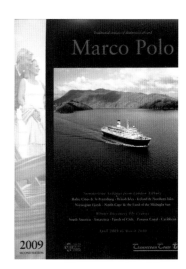

Left: CMS produced this Classic International Cruises brochure in 2003 to feature a summer season of thirteen cruises with the 300 passenger Arion. *(Richard Bastow collection)*

Right: The 2009 cruise season was Marco Polo's second year sailing out of Tilbury but the final one under the Transocean Tours banner. *(Richard Bastow collection)*

cruise staff, setting up shore excursion programmes and, most vitally, finding the required large number of British passengers in the very short period of time available.

CMS was now marketing a product under its own name for the very first time and quickly introduced the more user-friendly brand name of 'Cruise & Maritime Voyages' (CMV) for the new operation. A fresh logo was developed, which combined the blue and silver typeface and style of 'Cruise & Maritime Services' with a stylistic blue and silver sail that echoed the logo of GMG and represented the strengthening connection between the two companies.

New on-board stationery was still being unpacked and distributed as *Marco Polo* embarked her pilot for the Thames river passage on that January Saturday, with excited throngs of passengers lining the ship's rails looking forward to some Caribbean sunshine.

Watching proudly shoreside were a very contented set of individuals who had come together almost by default over these formative years but had put in an immense amount of hard work in a very short time to make CMV happen. Even the iconic bronze statue of Rudolf Nureyev up on Magellan Deck seemed to salute in silent admiration.

However, the first indication that the new CMV operation would not be limited to a year-round season of sailings from London Tilbury with *Marco Polo* actually had its seeds in the summer of 2009. CMS had been in prolonged negotiations with Transocean to secure the right duration period for their 2010 charter season. In midsummer Chris Coates and Richard Bastow prudently decided to cover their options by opening discussions with Majestic International Cruises in Greece for a possible summer-only seasonal charter of its vessel *Ocean Countess*, in what they then thought was the unlikely event that the Transocean arrangement might not materialise as planned

Chapter two

Early stages of growth and development 2010-2014

Ocean Countess meets *Marco Polo* at Eidfjord, Norway on 22nd August 2011. *(CMV Library)*

Ocean Countess had a rich history, as well as being well known in the UK market as the former *Cunard Countess*. Agreement was reached in principle with Majestic International Cruises for a three-year charter period: further discussions were due to be held but, as has been seen in the previous chapter, the situation was soon overtaken by the unfortunate events in Germany. Christian Verhounig, who at that time was the Director of Hotel Operations of GMG, joined the next set of talks in Athens and agreement was reached that CMV would operate *Ocean Countess* alongside *Marco Polo* in a two-ship operation from the UK.

Ocean Countess was contracted on a three-year 'deck and engine' charter from April until October requiring Majestic to provide the technical crew in the deck and engineering departments as part of the arrangement. This was ideal for CMV as it allowed them to contract GMG to run the hotel and passenger service operations. Apart from economies of scale, it ensured consistency of product delivery, with the same menu cycle, same bar stock, and a similar entertainment format.

This was a brave time for CMV to expand from a single-vessel summer season operation to becoming a full cruise operator with two ships offering nearly 600 trading days, with a global recession just beginning to take effect. The strategy, which set the formula for operations in subsequent years, was to support a London Tilbury home-ported vessel with a ship that could service what CMV considered to be a pent-up demand for cruises from regional ports that it simply had not been able to fulfil in previous years due to lack of suitable tonnage.

Marco Polo was based at London Tilbury for the remainder of CMV's first year of operation after her maiden sailing to the Caribbean. Her second cruise featured visits to the Amazon and Orinoco rivers, but plans to repeat this itinerary in 2011 were to be thwarted by the changing political situation in Venezuela. She settled into a familiar routine of established itineraries to Norway, the Baltic, around Britain, the Canaries, and Iberia. After a short break for a refit, she returned from London Tilbury to the Caribbean for a 35-night cruise over Christmas and New Year 2010/11.

With a nod to the 2004 and 2005 CMS programmes operated by *Arion* and *Funchal*, *Ocean Countess* was programmed to serve as CMV's regional vessel and move around the British Isles starting in London Tilbury on 18th April, then offering cruises from Hull, Newcastle (Tyne), Edinburgh (Leith), Glasgow (Greenock), and Liverpool. She finished her inaugural season at Plymouth to take advantage of the port's proximity to the Iberian Peninsula, the Canary Islands, and Madeira. Her season finished at the end of October. By the end of this 2010 maiden season,

37,115 passengers had sailed under the CMV flag; representing healthy growth on the 2009 figure, which bore out the feeling that consumer demand was actually supply-led. The coming recession would soon test that theory.

GMG were hugely supportive of the new CMV operation, and Richard Bastow and Chris Coates readily accepted an offer to sell a proportion of their equity to GMG during the year. It was very apparent that, with such a common interest, the two concerns could work even closer together.

There had long been a view that the company needed to establish new markets to supplement the UK and balance the risk of being dependent on a single market. But for the next couple of years, it was all that CMV could do to remain competitive in a global marketplace that had taken the brunt of an economic downturn. GMG established a small

Ocean Countess departs from London Tilbury on 18th April 2010 on her CMV maiden voyage. *(Neil Sutherland)*

sales office in Fort Lauderdale, Florida in 2011, from which it was hoped an increasing number of North American passengers would eventually flow.

A further development was the introduction of in-port promotional events as an additional marketing tool, whereby 'spare' days at the start or end of a season were used to offer prospective passengers the opportunity to sample the product by spending an afternoon or staying overnight in port on board the ship. These events were extremely successful and in 2011 over 5,700 guests enjoyed the hospitality that *Marco Polo* had to offer.

The pattern of sailings established in 2010 was repeated in 2011, with

Marco Polo home-porting in London Tilbury and *Ocean Countess* supporting the regional programme of departures. *Marco Polo* offered a full set of itineraries throughout the year, with just a short break in November. With just one transatlantic journey to the Amazon at the start of the year, *Marco Polo* was able to offer three successive 14-night itineraries to the 'Land of the Northern Lights', reverting to a creative but recognisable pattern of destinations that quickly proved popular as the year unfolded.

Ocean Countess had her season extended into March and November, to offer twelve departures from Hull during the spring, with her transfer to Newcastle not taking place until mid-June. The Scottish programme was much shorter this year as CMV responded to demand, with four sailings from Edinburgh (Leith) in August leading into an extended Liverpool programme of departures. Finally, *Ocean Countess* crossed to Dublin to open up three new opportunities to Spain, Portugal, and the Canary Islands for the Irish market, the last of which took her on to Nice for a final Mediterranean sailing in November.

Despite these bold efforts to broaden the client base, the 2011 and 2012 cruising seasons were challenging periods for CMV, with the UK market suffering strongly from the recession that brought pressure on margins. In summer 2011 it was deemed necessary to restructure the operation to ensure that it would be adequately funded to continue to develop the business. GMG increased its shareholding, and outside investors took financial positions that brought other businesses into a newly formed travel and leisure group of companies. Significantly the shareholders and the executive board was strengthened by Simon Weeks and Stephen Moore of South Quay Travel & Leisure, thus formally uniting the major 'movers and shakers' of the early business into a larger corporate structure known as CMV Holdings London Ltd. This action ensured that CMV would remain a significant player in the future UK cruise market.

Under the chairmanship of Nikolaos Tragakes, Christian Verhounig was appointed Chief Executive Officer, Simon Weeks the Chief Financial Officer and Stephen Moore, Chris Coates and Richard Bastow became executive directors, with each having his own responsibilities within either South Quay Travel and its associate Independent Coach Travel (ICT), and Viceroy Travel in the case of Stephen Moore; or in CMV for Chris Coates and Richard Bastow.

The two-ship fleet was retained into 2012 and the range of departures followed the pattern operated so successfully in the previous two seasons. *Marco Polo* again served London Tilbury throughout the year, with a break in November. Her itineraries included a special 'Britain's Maritime Heritage' cruise, during which 800 guests commemorated the centenary of the loss of the *Titanic* with calls at Cherbourg and Cobh, and a wreath laying to commemorate the sinking of the *Lusitania* off Cobh in 1915. Special menus on board recreated dinners enjoyed on classic liners of yesteryear and there were guest lecturers, exhibits, quizzes and auctions as *Marco Polo* also called at Belfast and Liverpool, two ports with strong *Titanic* connections. The rest of the season was both varied and familiar as *Marco Polo* visited destinations as far apart as Manaus, Valencia, St. Petersburg and Tromsø.

The season for *Ocean Countess* started in late April, but this year she was able to offer itineraries from Hull and Liverpool in the spring. She summered sailing from Glasgow (Greenock), offering a lengthy sea trip to Leixoes and the Canaries, before her mixed autumn departure programme saw her return to offer three sailings from Hull and six from Liverpool. One-night party cruises were offered as a sampler opportunity as she repositioned between Glasgow (Greenock) and Liverpool. Her final 'Farewell Voyage' for CMV saw *Ocean Countess* leave Liverpool on 9th October bound for Barcelona via the Canaries.

Whilst *Ocean Countess* was completing her third and final season with CMV, an interesting joint venture was being discussed with the All Leisure Group, owners of the Voyages of Discovery (VoD) brand, with a view to a cooperation in selling cruises on its vessel *Discovery* in 2013 and 2014. It was a radical concept for two rival companies broadly selling in the same market sector to work together, and it caught the imagination of the travel trade.

The arrangement was signed in August 2012 with the concept similar to *Ocean Countess,* with the technical operation of the ship lying with her owners and the hotel side of the operation being run by GMG, for the all-important continuity and consistency of product. The programme combined the best *Ocean Countess* itineraries with popular VoD sailings and resulted in *Discovery* being scheduled from Liverpool, Hull and Newcastle (Tyne) in addition to an early summer period from Harwich, one of her traditional home ports.

The arrival of *Astor* enabled CMV to address the departure of Classic International Cruises (CIC) from the Australian market. *Astor* found herself deployed in the German market for a TransOcean Kreuzfahrten programme, which began with a sailing from Lisbon to her new home port of Bremerhaven on 29th March. The range of cruises offered by Transocean would be familiar to British guests, and she took advantage of using Keil as a second home port to open up Baltic destinations. Her season took *Astor* as far as Montréal in August, before she headed to Lisbon and the Mediterranean in late September for a short autumn programme of departures, which culminated in her first 'Liner' voyage from Civitavecchia to Fremantle via the Suez Canal. Unrest in Egypt forced the cancellation of calls in Port Said and Safaga, but *Astor* arrived in Australia on time on 11th December, ready for her inaugural Australian season.

There were several new British ports for CMV in *Discovery's* first programme. She started the year sailing from Bristol Avonmouth in March, with a strong series of six departures, before a short season from Liverpool. From there she travelled to open up Harwich as a cruise port from 22nd May, whence innovative destinations included the White Sea. *Discovery* then headed north to Hull for three departures and on to her third new port for CMV at Newcastle (Tyne), for high season itineraries that took advantage of easy access to Norway and the Baltic. A further call in Harwich preceded an autumn programme of departures in the Mediterranean from Barcelona, Piraeus, Istanbul, and Bodrum, before *Discovery* finished her first season for CMV in Piraeus with a school cruise.

Marco Polo started 2013 with her now traditional January 42-night visit to the Amazon, which this year was again combined with calls in the West Indies and the Azores. She started and ended her domestic programme in London Tilbury but spent around six weeks from late May operating from Edinburgh (Leith) to serve the Scottish market, as CMV strongly enhanced their regional pattern of departures in 2013. Overnight party cruises were offered to link the two ports. She spent November undertaking a return 30-night trip to the West Indies before a Christmas sequence of short trips and festive events, which culminated in a 14-night Christmas and New Year cruise to the Canaries and Madeira. This was subjected to challenging weather conditions, but the schedule was adapted to make the best of the circumstances.

The 2014 programme settled into the established pattern of departures.

Astor wintered in the Australian summer for the first time, with a range of very short 2- to 5-night trips and much longer cruises, including

Top right: *Marco Polo* at anchor between Tresco and St. Mary's in the Isles of Scilly on the 20th April 2019. *(Andrew Cooke)*

Middle right: Captain Brian Larcombe, Master of *Discovery* with James Stangroom of the Port of Bristol and Mike Hall of CMV, at Avonmouth on 11th April 2013 exchanging mementoes to mark her inaugural season.. *(CMV Library)*

Bottom right: A spectacular send-off for **Ocean Countess** as she becomes the first ship to sail from Liverpool's new Cruise Terminal at Pier Head on 29th May 2012. *(Port of Liverpool)*

The elegant *Discovery* approaching her berth in Portsmouth. *(Andrew Cooke)*

the first 35-night 'Cruise Round Australia', and a 24-night 'Far East Delights' departure which headed as far as Singapore. *Astor* returned to Europe for the summer, leaving Fremantle on 1st April for a 40-night cruise via South Africa, which took her to Bremerhaven after a call in Harwich. Her Transocean itineraries took her back to Canada and Iceland, and offered the now established portfolio of Norwegian, Baltic and British destinations. She split the remainder of the summer between home-porting in Bremerhaven and Kiel, and completed her season in Bremerhaven on 15th October. *Astor* returned to Australia from London Tilbury on 5th November, again travelling via South Africa, before commencing a hectic Christmas programme 'down under'.

Discovery's season was brought forward to start from Bristol Avonmouth on 24th February and unusually her next two departures were from Liverpool, then Hull, where she settled in for a spring series of cruises. She was back in Bristol Avonmouth in May and undertook a special commemorative '70th Anniversary of D-Day' cruise during which she sailed off the Normandy beaches before returning to Plymouth. After three departures from Liverpool, she summered in Scotland, initially at Glasgow (Greenock) and then at Edinburgh (Leith), before returning to Liverpool, and then Bristol Avonmouth.

Meanwhile *Marco Polo* followed her 42-night Amazon Cruise with a lengthy period home-porting at London Tilbury with three 'Land of the Northern Lights' departures followed by a sequence of shorter cruises.

Like *Discovery*, she cruised the Normandy beaches during a D-Day commemoration on 6th June. She took a break from the Thames with a repositioning trip on 8th June to Newcastle for the early summer, but she returned to London Tilbury to deliver some CMV classic cruise destinations and itineraries, focussing particularly on the Baltic and Norway, until she took a short break in November. *Marco Polo* hosted an intense sequence of Christmas events and cruises at her home port before heading for Christmas and New Year in the Canaries and Madeira.

There were now the first signs in the 2012 booking figures that the investment in a US sales office was beginning to pay a return. As *Discovery* was the former *Island Princess* and she doubled, when required, for her sister ship *Pacific Princess* as the star of the TV series 'The Love Boat' (1977–1987), it was thought that this connection might also resonate with the North American market.

The year 2014 was to end somewhat eventfully. Firstly, the All Leisure Group chose to conclude the joint venture prematurely some two cruises early, as they had sold *Discovery*. Moving swiftly, CMV secured the slightly smaller, but recently refitted, *Funchal* from Portuscale Cruises in Lisbon for a month's service to ensure that passengers booked were not disappointed. Further business with Portuscale swiftly followed as their 550-passenger *Azores* (renamed *Astoria* in 2016) was secured on a long-term basis to operate the regional cruise programme in 2015, commencing from Avonmouth in January.

The first five years of Cruise & Maritime Voyages was not just a period of growth and development but also one of innovation. The concept of taking the ship to the market expanded the use of departure ports away from the traditional south-east England base to the extent that, by 2015, CMV passengers could cruise from any one of ten embarkation points around the UK, as can be seen in the Programme Summary in Chapter 10. It was undoubtedly a successful strategy, but brought challenges in the commercial repositioning of the vessels concerned between the ports in question. Two separate solutions were employed to address this issue.

Firstly there was the straightforward overnight cruise strategy, whereby a ship could position from, for instance, London Tilbury to Hull, or Glasgow (Greenock) to Liverpool by the operation of a mini-cruise often especially themed and including return coach travel to the departure port in the fare. The other method was to include two embarkation ports in a single itinerary. The requisite criteria was that the ports had to be repeated in the subsequent cruise(s) in order to provide the disembarkation point and they also had to be attractive enough destinations for the other passengers to whom they were the first, or the last, port of call on their cruise. Sailings that featured Hull then Rosyth the next day (*Discovery* 2014) or Newcastle (Tyne) and then Dundee (*Magellan* 2015), are excellent examples.

CMV has always been supportive of Britain's maritime heritage and it was particularly pleasing for the company to put its weight behind public relations exercises that, whilst informing prospective passengers of cruises and events, had the dual purpose of increasing people's awareness of the traditions of the country's great rivers. The Thames, the Humber, the Tyne, the Clyde, the Mersey, and the rivers Severn and Avon, which serve Bristol, have all benefitted from the extra publicity and promotion.

Whether the maritime tradition of the ports was in shipbuilding – John Brown on the Clyde, Swan Hunter on the Tyne, Cammell Laird on the Mersey and Harland & Wolff in Belfast spring to mind – or in being the departure points of famous liners of the past, CMV endeavoured to give their press releases a lighter touch and greater interest by cross-referencing. The transatlantic services of Cunard and Canadian Pacific from Liverpool and Greenock, the Orient Line and P&O's Australia and New Zealand service from London Tilbury all received subtle acknowledgement as indeed, going a little further back, did Brunel's SS *Great Britain* at Bristol. It is a sobering thought that a screw propeller ship built of iron was considered daring and radical, but then again it was 1843.

The men primarily responsible of getting the Cruise & Maritime Voyages message across are Mike Hall, the Head of Marketing and Paul Foster from the firm Paul Foster PR, which has handled the account since 2008 and is therefore also celebrating a first decade of collaboration. Paul has dealt with all the ups and downs of that period and, with Mike Hall, has been integral in CMV maintaining an almost constant presence in the national, local, and the travel trade press. He also freely admits to being responsible for some of the worst puns in press release headline history. The year 2015 produced some particularly fine examples of the genre: '*Easter Cruise Affordability*' (Norway Easter Cruise – March), '*Only Pools & Seahorses*' (TV Comedy Theme Cruise – July) and '*These Boats were Made for Walking*' (river cruise with rambler interest – September). When asked how he manages to keep the stories fresh he claims that, whenever possible, he likes to entertain as well as inform. Paul adds:

I still have the same excitement today as I did when I first assisted Cruise & Maritime over 10 years ago. It has never been boring, what with the various different embarkation ports coming on stream and the steady acquisition of new ships to promote. It's just been a joy.

Vessel schedules have also developed considerably over the decade, with the departure port and the time of year being major factors in deployment and it is fascinating to review the actual itineraries that have been operated by all the CMV vessels. These are shown in detail in Chapter 10 and it can be seen that primarily the company continues to concentrate on northern routings. The staple diet of the Baltic Capitals, Norwegian and Icelandic ports, however, has evolved to now encompass Spitzbergen, The White Sea, Greenland and the less well known towns and islands of the 'Hidden Baltic'.

Much to the delight of the port authorities and tourist organisations in the countries concerned, this enhancement, together with the advent and continued popularity of Northern Lights cruises and Christmas Market sailings, has seen CMV effectively extend the northern cruise season to almost ten months of the year from mid-February to December.

Planning winter cruise seasons has always been a challenge for British and European cruise lines and, for CMV, Caribbean, South American, and 'Round the World' itineraries have all had to be researched, developed and refined. The Australian operation has brought many maiden calls for *Astor* since 2013 and now *Vasco da Gama* will be exploring south-east Asia in February 2020 as she makes an elaborate northbound voyage to the UK.

These positioning voyages to and from the Antipodes are amongst CMV's collection of 'signature cruises' together with perhaps the 'Amazon Adventure', the 'British Isles Discovery' and the aforementioned sailings to the 'Land of the Northern Lights'. These last three all date back to the first season in 2010 and have been operated each year since, on broadly the same itinerary and duration with only minor tweaks.

However, the Australian voyages only commenced in 2013 and any thoughts that Chris Coates and Richard Bastow might have had about replicating the line voyages of their CTC days had to be swiftly dispelled. The November 1985 southbound voyage of the ill-fated *Mikhail Lermontov* followed effectively a straight line, and arguably the swiftest route, on a London Tilbury–Kingston–Panama–Tahiti–Auckland–Sydney schedule to position the ship in Australia in as short a time as possible. Whilst speed was of the essence in the 1980s (and indeed representing a healthy growth on the 2009 figure, which bore post-war decades) the more sophisticated traveller of the 21st century required something more substantial to persuade them that a long sea voyage could be a more attractive proposition than anything British Airways, Qantas or Singapore Airlines could offer. Therefore, both the southbound and northbound itineraries were treated as long cruises, rather than voyages, and an enticing selection of ports programmed whether the ship went via the Cape of Good Hope or the Panama Canal. Entertainment and catering were also elevated to a considerably higher standard than the 'Ten Pound Poms' would have experienced aboard their voyages when they sailed from London Tilbury to start a new life in Australia or New Zealand.

It was always CMV policy to offer the same, or very similar, cruises from different UK departure points and therefore a 'British Isles Discovery' cruise for example could be found sailing from Hull, Newcastle (Tyne), Edinburgh (Leith), Liverpool and Bristol Avonmouth, as well as London Tilbury with the necessary adjustments made for the navigation. It is worth mentioning that this cruise in particular has enabled thousands of CMV passengers over the years to enjoy parts of the British Isles that they might not necessarily have visited otherwise and these sailings also attract North American and Australian guests as well, often on a family reunion trip or even an ancestral research project.

This 'Britishness' also manifests itself in another growth area and that is the theme cruise. Whilst the concept is not unique to CMV, it has developed into a very slick operation and has supplemented the on-board entertainment programme considerably. As passenger tastes and preferences are entirely subjective, it was always a dilemma as to whether a particular theme would attract more passengers than it would repel, and in the same vein, a theme had to not be too intrusive or disruptive for those passengers who had little interest in the subject matter. The third point is whether a theme is to be used as a marketing tool to attract additional passengers or as an added value element for those who would book anyway.

It all started in a very small way as Sharon Bastow recalls:

In April 2008 we managed to secure 'Strictly Come Dancing' stars Vincent Simone and Flavia Cacace to sail with us aboard Marco Polo. *Vincent and Flavia performed their own show, gave dance classes and filled the lounge when being interviewed by the Cruise Director. The advertising that we did attracted a really good number of new passengers. It was a great success for our first attempt.*

Nowadays, the themes warrant their own section within the CMV brochures and the net has spread much wider in pursuit of new ideas, which have become more and more relevant as the number of repeat passengers increases year-on-year and they do not want to see the same thing too often. Notable themes centred around specific occasions, such as the centenary commemoration of the loss of RMS *Titanic* in 2012, the Diamond Jubilee cruise the same year that visited the four UK capital

cities, and the 70th and 75th anniversaries of D-Day in 2014 and 2019.

Other subjects that generated much interest on board were cricket, the circus and magic, various musical genres – Pop with 60s legends, Rock and Pirate Radio, and more recently Soul Legends, all featuring big name artists and personalities. One of the longest running ideas has been 'A Laugh on the Ocean Wave', which first broke into a chuckle in 2013 and showcased guest comedians on selected sailings.

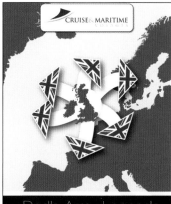

Dad's Army Legends
Springtime Fjordland

'Carrying on' that thread are the 'Carry On' Legends cruises, where cast members, and others who worked on those iconic film comedies, share their stories on board. British TV has also provided a wealth of opportunities such as Childhood TV Heroes and of course the long running serial dramas. So, leaving the last word on the subject to PR man Paul Foster, he tells us:

I wrote this in July 2016 for a Magellan theme cruise that had leading stars from those much-loved soap operas including 'EastEnders', 'Coronation Street', 'Emmerdale', 'Crossroads' and 'The Archers'. It has to be my all-time favourite press release headline – Soap and Water.

The themes are just one element of how the on-board product has developed in this first decade. The larger ships with their increased range of public rooms and amenities, plus the economic benefits that fleet-wide central purchasing provides, have enabled a greater variety of entertainment, a wider menu and bar stock, as well as speciality dining options. A popular development has been the Chef's Table, available on the larger vessels, where an exclusive dining experience is not only created but also hosted by the Executive Chef. Whilst there is an additional charge for dining in the speciality restaurants, some great value packages have been developed for purchase on board or, for even greater worth, prior to sailing. Acknowledging that an all-inclusive element and therefore knowing in advance what the on-board expenditure will be, has a decided attraction for today's cruise guest, the imaginative CMV Additions options, introduced in 2018, offer a whole raft

of benefits that have been really well received.

However, there is a considerably enhanced IT requirement to ensure that items such as the Columbus Club Membership data, as well as orders for the Additions Packages, are correctly conveyed to the relevant personnel on board.

The cruise industry, and indeed the travel industry as a whole, has never been slow to embrace the ongoing developments and enhancements that the digital age offers. Elements such as electronic ticketing, automated check-in, and the intelligent Cruise Card which is swiped every time you embark, disembark or make a purchase on board have become the norm. However, CMV is one of the few remaining lines where paper tickets and travel documents do still remain an option should a passenger not have access to an email account or a printer. Notwithstanding the march of progress, extensive brochures are nevertheless produced regularly, but communication by the company with its clientele, both for information and sales, is maintained on a far grander and more elaborate scale by the website (www.cruiseandmaritime.com), which was established in May 2010, and increasingly through social media. The CMV TV channel within the website is an ideal way to 'see before you buy' as all the ships and the cruise destinations are featured – many cleverly hosted in an entertaining and informative manner by Tyler Butterworth.

Social media in its turn has played a significant part in raising the company profile and at the same time providing a platform for CMV followers to comment and share views and information. The Facebook page was set up in October 2011 and Mike Hall, Head of Marketing, whose department oversees all the electronic content of the Facebook, Instagram and Twitter platforms explains that:

Social media enables us to stay in touch with our thousands of followers 24/7. When we started Facebook, for instance, only a small percentage of social media users were over-55s but now the largest growth area is among older users and this is very much our target market.

Top right: Cruise Director Richard Sykes interviews Vincent Simone and Flavia Cacace aboard *Marco Polo* in April 2008. *(CMV Library)*

Middle right: The extensive line-up of Carry On guests, including former cast members aboard *Columbus* in 2019. *(CMV Library)*

By the end of November 2019, CMV boasted over 30,000 'likes' on Facebook, 9,000 Twitter followers and almost 7,000 Instagram followers.

Whilst Mike Hall's team looks after the content of the website and the design and production of brochures, flyers, leaflets, and media adverts, his colleagues, Gary Hides as Head of Technology, and Dean Medley, the Information Security and Data Protection Officer, ensure that the technical delivery is at a consistently high level and keeps pace with technological developments. We're not sure that the broken Amstrad of 1996 would have coped!

19

Cruise & Maritime Voyages Ltd: The founder shareholders

The success of CMV owes much to the commitment and vision which the founder shareholders brought to the new venture.

Nikolaos Tragakes, Co-Founder of the Global Maritime Group (GMG). He established the privately owned company in 1987 and has a solid background in banking and specifically ship finance, which proved a very useful attribute for the new company. As well as having the vast experience of previously operating three other cruise ships, the Global Maritime Group brought technical management, crewing and recruitment, and hotel management expertise to the venture. Nikolaos' vision and foresight has greatly contributed to the successful growth and development of the business.

Anita Bistere, Co-Founder of the Global Maritime Group (GMG) Director of Entertainment. Anita runs the GMG entertainment division, which provides shipboard entertainment and social staff as well as fully costumed and choreographed production shows for CMV. Although headquartered in Greece, GMG has other offices in Bulgaria, Latvia, Romania, Serbia, and Ukraine.

Christian Verhounig, Chief Executive Officer (2011 to date). CMV's Chief Executive Officer is from Austria and discovered a love of the sea aboard *Astor*, where he joined the Hotel Department in 1997. He rose from bartender to Food and Beverage Manager to become Hotel Director on board before moving to shoreside positions. He held senior management positions with catering and hospitality companies in the cruise industry, taking on the role of Chief Operations Officer (COO) of Global Maritime Group in 2007, and CEO and Chairman of CMV Travel & Leisure Group in 2011. His areas of responsibility include the shipboard operation including the HR management for close to 4,000 employees, and control of costs and investments, as well as the SOLAS, MARPOL and ISO management of the fleet. In addition, he coordinates and oversees the worldwide sales and marketing operation as well as the strategic positioning of the group. When not travelling in between the offices worldwide he likes to dive in the summer and ski in the winter.

Christopher Coates, Group Commercial Director (CMV 2011 to date). Chris joined the cruise industry in 1983 in junior sales and marketing positions with Russian owned CTC Lines. Following a two-year spell with South African owned Astor Cruises as a National Sales Executive then Passenger Services Manager, Chris returned to the London based and renamed CTC Cruises Lines becoming a Sales & Marketing Director and executive board member at the age of 34.

Having moved on, in May 1996 he linked up with Richard Bastow to form Cruise & Maritime Services to provide ship brokerage and general sales agency services before being acquired and merged into the new CMV Group of Companies in 2011.

Chris's key responsibilities include market development, vessel deployment, programming and itinerary planning, pricing and yield management and all sales & marketing related commercial activities across the international network.

Simon Weeks, Chief Financial Officer **(CMV 2011 to date).** He began his career in travel in 1984 with the formation of a coach holiday company, Independent Coach Travel (ICT) recognised as leaders in the short-break market for many years. In 1989 Simon launched South Quay Travel & Leisure (SQT), a fully licensed tour operator, to offer ICT's product to a wider audience. In 2001 the group acquired Viceroy Travel with its retail agency accreditation and he began his involvement in cruise in 2002, helping Cruise & Maritime Services develop a tour operation to sell its programme. SQT is now the consumer facing side of the CMV Group and Simon has brought his industry expertise and financial acumen to the crucial role of Chief Financial Officer.

Stephen Moore, F Inst TT., Director **(CMV 2011–2015).** His background includes 43 years in the travel industry at Fred Olsen Lines, Townsend Thoresen Ferries and finally ICT/SQT. He was one of the founder members of British Association of Wholesale Tour Agents (BAWTA) and the Coach Tourism Council (CTC), now known as The Coach Tourism Association Ltd and towards the latter stages of his career sat as Chair of the ABTA Southern Region. Stephen's responsibility was to manage all of the non-cruise activities of the CMV group including the wholesale division (ICT), group retail operation (SQT) and retail and business travel agent Viceroy Travel. Stephen retired from the CMV Group in 2015.

Richard Bastow, Operations Director **(CMV 2011–2013).** Richard entered the passenger shipping industry in 1973 with Shaw Savill/Royal Mail Lines. He was with Chandris prior to joining CTC Lines in 1976 and steadily rose through the ranks to a senior management position. Appointed to the board in 1988, he served as Managing Director from 1992, and also served on the Council of Management of the Passenger Shipping Association. After CTC, in the Spring of 1996, he teamed up again with Chris Coates to establish Cruise & Maritime Services. At CMV he worked closely on operational matters with his GMG colleagues prior to retiring from his active career at the end of 2013.

Marco Polo passes Battery Point on the approaches to Bristol Avonmouth on 31st March 2016. *(Andrew Cooke)*

Chapter three

Building a truly international cruise line and brand

The golden anniversary of *Marco Polo's* launch took place on 26th April 2014 and plans were soon announced for her 50th anniversary season in 2015. It started with a specially commissioned 2015 calendar, which featured 12 different images of the ship throughout her career. The highlight was to be a special 36-night cruise to recreate her classic voyages across the Atlantic and recall her maiden visits to Québec and Montréal and other ports that formed part of her local programme of Soviet-era cruises from Montréal. The cruise sold out almost as quickly as it was advertised, prompting CMV to offer a repeat 34-night itinerary in the autumn. That too quickly sold out.

Richard Clammer researched and wrote an authoritative 96-page commemorative book to mark this rare anniversary in ship history. *Marco Polo: Celebrating Fifty Golden Years of Ocean Travel* was published by Ferry Publications, and quickly proved immensely popular with *Marco Polo's* wide range of admirers. CMV commissioned a special image depicting *Marco Polo* in her 2015 CMV livery, with a reflection of *Alexandr Pushkin* in Baltic Steamship Company black, sporting her original white funnel with a red band bearing the hammer and sickle insignia.

Marco Polo left London Tilbury on 24th July 2015 under some unseasonal grey skies, with 750 passengers crew on board for the 36-night 'Commemorative Canada and Greenland' cruise. On-board activities included themed nights and dinners, plus quizzes that took passengers back to the ship's early years of operation in the 1960s. *Marco Polo* headed through the North Sea to Lerwick (Shetland Isles), thence to Tórshavn (Faroes), where she met up with her older fleet-mate *Azores,* and Reykjavík (Iceland) for a long day's stay. Her passage across

the Atlantic continued, but her call at Tasiilaq (Greenland) had to be cancelled as there was a build-up of over three miles of thick ice outside the port, despite this being a midsummer call. In compensation, passengers were treated to the sight of numerous whales around the ship as *Marco Polo* hove-to off the ice pack.

Plans to take the Cape Farewell Passage also had to be amended due to ice conditions, so *Marco Polo* took the Prins Christianssund passage to Qaqortoq (Greenland), for a full day's anchorage. A call at Narsarsuaq (Greenland) followed transit of the Tunulliarfik Fjord Passage nestling in high mountains amidst seas with thousands of colourful icebergs, then *Marco Polo* made her first landfall in Canada at St John's, Newfoundland after a further two days at sea. There was time to visit Sydney (Nova Scotia), Charlottetown (Prince Edward Island) and Gaspé (Québec), before *Marco Polo* began cruising the St Lawrence River to reach Québec city, some 20 days after leaving London Tilbury on a more adventurous itinerary than her original crossing from Leningrad. A Gala Dinner on board was attended by Chris Coates and John Dennis of CMV and Montréal was reached the following day, where a traditional water tug welcome from *Ocean Pierre Julien* heralded an overnight stay on 13th/14th August. Crowds of sightseers and well-wishers amply illustrated the affection with which *Marco Polo* was held in Canada, and invited guests enjoyed a special luncheon on board on Thursday 13th August. As *Alexandr Pushkin*, *Marco Polo* had previously visited Montréal 114 times on her transatlantic runs, commencing over 49 years previously. Following a superb piece of research by port officials in Montréal, some special guests were located to be brought on board: these were a group of ladies who, over 35 years previously, had acted as

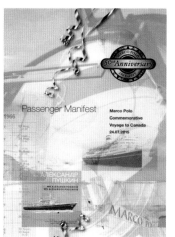

Far left: **The special Luncheon Menu for the event held in Montréal 13th August 2015.** *(CMV Library)*

Left: **A souvenir ship's manifest was given to all passengers to commemorate the voyage.** *(CMV Library)*

Itinerary and nautical mileage

Day	Date	Port	Distance
Friday	24/07/2015	London Tilbury	-
Saturday	25/07/2015	*At Sea*	-
Sunday	26/07/2015	Kirkwall, Orkney Islands	574
Monday	27/07/2015	Tórshavn, Faroe Islands	250
Tuesday	28/07/2015	*At Sea*	-
Wednesday	29/07/2015	Reykjavik, Iceland	547
Thursday	30/07/2015	*At Sea*	-
Friday	31/07/2015	Tasiilaq/Ammassilik, Greenland	414
Saturday	01/08/2015	*At Sea*	-
Sunday	02/08/2015	Qaqortoq, Greenland	390

Day	Date	Port	Distance
Thursday	13/08/2015	Montréal, Québec	139
Friday	14/08/2015	Montréal, Québec	-
Saturday	15/08/2015	Saguenay, Québec	303
Sunday	16/08/2015	*Cruising St Lawrence River*	-
Monday	17/08/2015	Sept Îles, Québec	253
Tuesday	18/08/2015	Havre Saint Pierre	120
Wednesday	19/08/2015	Cap-aux-Meules	268
Thursday	20/08/2015	Corner Brook, Newfoundland	215
Friday	21/08/2015	*Cruising Gulf of St Lawrence*	-
Saturday	22/08/2015	L'Anse aux Meadows, Newfoundland	224

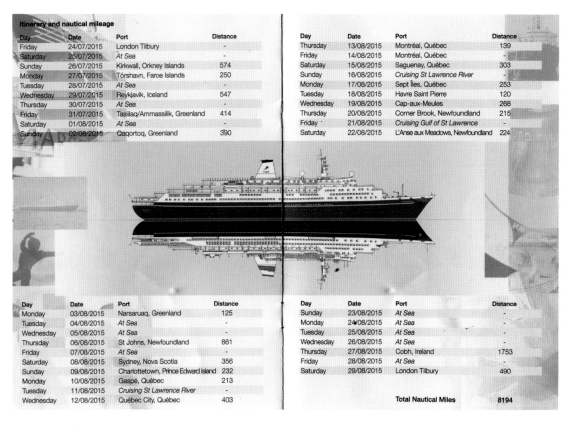

Day	Date	Port	Distance
Monday	03/08/2015	Narsaruaq, Greenland	125
Tuesday	04/08/2015	*At Sea*	-
Wednesday	05/08/2015	*At Sea*	-
Thursday	06/08/2015	St Johns, Newfoundland	861
Friday	07/08/2015	*At Sea*	-
Saturday	08/08/2015	Sydney, Nova Scotia	356
Sunday	09/08/2015	Charlottetown, Prince Edward Island	232
Monday	10/08/2015	Gaspé, Québec	213
Tuesday	11/08/2015	*Cruising St Lawrence River*	-
Wednesday	12/08/2015	Québec City, Québec	403

Day	Date	Port	Distance
Sunday	23/08/2015	*At Sea*	-
Monday	24/08/2015	*At Sea*	-
Tuesday	25/08/2015	*At Sea*	-
Wednesday	26/08/2015	*At Sea*	-
Thursday	27/08/2015	Cobh, Ireland	1753
Friday	28/08/2015	*At Sea*	-
Saturday	29/08/2015	London Tilbury	490
		Total Nautical Miles	**8194**

Top: The souvenir itinerary of the 50th Anniversary cruise wrapping around this wonderful line drawing of the ship with *Alexandr Pushkin* in reflection. *(CMV Library)*

Right: International brochures from France, Mexico, Australia and Germany. *(CMV Library)*

Montréal. During her anniversary year *Marco Polo* sailed 75,024 miles for CMV, a remarkable testimony to the quality of her build and the standards to which she had been consistently maintained throughout her subsequent career.

This voyage again demonstrated the extent of the international recognition enjoyed by *Marco Polo* and, since the corporate restructuring in 2011, helped restate the group's declared aim to take gradual steps to expand and strategically develop CMV's corporate presence in the wider international marketplace. The embryonic USA office had been opened in 2011, but during 2013 and 2014 there was more significant progress towards that goal.

Finding winter markets for their ships has always been a test for shipowners and cruise lines, but if the southern hemisphere could be brought into play, it would be feasible to link the austral summer from November to March with the European summer between April and October, and reposition the ships by what used to be known as 'line voyages'.

The Australian cruise market had long been in CMV's ambitions, but the lack of suitable vessels had precluded previous moves. However, when the opportunity arose to charter the stylish *Astor* from Premicon AG – the German owners that had acquired her following Transocean's demise – plans could at last be put in place. With the main cruise competition sailing from the east coast ports of Sydney and Brisbane,

hostesses in the port to greet and guide passengers aboard *Alexandr Pushkin* prior to her latest voyage or cruise. CMV felt very honoured to host them on board.

Marco Polo cruised back down the St Lawrence River to Saguenay (Québec), where a further event was held for invited guests, and Sept Îles (Québec), prior to a half-day call at Havre Saint Pierre. She anchored off Cap-aux-Meules (Îles de la Madelaine) and managed an overnight stay at Corner Brook (Newfoundland) then reached L'Anse aux Meadows (Newfoundland). The remaining crossing of the Atlantic took four days before *Marco Polo* arrived at Ringaskiddy for Cobh. She finally arrived back at London Tilbury on 29th August after an epic 8,194 nautical mile journey, having visited 19 ports en route.

All passengers were given special mementoes of this memorable cruise in the form of limited-edition pin badges, a commemorative passenger manifest booklet, and a personal copy of the DVD celebrating *Marco Polo's* 50 years of service, which was premiered on board in

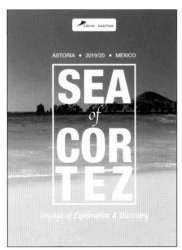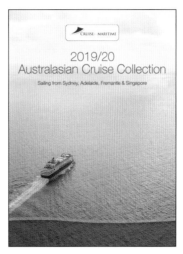

CMV's concept was to echo the CTC operations of the early 1990s and offer the Western Australian market a summer season of cruises from Fremantle, topped and tailed by southbound and northbound voyages. A CMV Australia office was established in Sydney in February 2013 with the inaugural programme of 14 sailings, running from December through to April 2014, going on sale shortly after.

The initial deal with *Astor* was for a three-year charter period intended to cover the austral summer seasons with a European summer deployment in the German-speaking market, where Premicon AG had sold cruises from Bremerhaven and Kiel through their TransOcean Kreuzfahrten tour operation. However, in December 2014, the Global Maritime Group purchased *Astor* and she became the second fully owned vessel of the company. This was a nostalgic move for Chris Coates in particular who, between 1986 and 1988, had served as Sales Executive Manager for Astor Cruises in the UK, during a break in his CTC career. He commented:

I am personally delighted to renew my acquaintance with Astor *– she has always been such an elegant and stylish vessel and I will not be at all surprised if she becomes as much-loved and popular in Australia as she has been in Europe.*

The Australian market did indeed take to *Astor* and she was to spend six consecutive summers in the southern hemisphere. She scored heavily as a premium cruise product, offering a credible alternative to the large resort ships of the mainstream fleets that saw Australia as the final

destination for their older tonnage. Dean Brazier joined the company as Managing Director, Australia, in 2017 and oversaw the transfer of the CMV operation from Sydney to Adelaide, which along with Fremantle makes an efficient home port for the cruise programme. From summer 2019–2020 this will be undertaken by the company's new flagship *Vasco da Gama*, a decision that is, in itself, testimony to the faith and confidence that CMV have in the Australian market. He comments:

We have worked very hard to be innovative in our itineraries, discovering and researching new ports of call and then to be supportive of local suppliers in both South Australia and Western Australia to ensure that our passengers can enjoy their familiar brands on board. My staff and I have also enjoyed being a little inventive with some enhancements to the on-board entertainment programme – celebrity chefs, war historians and the Perth Fringe theatre have all featured recently. We are proud to consider ourselves as Australia's leading independent cruise line.

Scenic river cruises were operated by *Vienna I* seen here in October 2013. *(CMV Library)*

The successful establishment of a consistent summer cruise presence in Australia enabled the UK and USA offices to feature these cruises in their own programmes, and increasing numbers of British and North American passengers began to enjoy the opportunity to cruise 'down under'.

Upon return from the southern hemisphere, *Astor* and now *Vasco da Gama* operate mainly from Bremerhaven and Kiel for the German market under CMV's TransOcean Kreuzfahrten brand. The company's presence in Germany commenced in 2013 with the establishment of a ship management office by the Global Maritime Group, but direct involvement in Germany followed successful negotiations with Munich-based Premicon AG. In January, CMV took over TransOcean Kreuzfahrten including the 600-passenger *Astor's* 7,000-summer-capacity German programme and the company's 17,000-capacity river-cruise programme. The four-ship river-cruise fleet included the 176-passenger *Belvedere*, the 150-passenger *Bellefleur*, the 180-passenger *Bellejour*, and the 80-passenger *Sans Souci,* which collectively operated a comprehensive programme of river cruises on the Rhine, Main, Danube, Mosel, Neckar, Elbe, Oder, Havel, Rhône, and Saône rivers. The river-cruise programme dovetailed with CMV's own river vessel, the 160-passenger *Vienna I,* which operated under the new premium-plus 'Signature River Cruise'

brand. *Astor* was still programmed to operate on the Australian market for CMV during the November–May winter season, based in her home port of Fremantle with capacity for 10,000 passengers.

The new alliance brought together two established cruise lines with popular premium brands and was designed to provide valuable synergies, enhanced distribution, and competitiveness through coordinated and measured sales initiatives. The existing Offenbach-based sales team, headed by the highly respected Klaus Ebner as Director of Sales and Marketing, was retained as part of the new arrangements.

This was a key step, as it gave CMV a presence in Germany, the fastest growing and highest-yielding cruise market in Europe, strengthening international presence in line with the group's strategic development and growth plans. The combined ocean fleet passenger carryings were projected to exceed 70,000 passengers, representing almost 100% growth in volume since the establishment of the company in 2010.

This position in Germany was further strengthened on 31st March 2014 when CMV announced the takeover of the shoreside commercial sales and marketing management of Passat Kreuzfahrten Gmbh through a strategic alliance to facilitate expansion into the growing German cruise market. The following day CMV assumed full control and responsibility for the distribution, marketing, and commercial shoreside management of Passat's premium-rated cruise vessel, the 470-passenger *Delphin,* and her 13,000-capacity year-round cruise programme.

After over 30 years of sterling service to the German market, *Astor* will say 'Auf Wiedersehen' to the German market with a 10-night cruise from Bremerhaven on 14th May 2021.

The 16,631grt *Delphin* was owned by Vishal Cruises Pvt Ltd, and chartered to Passat Kreuzfahrten. She boasted 237 cabins, with a wide range of well-appointed public facilities across seven passenger decks, and was well-equipped for worldwide ocean cruising in the premium sector. Her destinations included Scandinavia and Russia, the British Isles, Greenland, Iceland and the Arctic Circle, the Mediterranean, South America, Antarctica, and Africa. During the summer, *Delphin* operated from the dual home ports of Kiel and Bremerhaven in northern German, but that arrangement only continued until 2015 allowing efforts to be concentrated on the expanded seasonal programme of *Astor* and the river cruises.

Another European cruise market that was of considerable interest to the increasingly acquisitive directors of CMV was France. French cruise passengers have always displayed a strong preference to sail on a specifically French product and, since the demise of the much-loved premium cruise line Croisières Paquet in late 1996, this has only been offered by tour operators chartering international vessels to meet demand on a seasonal basis. One such is Rivages du Monde, a specialist cruise and tour operator from Paris, and in April 2015 it was announced that, from the following summer, CMV's *Azores* was to be sub-chartered to the French operator. The opportunity was also taken to announce that the vessel would be renamed for the 2016 season and therefore the more aptly titled *Astoria* would launch the new cruise programme, based on sailings from Le Havre, Dunkirk, Ostend, Bordeaux, and Marseille. After five years of successful cooperation, *Astoria* will bid adieu to Rivages du Monde, and indeed to France, in September 2020 upon completion of her final summer season of the sub-charter arrangement.

However, CMV has consolidated its French market presence with the announcement in November 2019 that it has established its own sales office in Marseille. A 15-strong team, under Directeur Général Clément Mousset and Director of Marketing and Operations Cedric Rivoire-Perrochat, opened for business on 2nd January 2020. In keeping with the home-market preferences of the French cruise passenger, following her departure from the German market, *Astor* will be renamed and allocated on a year-round schedule of sailings from Le Havre and Marseille, commencing with a 'French Maritime Cities' cruise from Le Havre on 1st May 2021. She will henceforth be known as *Jules Verne*, after the prolific French author (1828–1905), in only the third name-change of her career, stretching back to 1987. Apart from two spells as *Astor*, she was *Fedor Dostoevskiy* in her Soviet and Russian days between 1988 and 1995. Her decks and public rooms are also to be renamed with doubtless some suitable Gallic flair.

In December 2017, Christian Verhounig, CEO and Chairman of CMV, explained that CMV specialised in developing dedicated source markets and, following those already established in the UK and Ireland, Australia, Germany and France, the company was launching an innovative cruise programme aimed exclusively at the Mexican domestic market. Cruceros Marítimos Vacacionales subsequently commenced operations in Mexico and the first sailing with *Magellan* departed from Acapulco in February 2019. A series of eight 7-night cruises followed this inaugural sailing,

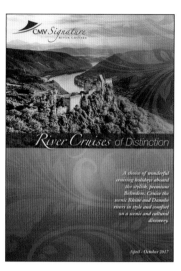

The TransOcean Kreuzfahrten brochure for the 2019/2020 World Cruise of *Astor*. *(CMV Library)*

The Signature River Cruises of Distinction brochure 2017. *(CMV Library)*

topped and tailed by transatlantic positioning voyages.

John Dennis, Vice President Sales and Marketing of the CMV North American sales office had the responsibility for the commercial management and business development of the new Mexican operation, and in April 2019 he was able to announce that a series of 11-night cruises in the Sea of Cortez (also known as The Gulf of California) would be operated by *Astoria* from December 2019. He added:

This is an exciting project that we have been very much looking forward to announcing in close cooperation with the Mexican states of Baja California Sur and Sonora and the (US) State of Arizona – the first opportunity to cruise from Puerto Peñasco. We are thrilled. Not only to be Arizona's de facto cruise line, but also to welcome guests throughout the country and internationally to enjoy the Sea of Cortez experience. With superb airlift into Phoenix and Tucson, we anticipate considerable interest from our international markets.

By the end of this first decade, the stated corporate aim of building a solid, vertically integrated business encompassing a full in-house ship management service offering a high-quality product linked to a strong, recognisable, international brand had come a long way towards fruition.

Chapter four

Magellan
the game changer

By the end of the 2013 season CMV's business had grown consistently in line with expectations since the inaugural year, with strong forward bookings for the 2014 season. Fleet mileage had increased by 54% from 118,267 miles in 2010 to 182,663 in 2013. This track record gave CMV the confidence to maintain the momentum of a growing business by matching capacity to customer demand. The nature of the cruise business is such that long-term planning is required to deliver new ships at the right time to meet growth: contracts have to be agreed, operating plans formulated, itineraries negotiated, pricing fixed and marketing proposals delivered before a cruise can go on sale, so there is a lag between agreeing to acquire a new vessel and her entry into service. It was evident to CMV that additional larger tonnage would be needed from 2015 if growth was not to stall. The search began for an additional vessel to expand the fleet.

At the time the strategy of other cruise lines was evolving to move away from small to mid-sized ships towards significantly larger vessels, bringing economies of scale but offering a very different cruising experience to that enjoyed by CMV's passengers. In autumn 2014 Costa Crociere, part of the Carnival Cruises Group, was in the process of absorbing management of the Spanish Iberocruceros fleet into their structure. Costa Crociere embraced the trend towards larger ships, and deemed *Grand Holiday,* one of their now expanded fleet, to be surplus to requirements as they closed down the Iberocruceros brand. This was an extraordinary opportunity for CMV. *Grand Holiday* had undergone an extensive €55m refit in April 2010 before moving from the USA to join Iberocruceros. Her deployment in the Spanish family holiday market was for a different style of cruise programme to that sought by CMV's loyal passengers, and her internal décor reflected the Mediterranean holiday experience. But she offered the larger capacity that would allow CMV to expand and was in excellent condition. Looking beyond the brasher style of the Iberocruceros product, it was evident that *Grand Holiday* could easily be adapted to the very different tastes of CMV guests.

CMV announced on 3rd November 2014 that *Grand Holiday* would be joining the British fleet as *Magellan* in Spring 2015. Her first season's programme was released the following day.

The new addition to the fleet was named after the Portuguese explorer Ferdinand Magellan, who launched the Armada de Molucca, a Spanish expedition to find a western route to the Spice Islands, on 20th September 1519. After crossing the Atlantic, Magellan discovered the strait that now bears his name before continuing round South

Magellan alongside in the popular port of Eidfjord on 30th August 2015. *(CMV Library)*

America into an ocean he named the Pacific. His fleet was the first to cross the Pacific, calling in the Philippines before reaching his objective, the Spice Islands. The surviving crew finally returned to Spain on 6th September 1522, after completing the first circumnavigation of the world.

The acquisition of *Magellan* was a game changer for CMV. The fleet was already undergoing significant change at the end of 2014 following the premature withdrawal of *Discovery* by her owners in October. *Azores* was earmarked as her more permanent replacement, but her passenger capacity was slightly smaller at 580 compared to the 698 of *Discovery*. The 1985-built *Magellan* was a different proposition altogether.

Magellan had been one of the largest cruise ships in the world when built, but was now seen as a mid-sized ship, although twice the tonnage of *Marco Polo*. *Magellan* offered more cabins than *Astor* and *Marco Polo* combined, and her maximum capacity for 1,452 passengers was almost as much as the two established vessels put together. But CMV saw her as an adults-only ship so in practice the capacity would be around 1,250 passengers. Despite her size, *Magellan* retained the ability to offer the core hallmarks of the CMV brand. Her design was radical, at the cusp of the transition from classic cruise liner to the modern convention, with main restaurants placed immediately below the main passenger deck. Yet she still boasted a starboard promenade, was built as a spacious vessel with exceptionally wide corridors relative to more modern ships, and had plentiful outside seating areas on the traditional wooden decks. Thus, she encapsulated the spirit of the brand in a perfect balance between tradition and modernity, offering the capability of sailing from smaller ports around Britain whilst retaining the characteristic cosiness and intimacy on board.

Magellan would accommodate expansion of the business, but there was still a need to replace the capacity lost through the premature departure of *Discovery* from the fleet in autumn 2014. *Funchal* was not a long-term replacement, but fortunately CMV was able to source *Azores* from Portuscale Cruises of Lisbon. *Azores* was familiar to the German market, having been chartered by Ambiente Kreuzfahrten during 2014, but had been laid up at the end of the season. Although dating back to 1948, *Azores* had previously undergone a radical rebuild to emerge as a boutique cruising vessel, and therefore matched the CMV philosophy perfectly. At 650-passenger capacity she was a different scale to *Magellan*, but a perfect replacement for *Discovery*. Further, she was immediately available and was scheduled to take up her maiden sailing for CMV on 26th January 2015 with a 30-night itinerary from Bristol Avonmouth to the West Indies.

The arrival of *Azores* and *Magellan* would transform CMV's capacity and allow the expansion of the regional programme of sailings, so the benefits could be felt around the country. The introduction of *Magellan* enabled CMV to reprogramme two extra Hull cruises and an additional Bristol Avonmouth sailing, plus a new summer season of sailings from Liverpool and an autumn Mediterranean fly-cruise programme offering a choice of 11-night sailings from Nice and Venice to visit nine classic ports in Greece, Italy and Turkey. The most dramatic expansion was from London Tilbury, where the number of cruises on offer grew from 33 in 2014 to 58 in 2015.

The programme saw *Azores* operating alongside *Marco Polo* for the British market including the seasonal programmes from Liverpool, London Tilbury and Hull, and the experimental 11-night autumn Mediterranean fly-cruise series from Rome and Venice. There would be a second *Marco Polo* 34-night autumn commemorative voyage to Canada. For the winter 2015–2016 season, *Magellan* was earmarked to cruise to the Amazon whilst *Marco Polo* would embark on a new 54-night voyage to Brazil, Argentina and Chile, and Tierra del Fuego. A new 2015 special launch-edition brochure was released on 4th November 2014 with details of *Magellan's* inaugural CMV summer 2015 and her winter 2015–2016 programme, and special introductory fares with savings of up 50% plus a 25% single supplement deal for the solo traveller. This gave the new programme a highly competitive position in the market.

The year began with *Astor* in Australia in the midst of her winter programme, *Marco Polo* heading for her 42-night annual Amazon Cruise from London Tilbury and *Azores* coming out of her lay-up in Lisbon. In the event *Azores* was slightly delayed leaving Lisbon and her maiden departure to the West Indies was switched to Plymouth. She was scheduled to arrive back in Bristol Avonmouth on Wednesday 25th February but was sensibly diverted for an unscheduled call in Lisbon, due to adverse weather and sea conditions. She was able to return on Friday 27th February when sea conditions improved, but the cruise terminated in Portland due to very tight tidal restrictions at Bristol Avonmouth. Unusually her maiden voyage had neither started from, nor returned to, the planned port. The operations team responded to a tricky challenge to get *Azores'* subsequent cruises back on schedule.

Meanwhile, *Magellan* was re-livered with preparatory works being undertaken in Greece prior to sailing to the UK for her naming ceremony at her new home port of London Tilbury. On Wednesday 11th March she took a pilot on board whilst off the Essex coast at around 04:00 and cruised slowly westward up the River Thames to reach her berth at London Tilbury at 08.00, where she was to remain for her four-day

Magellan – the game changer

Top left: The lovely Lido Bar on Columbus Deck 10. *(CMV Library)*

Top right: The spectacular Magellan Show Lounge Decks 8 and 9. *(CMV Library)*

Above: Just the place on a sunny afternoon - the Pool on Columbus Deck 10. *(CMV Library)*

Left: Stylish Captain's Club Lounge on Magellan Deck 9. *(CMV Library)*

Magellan and *Marco Polo* together at London Tilbury on 9th December 2018. *(CMV Library)*

christening celebrations.

The main christening event was held on Thursday 12th March 2015. Cruise Director Richard Sykes introduced and welcomed over 1,200 customer and travel trade guests to the ceremony in *Magellan's* Show Lounge. CMV Chief Executive Christian Verhounig said the growth of the company would not have been possible without the support of assembled guests. He noted that:

Our cruise teams around the world will continue to provide an exceptional service to the travel trade and our colleagues on board will deliver a first-class product and service.

Christian went on to note that *Magellan* was larger than other ships in the fleet, but she retained the intimate feel that had become the trademark of the CMV brand. He concluded:

This is a new, exciting chapter of the CMV success story.

Commercial Director Chris Coates observed that CMV had grown from a base-zero position to having more than 100,000 guests in 2014 and becoming:

...an internationally recognised organisation of considerable substance. Despite a touch economic climate, we have a strong base in the British, German and Australian markets, backed up by a flourishing North American sales office.

Over 75% of *Magellan's* debut 2015 season was already sold out.

Members of the ship's crew and shoreside staff were introduced and welcomed onto the stage. The Master of *Magellan*, Captain Emmanouil Psarrakis, also gave a short speech before the ship's godmother, Gloria Hunniford, was welcomed to the stage for the ship to be blessed and officially renamed. The popular television presenter fitted perfectly with the profile of CMV's customers. She joked:

It's been a big week for cruising and I just want to say a big thank you to Her Majesty the Queen for being my warm-up. THIS is the main event! [referring to the naming ceremony of the *Britannia* two days earlier] *I've even offered to live on board and be a proper godmother.*

A dance performance from Luke Miller and Laura Robinson, the fastest-rising Latin American dance stars in the UK followed the renaming. The dance performance was followed by classical singer Yvonne Howard, hailed by the international press as 'one of the finest singing actresses the country has produced' and pianist Juliet Edwards. The evening culminated in a spectacular firework display, which lit up the Thames, and guests continued to party with the ship's band until well into the night.

Magellan made a hugely positive impression on the visiting guests, who found their cabins to be very spacious and well laid out. Her interior felt modern and stylish, yet she could still offer the traditional British cruising product that lay at the heart of the CMV brand. Although a sizeable vessel with plentiful facilities, she was easy to navigate and not too exhausting to explore.

After two further evening celebrations for invited guests which raised funds for comic relief, *Magellan* sailed on her inaugural cruise from

London Tilbury on 15th March 2015, heading for the Faroe Islands in anticipation of witnessing a total eclipse of the sun on 20th March. *Marco Polo* followed *Magellan* out of Tilbury on 16th March for the pair to rendezvous with fleet sister *Astoria* off the Faroes during the 'Solar Eclipse and Northern Lights Spectacular'.

As *Magellan* headed north on her inaugural sailing, *Astor* was completing a successful winter season in Australia. She largely operated a series of relatively short cruises from Fremantle but had also found time to venture on a 33-night 'Grand Round Australia Voyage' on 27th January. Her 38-night 'Northbound Voyage via Africa' left Fremantle on 16th March and she headed straight out across the Indian Ocean for Cape Town, reaching there on 2nd April. She continued via Namibia, Cape Verde, Casablanca and Lisbon on her way back to London Tilbury. *Astor* was able to offer one 8-night 'Round Britain Discovery' itinerary before she repositioned to Bremerhaven for her summer programme of sailings for TransOcean Kreuzfahrten. This offered the full range of popular CMV itineraries to Britain, the Fjords and the Baltic, with several sailings operating from Kiel. Her season finished in Antwerp on 6th October and she was laid up in Vlissingen two days later.

CMV's strong links with the travel trade were enhanced by the opportunities to partake in one of 15 ship visits at seven different ports featuring *Azores*, *Magellan* and *Marco Polo* during 2015.

Magellan spent a short spring season operating a joint programme of itineraries from Newcastle and Dundee, before returning in June to home port at London Tilbury for the remainder of the year. During the summer she celebrated her 30th birthday with a visit to her build site at Aalborg on 16th July as part of a 'Scandinavian Cities & Fairy Tales Cruise'. She was greeted by a cannon salute as hundreds of Danes turned out to greet her. It was the first time *Magellan* had returned to her birthplace since she was built. Some 3,800 local people had been involved in her construction as the then most expensive passenger ship ever constructed. The Mayor of Aalborg organised an emotional reunion for some 200 of her builders, engineers and architects, which included a ship tour and lunch on board hosted by Chris Coates. Whilst her design and hull form remained unchanged, *Magellan's* interior was largely

Top right: **Astor** heading northbound after a successful season in Australian waters. *(CMV Library)*

Middle right: **Magellan**'s elegant Waldorf Restaurant located aft on Amundsen Deck 8. *(CMV Library)*

Bottom right: For those "Wee Small Hours of the Morning" - Sinatra's Lounge Magellan Deck 9. *(CMV Library)*

A superb aerial view of *Magellan* showing her extensive deck space. *(FotoFlite)*

unrecognisable to those who had built her.

Azores was able to pick up *Discovery*'s itineraries from Bristol Avonmouth, Hull, and Liverpool, and ended her maiden season with an 11-night 'Mediterranean Classics & Treasures' itinerary that took her from Livorno and round the Adriatic to Venice. When *Magellan* switched back to London Tilbury, *Marco Polo* was released to enhance the regional programme of itineraries from Newcastle (Tyne) and Leith/Rosyth, before she returned to finish her season at London Tilbury.

After returning from her maiden cruise, *Magellan* sailed north to spend the spring operating from Newcastle (Tyne), taking advantage of proximity to the Fjords with a series of 'Majestic' cruises. She then underwent a short refit so that her facilities could be upgraded to include a well-stocked library, a purpose-built bridge and cards room and an outside garden area on the Magellan Deck.

Marco Polo retained her role as the London Tilbury-based vessel for the early part of 2015, undertaking her annual 42-night 'Amazon Cruise' before returning for a full spring programme of classic itineraries from the port. She repositioned to Newcastle at Whitsun for a short sequence of three cruises, which omitted the call at Dundee as CMV matched capacity to demand from Scotland. *Marco Polo* still offered three itineraries from Leith and Rosyth, before she returned to Tilbury for her 36-night 'Commemorative Canada & Greenland Cruise', marking the 50th anniversary of her original transatlantic crossing for the Baltic Steamship Company. Demand was sufficient to justify a repeat of this trip in the autumn, as many Columbus Club members sought to celebrate a momentous anniversary for one of their favourite ships. At the end of the season *Marco Polo* retired to Vlissingen for a short refit, where she had new carpets fitted and furniture reupholstered.

After a 15-night voyage to the 'Canary Islands & Madeira' on 23rd October, *Magellan* returned to London Tilbury for her first long cruise for the company – a 35-night 'Treasures of the West Indies' itinerary, which included 10 nights at sea with a call in the Azores on the outward journey, and nine calls on successive days in the Caribbean Islands.

Magellan was chosen to host the prestigious Cruise Lines International Association (CLIA) Annual Dinner at London Tilbury on Thursday 10th December 2015. Demand was high for this highlight of the CLIA annual calendar. The event comprised a Cruise Forum featuring key travel agents, and a Cruise Networking Forum for CLIA Executive Partners, ports and cruise executives. A cocktail reception in the Captain's Club preceded a formal black tie six-course dinner for 500 guests in the Waldorf and Kensington dining rooms. The formal agenda concluded with the annual Cruise Excellence Awards presentation ceremony, which was held in the Magellan Show Lounge. The River Thames was closed for 20 minutes for a celebratory firework display which finished a memorable evening in spectacular style.

The addition of *Azores* and *Magellan* enabled CMV to radically increase capacity from London Tilbury in 2015, but at the same time improve itineraries from regional ports so that all customers benefitted.

Magellan left London Tilbury for the first of her longer winter cruises on 5th January 2016 for a 42-night cruise to the Amazon. This trip promised to be a real adventure, away from the cold and wet of a British winter. She headed for Lisbon and then out into the Atlantic, calling at Madeira before reaching the Amazon basin. From here she sailed up the river, visiting Manaus, Parintins, Santarém and Boca da Valéria, giving guests the unique opportunity to take in the tropical rainforest wildlife. The Caribbean was next on the itinerary, with Grenada, St. Vincent, Bequia, St. Lucia and Barbados featuring on the agenda, before *Magellan* headed for home with the transatlantic crossing broken by two calls in the Azores.

Magellan had already proved to be a popular success for CMV in 2015, and by March 2016 bookings for the year were already at 85% of available capacity. Increasing recognition of the quality, value and variety of the CMV product, with an unmatched range of regional departure ports, put the company in a position of strength. This positive outlook encouraged the company to consider the early provision of additional tonnage for 2017 to accelerate their midterm growth plans. The statistics provided further impetus to expansion. Record numbers of passengers took cruises from the UK and Ireland in 2015, with the highest growth rate of any European market, and this growth showed no sign of letting-up. And CMV's prime target market was expanding, as 17,000 people reached the age of 50 each week. It was hugely important to CMV that capacity kept pace with this growing market, without sacrificing the core characteristics that had made the brand so successful. CMV's growing international recognition and sound business model had encouraged the group to invest confidently in a rapidly growing market and build the business as a strong value-based 'independent' alternative.

The search for a suitable ship took CMV back to Carnival Corporation, from whom they were eventually able to acquire the 1989-built 63,786grt *Pacific Pearl*, then sailing for their subsidiary, P&O Cruises Australia. She was already a popular vessel in the UK market having previously cruised in local waters for some 13 years for P&O Cruises and Ocean Village. This familiarity made her a very attractive proposition for CMV and would significantly aid the marketing and sales effort. Developing the 'Explorer' theme further, *Pacific Pearl* was to be renamed *Columbus* and join the

fleet in April 2017. *Columbus* would be dedicated to the UK cruise market and home port in London Tilbury to further enhance the CMV reputation for delivering a more traditional scenic British cruising experience. At 63,786grt and with an impressive space ratio, she could carry about 1,400 mainly British passengers, accommodated in 775 cabins (including 150 dedicated single-occupancy cabins) and become the new flagship of the CMV ocean fleet. Her arrival would allow CMV to increase its presence in UK and international markets and help the group deliver overall capacity of 120,000 passengers in 2017. Although primarily sailing as an adults-only vessel she would offer two experimental multi-generational sailings in August 2017 for all age groups.

The acquisition of *Columbus* was announced on 7th March 2016 and bookings for the 2017 season went live on 31st March with a special 2017 launch-edition preview brochure released on 7th April.

After her winter docking period in Greece, *Azores*, now renamed *Astoria* to bring her in line with CMV's smaller ship offering alongside *Astor*, headed to Bristol Avonmouth on Thursday, 10th March 2016 to begin her spring programme of departures. Her first sell-out Easter trip departed on 21st March for a 7-night 'Scottish Islands & Emerald Isle' cruise. A week later she headed south for a 15-night cruise to Leixoes (for Oporto), Lisbon, two popular islands in the Azores, and the Spanish port of La Coruña before returning to Bristol.

With the enhanced additional capacity offered by *Magellan* there were opportunities to deploy the fleet more creatively in 2016. The French cruise market was underdeveloped relative to that in the UK and Germany. French operator Rivages du Monde was strongly established in the river-cruise market, offering a range of itineraries in Europe, Burma, Russia, and South America. Looking to expand into the maritime cruise market, they agreed to take *Astoria* on charter for the summer season from 11th May. She spent the first two months sailing from channel ports before heading up to Norway for the high summer and the Mediterranean for the autumn. *Astoria's* travels took her around Italy, Greece and the Aegean before she competed a lengthy autumn programme in Barcelona

The Taverner's Bar stands ready to provide enjoyment for another evening's guests. *(CMV Library)*

on 10th November.

Astor followed her well established and popular itineraries in Australia during the winter before her 38-night journey from Fremantle to London Tilbury via South Africa positioned her for a summer season with TransOcean, where she home-ported at Bremerhaven, Hamburg and Kiel, but also found time to offer two cruises from Genoa.

Magellan split her year between sailings from London Tilbury and a short spring season from Newcastle with linked itineraries from Dundee, again enabling Marco Polo to cover London Tilbury during the spring and Hull, Newcastle and Leith during the summer. Marco Polo was able to add sailings from Greenock, Liverpool and Bristol Avonmouth in an expanded autumn regional programme. CMV celebrated the 50th anniversary of Marco Polo's first transatlantic crossing as the Russian liner Alexandr Pushkin on 13th April 2016. That historic trip from Leningrad (now St. Petersburg) for Québec and Montréal via Helsinki, Copenhagen and London Tilbury was the first regular Russian transatlantic service since

1909 and also the first to Canada. Alexandr Pushkin was transformed into Marco Polo in 1993 and was still a regular visitor to St. Petersburg, with her visit after the anniversary on 8th May during a 'Baltic Cities and St. Petersburg' cruise from London Tilbury.

By November 2016, the 2017 programme of cruises was more than 70% sold. Magellan and Marco Polo took a break from their schedules and went to Amsterdam for dry-docking as part of their routine maintenance programmes. Magellan had a brand new Taverner's Pub added to her facilities – a traditional British-style pub capable of screening sports events and featuring Fosters, Spitfire, and Double Stout on draft. The Taverner's Pub would be open throughout the day and evening, as the perfect venue for a drink and conversation, or for a nightcap. It replaced the former Scott's Nightclub, with the late-night disco moved to the Captain's Club. Both returned to sell-out festive programmes, with Magellan heading for London Tilbury and Marco Polo to Bristol Avonmouth.

Chapter five

The maiden world cruise

The addition of *Magellan* to the fleet enabled CMV to plan the first 'Grand Round the World Cruise' for January 2017. Long-distance itineraries were not new. CMV was by now well-experienced in offering a more relaxed recreation of the traditional 'Liner' sailings between London Tilbury and Fremantle at the start and end of the Australian summer with *Astor*. Guests could make a complete circumnavigation of the globe by combining the outward and return journeys with an extended stay in Australia. And *Marco Polo's* popular winter itineraries to the Amazon were an established fixture in the calendar, dating back to the company's first season in 2010, with *Magellan* adding to this series in January 2016. A full-world cruise represented a very different scale of venture in terms of sales, management, on-board organisation and the entertainment proposition for a journey of 120-nights duration.

The flagship *Magellan* was allocated to the new adventure, and the sales and promotional effort began some 18-months before her scheduled departure from London Tilbury. This was not a spontaneous cruise decision, but with prices starting from £8,999, or just £75 per person per night, the four-month cruise represented excellent value for money. Nine shorter cruise sector options were also made available, based on itineraries from Auckland, Sydney, Hong Kong and Singapore.

Those opting for the full *Magellan* 'Maiden Grand Round the World Cruise' would circumnavigate the globe via the West Indies, a transit of the Panama Canal, French Polynesia, Australasia, South East Asia and the Far East, India, the Red Sea, Suez Canal, the Holy Land, and the Mediterranean, before returning to London Tilbury on Friday 5th May 2017. There were also options for European customers to join *Magellan* at Amsterdam and return there at the end of the cruise.

The extent of the heightened activity required showed itself particularly in the Shore Excursion Department, where Michelle Lupino, Head of Shore Excursion and Itinerary Planning, together with her five staff, commenced the planning in Autumn 2015 for the extensive shore excursion programme that would be offered to passengers throughout the 38-port itinerary. Having considerable experience producing Round World and Grand Voyage tour schedules in her previous life at P&O, prior to joining CMV in 2009, Michelle was able to reactivate contacts with a network of agents worldwide and was especially keen to provide Magellan passengers with overland tour opportunities. A three-day visit to Angkor Wat, Cambodia from Chan May in Vietnam on 26th March 2017, which had participants re-joining the ship in Phu My was the first to be offered. Of the 168 excursions available, the best sellers were The 'Lost' City of Petra from Aqaba and Luxor & The Valley of the Kings from Safaga. A special 20-page advance mini-edition 'World Cruise' brochure promoted the World Cruise and highlighted options available in conjunction with *Astor's* 2016 and 2017 voyage programme between the UK and Australia.

Astor would leave London Tilbury on 16th October 2016 for her traditional 46-night voyage via the West Indies, a transit of the Panama Canal, French Polynesia and New Zealand to arrive in Sydney on 1st December, and passengers had the option to return on *Magellan* as she began to head north from the midpoint of her circumnavigation from Sydney on 23rd February 2017. As an alternative, *Magellan's* 49-night southbound World Cruise voyage sailed from London Tilbury on 5th January 2017 to arrive in Sydney on 23rd February, giving the option to return on *Astor's* northbound voyage from Fremantle via South Africa on 15th March 2017 to arrive back at London Tilbury on 23rd April 2017. Combination early booking fares started from £6,079 or just £69 per person per night, for an 88-night voyage coupled with the chance to spend three weeks in Australia.

In August 2016 CMV announced that the World Cruise would be repeated in 2018, with *Columbus* being the new flagship vessel of choice. *Columbus* had specifically been built for deep-sea ocean cruising and offered the space and comfort that made her the ideal ship for such an epic circumnavigation of the globe.

The 121-night itinerary would leave London Tilbury on 5th January

Top right: **Angkor Wat, Cambodia (CMV Library)**

Middle right: **Petra, Jordan (CMV Library)**

Bottom right: **Sydney Harbour bridge (CMV Library)**

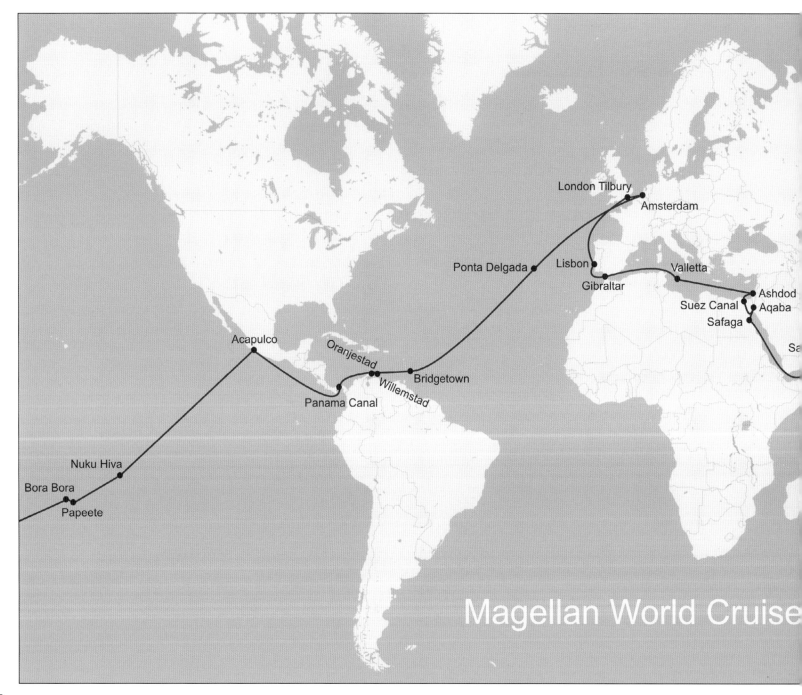

London Tilbury

Amsterdam

Ponta Delgada

Lisbon

Valletta

Gibraltar

Ashdod

Suez Canal

Aqaba

Safaga

Acapulco

Oranjestad

Willemstad

Bridgetown

Panama Canal

Nuku Hiva

Bora Bora

Papeete

Magellan World Cruise

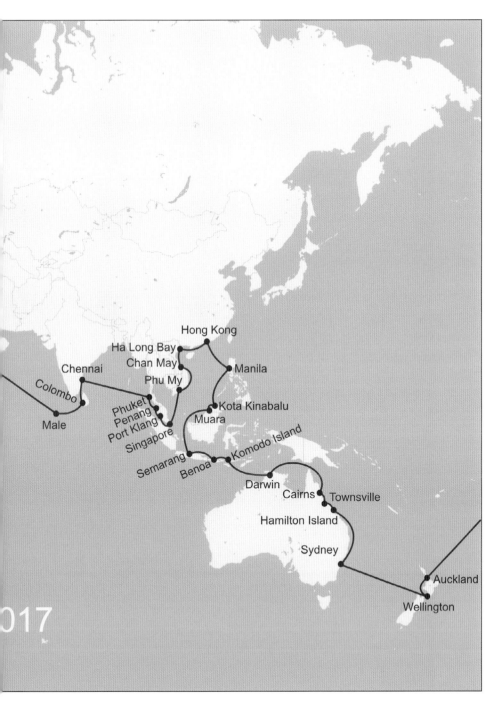

Hong Kong
Ha Long Bay
Chan May
Chennai
Phu My
Colombo
Manila
Phuket
Penang
Kota Kinabalu
Male
Port Klang
Muara
Singapore
Komodo Island
Semarang
Benoa
Darwin
Cairns
Townsville
Hamilton Island
Sydney
Auckland
Wellington
017

2018 and visit four continents, three oceans and 40 ports of call including Tahiti, Auckland, Sydney, Shanghai, Hong Kong, Singapore and Dubai, with transits of both the Panama and Suez canals. *Columbus'* departure would mark the 20th anniversary of her inaugural world cruise as *Arcadia*.

Michelle Lupino, ironically, had worked on the excursion programme for that cruise in 1998 and so especially enjoyed putting together a next generation of tours for *Columbus* passengers. The overland options had expanded and additionally featured a four-day tour from Shanghai on 17 March 2018 that covered Shanghai, the Terracotta Warriors at X'ian and Beijing and returned to the ship in Hong Kong. Also offered was a three-day excursion taking in the Taj Mahal at Agra in India which left in Cochin on 8th April and reunited the participants with *Columbus* in Mumbai on 10th April.

The 2018 World Cruise went on sale on 19th August 2016 and again offered exceptional value. With an early booking 'save up to 25% plus buy one get one half price' offer, guests seeking to escape the British winter in style and comfort could sail for as little as £8,275 per person, the equivalent of around £68 per day. There were also free twin-cabin upgrades for early bookers. This fare, based on two people sharing a twin cabin, included delicious full-board cuisine, afternoon teas and late-night snacks, Captain's cocktail parties, deck parties, self-service tea and coffee between 06:00 and midnight, big show entertainment, cabarets and classical interludes, daytime activities and leisure facilities, guest speakers and arts and crafts, porterage of luggage from port to cabin and port taxes. And there were 150 cabins available on board *Columbus* for solo travellers with just a 25% supplement on the equivalent category twin-share prices as CMV continued their policy of not penalising independent single travellers

An interesting footnote is that the overland excursion options continue to expand and are now included on the southbound and northbound voyages between the UK and Australia whilst the Grand Africa and Indian Ocean Voyage aboard Marco Polo in January 2020 had ten such tours, including safaris, all of which sold out rapidly.

Chapter six

Introducing Columbus

Columbus alongside in Amsterdam on 26th August 2017. *(CMV Library)*

CMV took delivery of their new flagship *Columbus* in Singapore on Wednesday 12th April 2017. She arrived at the Singapore Cruise Centre in her P&O Cruises Australia livery as *Pacific Pearl* at the end of her farewell voyage from Australia, before transferring to the Sembcorp Marine Shipyard to complete the required handover formalities as the renamed and reflagged *Columbus*.

Over 300 crew members and 100 specialist outfitters joined *Columbus* for her scheduled departure from Singapore on 19th April. They completed the required maritime formalities, including reclassification and provisioning works, before embarking on an empty ballast voyage via the Suez Canal to the Damen Shipyard in Rotterdam. Much of the refurbishment and modification work was completed on the voyage before *Columbus* reached Rotterdam on Saturday 13th May, to undertake a three-week dry dock and complete her extensive upgrade.

The works included adapting *Columbus'* lounge configuration to match her new role as an adults-only ship. The existing children's areas and teenage centre were converted into the Columbus Observation Lounge, Trumps & Aces Card and Bridge Room, the Ship's Library, and a Crafter's Studio. The existing large casino was also scaled down into a combined Captain's Club and Casino, whilst the existing Captain's Lounge was converted into the Taverner's Pub.

Columbus crossed the North Sea on completion of the works, arriving in London Tilbury on Monday 5th June in readiness for her renaming ceremony. Angela Rippon CBE accepted the invitation to be godmother for the new addition to the fleet. She was a highly appropriate choice, popular with guests as one of the most recognisable British journalists from her broadcast career of over 50 years. Angela received her CBE for her charity work in the field of Alzheimer's Disease and dementia.

The glittering naming ceremony was held at *Columbus'* new home port at the London Cruise Terminal, Tilbury on Thursday 8th June. There was no champagne wasted as Angela Rippon pulled a cord to unveil a plaque in the Palladium Show Lounge with the traditional words:

I rename this ship Columbus. May God bless her and all who sail in her.

Acknowledging the vessel's long and colourful past with many cruise lines, she said:

This beautiful ship Columbus is named after a man whose courage, sense of adventure and perseverance led him to discover the Americas in 1492. He didn't just see the world, he opened up the New World to travel and to commerce. And this Columbus will do the same – opening up new horizons, new destinations for travellers, leaving its own footprint in the places that it visits, making a lasting impression on the lives of those who share their time and experiences with each other aboard this very special and quite superb flagship of the Cruise & Maritime Voyages line.

She told a delighted audience of the media, travel trade and VIP Columbus Club customers:

I look forward to offering Columbus the same respect as my own godchildren.

Angela reminded the audience that Columbus discovered the New World of America on 12th October 1492, noting that 12th October was her own birthday. The evening culminated in a spectacular firework display, with *Columbus'* decks crowded with guests taking in the spectacle. More than £4,200 was raised by guests for the Essex-based charity Havens Hospices.

Commercial Director Chris Coates, noted that the arrival of *Columbus* allowed CMV to be on course to carry close to 120,000 passengers cruising from the UK in 2018, which gave the company a remarkable 10% share of the market. With strong support from the UK travel trade, over 95% of *Columbus'* 2017 cruise programme had already been sold, as had an extraordinary 40% of 2018 capacity.

Columbus left London Tilbury on her maiden 3-night cruise to Amsterdam and Antwerp on Sunday 11th June, in glorious sunshine to the accompaniment of a brass band and confetti cannons. She was based at London Tilbury for the remainder of 2017, offering a classic mixture of popular CMV itineraries from 3 to 15 nights duration, with the highlight being a new 47-night 'Cuba, Belize & Central Caribbean' departure on 29th October which included calls at 15 Caribbean ports in addition to the Azores and Madeira.

The company's adults-only stance was a popular characteristic of the fleet, but many regular guests stated they wanted to show their families why a cruise with CMV was so special for them, and asked if they could bring their family away with them during the school holidays. CMV responded with two multi-generational cruises during the school holiday period, with an emphasis on family fun to enable families to spend quality time together. Life was made a little easier for families with special drinks packages, popular films, games and competitions. The response to the 2017 experiment on board *Columbus* was highly supportive, with 150 children joining a 7-night cruise to the Norwegian Fjords on 4th August and 180 heading to the 'Canary Islands and Madeira' a week later. So the

programme was expanded in 2018, to include eight such cruises from London Tilbury, Liverpool and Bristol.

The programme of themed cruises for 2017 included a 15-night Easter Cruise from Bristol Avonmouth on board *Marco Polo* to the Azores and Madeira, featuring 'Dad's Army' vicar Frank Williams and TV funny man John Archer. *Magellan* sailed from London Tilbury for three nights to Amsterdam and Antwerp with sixties pop legends 'The Swinging Blue Jeans', 'The Dreamers' and top Beatles tribute band 'The Cheatles'. She followed this with a 5-night Medieval Cities trip which cruised the River Seine up to Rouen with 'Carry On' stars of yesteryear Anita Harris, Valerie Leon and Jacki Piper. *Columbus* got in on the action with a 7-night cruise from London Tilbury for lovers of antiques, who could join experts Henry Sandon and Caroline Hawley to visit the Scottish Islands and Faroes. The final themed cruise was a trip back to childhood with TV Legends Valerie Singleton of 'Blue Peter', Mick Robertson of 'Magpie', and Floella Benjamin from 'Play School' and 'Playaway'. This cruise was once more on *Columbus* from London Tilbury for 15 nights to the Canary Islands and Madeira. Passengers and crew were astonished, alarmed and finally delighted when a Dalek made a surprise appearance on board, introduced with smoke and lighting effects. The Dalek had been smuggled on board in great secrecy, but Mike Hall noted that although CMV was happy to take extraterrestrials on board, in future they must pay the fare and have the right documentation. Mike expressed sympathy for the Dalek's cabin steward.

Magellan hosted a 'Cricket Legends' theme during a 6-night 'Medieval Cities and River Seine' cruise from London Tilbury on 24th October. The strong line-up fielded former England and past county cricket legends from Essex and Kent, with popular TV presenter Nick Hancock on hand to see fair play. Guests watched big-screen cricket highlights, a 'Question of Cricket Challenge' with team representatives of former players from Essex and Kent (including Chris Cowdrey, Alan Wells, John Lever, Ray East, Don Topley and Ken McEwan), and Chris Cowdrey was interviewed about his experiences by Nick Hancock during a popular 'audience with' session.

Astor arrived in Fremantle on 8th December 2017 and immediately embarked on her established winter programme of cruises from the port, including two long trips to Bali. Passengers and crew on board *Astor* honoured the memory of ANZAC soldiers during a 4-night 'WW1 Memorial' themed cruise, which departed from Fremantle on 21st January 2018. *Astor* sailed into King George Sound, Albany, on Tuesday 23rd January in

Top left: **Raffles, an attractive lounge bar on Promenade Deck 6.** *(CMV Library)*

Middle left: **Club Oasis aft on Columbus Deck 8.** *(CMV Library)*

Bottom left: **Lido Deck 12 for the sun lovers.** *(CMV Library)*

time for guests to witness a special dawn service from a unique vantage point off Middleton Beach. Captain Andrey Lesnichiy and the ship's officers joined passengers for the laying of a wreath and a minute's silence between 04.00 and 05.30 in the vicinity of the Mount Clarence national memorial and Middleton Beach. Passengers had the option to attend a dusk memorial service, complete with the playing of 'The Last Post', on Mount Clarence and a 'Firing of the Cannon' ceremony. *Astor* repositioned to Adelaide from 17th February before returning to Fremantle on 12th March for the 40-night northbound journey to London Tilbury via South Africa. An overnight 'Welcome Europe' cruise took her to Bremerhaven for the TransOcean season, which also featured departures from Hamburg and Kiel, with three charters in the high season from the latter port. Her itineraries concluded with a short cruise to Antwerp so she could enter dry dock at Vlissingen at the end of September.

CMV's original plans had been to withdraw *Astoria* at the end of the 2017 season following the arrival of *Columbus*, but when the opportunity arose to combine a spring and autumn programme for CMV with her second season of summer programmes for Rivages du Monde there was great enthusiasm for her retention. Her spring home was London Tilbury, whence *Astoria* commenced a programme of six departures on 8th March with a 6-night 'Springtime Break and River Seine Experience' cruise. *Astoria* became the first vessel to use the new cruise terminal at Visby, also known as the Copenhagen Malmo Port (CMP), when she called on 16th April during a 9-night 'Hidden Baltic Treasures and Kiel Canal' cruise from London Tilbury. Construction of the new 340 metre berth had begun in 2016, and CMV became regular visitors after this maiden call. This groundbreaking trip was followed by a maiden two-day call for *Astoria* in Fort William during a new 14-night 'Scottish Lochs, Glens, Islands and Ireland' itinerary from London Tilbury on 25th April. She was the first cruise vessel to berth at the port at the start of the 2018 season, and a special plaque exchange ceremony was held on 26th April to commemorate the occasion. Passengers were greeted by pipers, a Scottish Country Dancing demonstration, and a talk on Lochaber Geopark to make this a truly special welcome.

Astoria repositioned to Le Havre on 6th May and spent the summer with a succession of European departures from ports as diverse as Dunkirk, Tromsø and Reykjavík. Increasing market demand encouraged CMV to add a new late summer and autumn 2018 programme from Poole and Portsmouth on *Astoria*. *Astoria* made her maiden call at Poole on 31st August to inaugurate the new programme, and in doing so became the largest cruise ship ever to use the new South Quay cruise berth. The schedules featured three departures from Poole plus two 'open jaw' cruise

combination options with return coach transfer back from Portsmouth to Poole. Highlights included the chance to watch the Bournemouth International Air Show from anchor during a 3-night weekend cruise to Rouen, and a special overnight Captain's Gala Cruise to Portsmouth, which included a rare circumnavigation of the Isle of Wight. The programme of sailings from Poole and Portsmouth was supported by special Pullman Express coach services from pick-up points across Dorset, Hampshire and Sussex, together with a direct link from London Victoria. After a final 12-night 'Land of the Northern Lights' cruise from Portsmouth, *Astoria* was laid up for the winter at the Damen Shipyard in Vlissingen.

Columbus departed from London Tilbury on Friday 5th January on her first 121-night 'Grand Round the World Cruise' for CMV, marking the 20th anniversary of her first circumnavigation of the globe as *Arcadia*. She enhanced the CMV brand further in the long cruise market as she had been built specifically for this kind of voyage. Her itinerary would take in a lot more of the world than Christopher Columbus himself had envisaged when he crossed the Atlantic in 1492.

Columbus' 2018 itinerary differed from that offered by *Magellan*. The transatlantic journey still started from London Tilbury and Amsterdam, with calls in Lisbon and Funchal in 2018 replacing the more northerly route via the Azores of 2017. Bridgetown was again the first port of call in the Caribbean before *Columbus* headed for the Panama Canal. But *Columbus* sailed straight out into the Pacific after the canal transit, with broadly the same route across the Pacific, but with an additional call in Moorea Island in 2018, before making landfall in Auckland in New Zealand. *Columbus* omitted Wellington from her antipodean itinerary, but on the northbound leg was able to add calls in Shanghai and Dubai to established visits to Hong Kong, Manila and Singapore, as she took a more direct route through South East Asia. The 121-night 38-call programme of 2018 compared to the 120-night 42-call itinerary of 2017.

The return of *Columbus* released *Astoria* to head for her Continental summer with Rivages du Monde, as *Columbus* became the London Tilbury-based vessel for the remainder of the year. She offered a sequence of classic 7- to 15-night CMV itineraries throughout the season, with three more 'multi-generational' trips during the school summer holidays. Demand was sufficiently strong to sustain regular departures from London Tilbury right through the autumn. Tapping into the pre-Christmas market, *Columbus* ventured to Europe with a succession of highly popular 'Christmas Market and Festive Getaway' short breaks. Her Christmas was spent on a 15-night cruise to the Canaries and Madeira.

Magellan began her cruise season from London Tilbury on 8th December 2017 with a series of festive events before spending Christmas and New Year on a 21-night 'Cape Verde, Madeira & Canaries' itinerary. With the world cruise now picked up by *Columbus*, *Magellan* ventured to the Amazon, West Indies and Azores on a 42-night itinerary, which included cruising deep up the River Amazon. She then settled into a programme of cruises from London Tilbury and Amsterdam, including a multi-generational Easter trip to the River Seine where she passed *Marco Polo* early on 5th April, until the return of *Columbus* enabled *Magellan* to reposition to Newcastle to become the springtime vessel sailing both from the Tyne and Dundee. The summer was spent offering six departures from Liverpool and Dublin, before *Magellan* continued her anti-clockwise route round Britain to serve Bristol Portbury from 27th August. At the end of October she made one further sailing from London Tilbury as she departed in search of the Northern Lights, leaving in tandem with *Columbus* on a cricket-themed sailing to Antwerp, before heading to the Damen Shipyard in Amsterdam for her annual dry-docking in anticipation of a busy festive season ahead.

Regional ports were also served by *Marco Polo* in 2018, emerging from winter dry dock in Amsterdam to pick up an early season programme from Bristol Avonmouth on 31st March, which included a trip to Spain for the Seville fiesta. A couple of departures from Cardiff maintained the Welsh connection, until *Marco Polo* repositioned round to Harwich and then Hull for an early summer programme from 17th June. A 21-night itinerary for an 'Arctic & Greenland Expedition Voyage' from Harwich was perfectly matched to *Marco Polo's* small-ship cruising capabilities, and this was followed from London Tilbury with an imaginative 17-night 'North Cape, White Sea & Murmansk' departure. *Marco Polo* was not finished with long itineraries as she headed west for a 30-night 'Canada in the Fall' cruise on 5th September and a similar length journey to the West Indies and Azores, before ending the as she had begun, at Bristol Avonmouth.

CMV used the opening of the ITB Berlin Travel Show and the Seatrade Cruise Global conference in Fort Lauderdale to announce the addition of sixth ship to their fleet on 7th March. The company had again agreed a deal with Carnival Corporation to take *Pacific Eden* from P&O Cruises Australia to be deployed and dedicated to both the German and Australasian cruise markets from 2019. The ship would operate under CMV's German brand, TransOcean Kreuzfahrten, between May and October, home-porting from both Bremerhaven and Kiel. After a classic 'Liner' voyage to the southern hemisphere she would spend the Australian summer from December to March sailing from Fremantle (Perth) and Adelaide, offering a more traditional scenic cruising experience. The 'Liner' voyages would be open to international guests and marketed by CMV's UK, North American and wider global marketing teams. *Pacific Eden* would join

CMV's fleet with delivery in Singapore in early April 2019, followed by a short docking period to include livery change, rebrand and some preparatory works, before she positioned westbound to Northern Europe via the Suez on her inaugural voyage.

Pacific Eden came with a rich heritage and a strong maritime pedigree. She was launched in 1994 by Holland America Line as the innovative *Statendam*, the first of a series of vessels of this design. At 55,820grt and with an impressive space ratio, she could carry 1,150 passengers accommodated in 630 cabins (including 100 singles and 149 balcony suites and cabins with an 80% ocean-view ratio). Her stylish, traditional design fitted well with the CMV brand and she had the benefit of having undergone a major refurbishment in 2015. The planned deployment would absorb the growth potential in the German and Australian markets as part of CMV's strategy of expanding international business and increase overall capacity to just below 150,000 ocean-cruise passengers in 2019.

Klaus Ebner, Head of Marketing and Sales at TransOcean Kreuzfahrten, saw the ability to significantly increase capacity for guests with the new ship and her wide range of facilities, and to be able to offer even more exciting and varied itineraries. Dean Brazier, Managing Director of CMV Australia, observed that *Astor* had been an enormously successful and very popular cruise product in Australia and the new ship would significantly broaden CMV's distribution base, raise corporate profile and service growing demand with the capacity increase. He saw exciting times ahead.

Continuing the established naming theme, four distinguished explorers were shortlisted for the ship's new name, with travel trade and Columbus Club members invited to cast their vote. The shortlist included *Vasco da Gama, Pytheas, Henry Hudson* and *Amerigo Vespucci*. Christian Verhounig, CEO and Chairman, announced on 20th March that the winner was *Vasco da Gama* with 46% of the thousands of votes received.

Vasco da Gama was a Portuguese nobleman, navigator and explorer, famous for being the first European to reach India by sea. After thousands of lives and dozens of vessels lost in shipwrecks and attacks in search of this passage, da Gama successfully landed in Calicut on 20th of May 1498. In doing so, he connected the Atlantic Ocean with the Indian Ocean and the Western World with the Orient, paving the way for an age of global commerce and European establishment in Asia. His outward and return journey around the Cape of Good Hope was at the time the longest ocean voyage ever undertaken, a distance equal to the equatorial circumference of the Earth, being about 24,000 miles. He successfully conducted three such voyages, and also served as the Second Viceroy of Portuguese India.

The style of Columbus

Top left: **The Pool and Big Screen on Lido Deck 12.** *(CMV Library)*

Top right: **The Waterfront Restaurant on Promenade Deck 7.** *(CMV Library)*

Above: **The Dome Observatory and Nightclub is perched high up on Sun Deck 14.** *(CMV Library)*

Left: **The spacious Atrium is the centre of the ship and ranges through three decks.** *(CMV Library)*

Chapter seven

Continued growth in 2019 as Vasco da Gama joins the fleet

Vasco da Gama inbound to London Tilbury on 6th June 2019. *(CMV Library)*

Demand for the UK cruise season was sufficiently buoyant to encourage CMV to offer five new cruises in the 2019 programme, as the operating seasons of *Magellan* and *Columbus* were extended into April and November respectively. With many popular destinations having a waiting list of passengers, the time was right to offer additional opportunities to travel during the early and late season.

The 2019 programme of sailings from the UK embraced departures from Avonmouth (Bristol), Bristol Port, Cardiff, Cobh (Ringaskiddy), Dublin, Dundee, Edinburgh (Rosyth), Hull, London Tilbury, Liverpool, Newcastle (Tyne), Poole, and Portsmouth. No other cruise operator came close to offering such comprehensive coverage of the UK and Ireland market, placing everyone within easy reach of a CMV cruise departure.

Astor began the year in Australia on her winter programme of short Australian coast cruises from Fremantle and Adelaide, combined with two longer round-trip voyages to Bali. Her season 'down under' finished on 10th March when she began her return northbound voyage to the UK, sailing on a 14,095 mile 43-night journey across the Indian Ocean to Durban and Cape Town, before heading up the Atlantic to Casablanca, Lisbon, Leixoes, and Tilbury. After a short repositioning trip to Kiel, *Astor* embarked on her summer programme of German cruises for TransOcean, spending much of the summer at Bremerhaven but also offering sailings from Wismar, St. Nazaire and Hamburg. The programme was as popular as ever, covering itineraries in the Baltic, Norway, Greenland, Iceland, around Britain, and French river cruises, and included two long trips – a 19-night venture to the Canaries from St. Nazaire and a 20-night trip to the Azores from Hamburg. The TransOcean season concluded with a cruise from Hamburg to Tromsø in search of the Northern Lights, before *Astor* retired to Antwerp for the winter.

Astoria started her spring schedules from Poole with a trip from winter lay-up at the Damen Shipyard at Vlissingen. She undertook a programme of six cruises across the full range of CMV destinations, including a double-transit of the Kiel Canal during an 11-night 'Hidden Baltic Treasures and Kiel Canal' itinerary. After repositioning to Le Havre, *Astoria* took up her summer programme of sailings for Rivages du Monde, with a particular focus on Scotland and Norway, sailing initially from Le Havre, Dunkirk and Zeebrugge. Three Iceland- and Greenland-originating cruises from Reykjavík and Kangerlussuaq occupied the main summer period, before *Astoria* repositioned from Dunkirk to Portsmouth for her short autumn programme of two departures. Hull was next on the agenda for a full September and October programme, with a 'British Isles Discovery' itinerary and trips north to Norway, Iceland, and across to the Baltic.

Marco Polo had a particularly busy year, offering departures from six British ports. She wintered at Bristol Avonmouth, whence she began her 70-night 'Grand Circle South America' voyage on 6th January. This represented an extraordinary opportunity to visit all the highlights of the continent during one clockwise trip, visiting Rio de Janeiro, Buenos Aires and Montevideo, before heading back out to sea to call at Port Stanley in the Falkland Islands. The Straits of Magellan and Punta Arenas followed, then *Marco Polo* headed through the Chilean Fjords, along the coast to Valparaiso and calls in Ecuador, before transiting the Panama Canal and visiting the Caribbean Islands and Ponta Delgada on her way across the Atlantic back to Bristol Avonmouth. A short season to Norway, round Britain, and France followed from Bristol before *Marco Polo* repositioned across the Bristol Channel to serve Cardiff. Three cruises from Cardiff followed, then *Marco Polo* headed for Portsmouth for commemorating the 75th anniversary of D-Day, visiting Honfleur, cruising the Normandy beaches on 6th June and sailing up the River Seine to Rouen. She provided a wonderful vantage point to watch the Rouen Armada, before concluding a memorable Portsmouth season with a trip to Iceland. Two lengthy cruises to the Arctic and Greenland followed from London Tilbury, then *Marco Polo* headed up the east coast to Newcastle (Tyne) and Rosyth for a summer programme of short voyages. Highlights of the autumn programme were a 30-night 'Canada in the Fall' cruise from London Tilbury and two trips north for the Northern Lights.

For *Columbus*, the Christmas and New Year period was spent in the warmth of the Canaries and Madeira. She returned to London Tilbury in anticipation of her 120-night 'Grand Round the World Cruise' which left on 5th January with 1,207 passengers and 617 crew members on board. This epic 36,306-mile journey headed out across the Atlantic after calling in Amsterdam to pick up European passengers, before transiting the Panama Canal and visiting the Mexican coast. From here *Columbus* sailed out across the Pacific. She diverted from her scheduled route whilst en route to Tahiti and Bora Bora on 4th February to assist a sailing boat in distress after an emergency call from the Joint Rescue and Coordination Centre in Tahiti. *Columbus'* crew successfully assisted the sailing boat and were able to ensure the safety of all her passengers and crew.

Columbus sailed on to Auckland and Sydney, reaching there on 24th February. There was time for an overnight call at Yorkey's Knob for Cairns as she headed north to visit Yokohama (for Tokyo) and Kagoshima in Japan. Passengers could visit Beijing from Tianjin, then have a night in Shanghai before reaching Hong Kong. As *Columbus* headed west she paused in Singapore, Cochin and Mumbai, then sailed across the Indian Ocean to reach Salalah in Oman. 'Bucket list' destinations continued to

be ticked off as *Columbus* called in Egypt and Jordan prior to her transit of the Suez Canal, which brought her into the Mediterranean. With calls in Ashdod, Valletta, Gibraltar, and Lisbon she completed her world tour in London Tilbury on 5th May. There was no rest for *Columbus* as she headed straight into her season of cruises from her home port. Her main itineraries featured predominantly 10- to 15-night cruises to the classic CMV range of popular destinations. *Columbus* underwent repairs at the Damen Shipyard at Rotterdam during the season, which caused the cancellation of a small number of cruises, but she recovered to complete her summer and autumn schedules. *Columbus* offered a new departure from London Tilbury on 3rd November with a 6-night cruise to Southern Norway including visits to Oslo and Stavanger, then on 10th November she headed for the Canary Islands and Madeira, with bonus calls in Casablanca and Cadiz.

Magellan's year began on a Christmas and New Year trip to Mexico and the Caribbean on a 25-night cruise from Tilbury to Cozumel, as she headed west for her new deployment to support the launch of Cruceros Marítimos Vacacionales' new Mexican Riviera cruise programme targeted at the Mexican domestic market. She commenced operations on 3rd February 2019 with a debut series of eight 7-night sailings home-porting from both Acapulco on Sundays and Manzanillo on Fridays. The itinerary included calls to Manzanillo and Cabo San Lucas in the Baja California peninsula, plus two days at sea. Acapulco is the primary gateway port serving the region of Guerrero and Mexico City. Mazatlán and Puerto Vallarta, apart from being transit calls, also provided secondary gateway ports to the cities of Guadalajara, Leon, and the northern Mexico States. The tailored Mexican programme was the only exclusive Mexican cruise product available in a domestic leisure market, which offered great potential for expansion as CMV continued to develop their strategic international development plan. The season offered capacity for 12,000 passengers and was targeted at the affluent ABC1 middle class sector, 30–55 age group, couples, families, solo travellers, groups, and the honeymoon market.

This positive development followed extensive negotiations with key stakeholders and Government officials and facilitated the opening of a dedicated sales office in Mexico City and big trade launch events.

Top left: Hollywood's - a two tier show lounge on Boat Deck 7 and Upper Deck 8. *(CMV Library)*

Middle left: The Lido Pool with a retractable roof for all weather bathing on Lido Deck 11. *(CMV Library)*

Bottom left: Located aft on Navigator's Deck 10, the Oasis Pool. *(CMV Library)*

This inaugural season finished on 31st March when *Magellan* commenced a 14-night 'Trans-Panama' itinerary, followed by a 19-night 'Caribbean & Azores Experience' from Montego Bay, which brought her back across the Atlantic to London Tilbury, arriving on 3rd April. *Magellan* offered three new cruises from London Tilbury in April 2019: on 3rd April she undertook a 10-night cruise around the British Isles, including a journey along the River Seine to Rouen and visits to Amsterdam and Honfleur; on 13th April she visited the Norwegian Fjords with calls into Geiranger, Flåm and Eidfjord; and on 20th April she took an 'Easter Hidden Baltic' cruise to visit Scandinavia, Germany and some of the more

arrived in London Tilbury for a gala event on 6th June for media, trade partners and key suppliers, who were invited on board along with more than 130 of CMV's most loyal passengers. Adverse weather conditions prevented a similar event being held in Amsterdam the following evening, so *Vasco da Gama* headed directly to her new home port of Bremerhaven in readiness for her christening event on Sunday 9th June.

The christening was spectacular. *Vasco da Gama* left her berth on the Columbus Quay and manoeuvred the River Weser up to the Seebäderkaje and anchored in the middle of the river, in front of thousands of spectators. Following a welcome speech by the Lord Mayor

Vasco da Gama speeds along on her maiden voyage from Singapore in April 2019. *(CMV Library)*

The Jade Wellness Centre forward on Lido Deck 11. *(CMV Library)*

unusual ports in Lithuania and Poland.

Pacific Eden was handed over to CMV on the evening of 8th April as she shared a quay with *Columbus* in Singapore, whilst the latter was in the midst of her 'Grand Round the World Cruise'. She only required a short docking period to allow for a livery change, rebranding and some technical work before she left Singapore as *Vasco da Gama* on her maiden voyage for CMV on Wednesday 24th April 2019. Her route to Europe was a spectacular 46-night adventure across South East Asia, the Indian subcontinent, Egypt, Jordan, a transit of the Suez Canal, Israel, and the Mediterranean. Highlights included: the beautiful beaches of Malaysia and Thailand, the Taj Mahal in India, the lost city of Petra from Jordan, shrines to ancient Pharaoh's in Egypt, some of the holiest sites on earth in Israel, the eternal city of Rome and the souks in Marrakech. She

of Bremerhaven, Melk Grantz, and the traditional plaque exchange to mark her first arrival in port, *Vasco da Gama* was christened by her new godmother, the popular German singer Annett Louisan. The sky above Bremerhaven was lit by a spectacular firework display as the champagne bottle hit the hull. On board, Kai Wingenfelder and Christof Steinschneider of the band 'Fury in the Slaughterhouse' rocked the ship to continue the good mood on board. This was the first time a cruise ship had been baptised in Bremerhaven. *Vasco da Gama* embarked on her maiden voyage the following day, visiting the Sogne, Aurlands, Hardanger, Lysse and Geirangerfjord, in Southern Norway.

For her first season TransOcean included a number of special event cruises within the programme. Annett Louisan returned to *Vasco da Gama*, together with Nico Santos and Matthias Reim, for a five day 'Stars at Sea' cruise to Copenhagen in August. An innovative culinary cruise was undertaken to the Baltic in late July with a vegan cruise offering exclusively vegan cuisine. On completion of her German season, *Vasco da Gama* returned to London Tilbury for her second departure, on 9th October 2019, to sail to Barbados, transit the Panama Canal, and then visit Acapulco, the islands of the South Pacific, and Auckland before arriving in Sydney some 53 nights later. There was strong interest in the journey from those wishing to take the opportunity to visit friends and relatives in Australasia and tick off a sequence of 'bucket list' destinations on the way.

Building on the success of the winter 2019 programme of cruises from Acapulco with *Magellan*, CMV introduced a new programme of 'soft

programme was operated in close cooperation with the Mexican states of Baja California Sur and Sonora, and the US state of Arizona.

This was the CMV group's first foray into the soft expedition cruise sector, inaugurating a new 'Voyages of Exploration' collection. *Astoria* was chosen for this programme as she could offer a unique, classic boutique style in an authentic cruise experience, supported by an enrichment programme and supplemented by classical and more popular themed entertainment. Her cruises carried a compliment of just 500 mainly North American and Mexican guests, and was structured as an 'inclusive' sailing, with gratuities and house wine/beer with lunch and dinner included, thereby providing attractive price points and a great value. The international market was served through the airlift potential of

The Study, an intimate area on Upper Deck 8. *(CMV Library)*

The luxurious Royal Penthouse Suite located on Navigator's Deck 10. *(CMV Library)*

expeditions' to Mexico's Sea of Cortez in January 2020. *Astoria* was dedicated to this programme, sailing from Puerto Peñasco (Rocky Point) on the Mexican coast to eight contrasting ports during an 11-night cruise itinerary visiting Topolobampo, Mazatlán, Cabo San Lucas, La Paz, Bahia Loreto, Santa Rosalia, and Guaymas. Puerto Peñasco is accessible to the American market through Phoenix, Arizona, some 200 miles distant.

The Sea of Cortez (Gulf of California) is one of the most ecologically diverse places on the planet, described as a 'living aquarium' by French explorer Jacques Cousteau. From exotic islands to world-renowned vacation destinations, it presents a chance to discover truly breathtaking natural experiences, infused with a distinctive Mexican culture. The

Phoenix and Tucson and coach transfer to Puerto Peñasco.

Astoria operated as a 'child-free' ship, with all passengers required to be 16 years old or above at the time of sailing, and particularly accommodated solo passengers. On her Mexican programme she offered a full American breakfast, with a blend of traditional cuisine and international specialities for lunch and dinner. Seating is on an informal basis for breakfast and lunch, with flexible dining in the evening between 17:30 and 20:30, except on gala nights when there is one sitting for all guests, usually at 19:30. Pricing included CMV house wine and beer at lunch and dinner, but the ship's extensive wine list added further temptation.

Vasco da Gama seen in Gravesend Reach during her maiden 2019 season. *(CMV Library)*

Chapter eight

Further expansion in the second decade

...ates the Geirangerfjord during a 12-night North Cape cruise from Kiel in July 2013. *(CMV Library)*

As CMV entered its second decade of operations in January 2020, the founders could look back with pride at the remarkable achievements of the first 10 years. The company had expanded from the early two-ship operation to a fleet of six vessels in 2019, with two further additions announced for 2021. Capacity had grown incrementally to match increasing demand for the CMV product in a rapidly growing and highly competitive cruise market. The brand had grown from carrying 37,115 passengers in 2010 to approaching 150,000 in 2019, and employing almost 4,000 staff.

CMV had become a truly international brand, building the core business in the UK but also offering cruise programmes in Australia, France, Germany and Mexico, as well as extended winter itineraries around the globe. The company had recreated the classic voyages linking London Tilbury with Australia each autumn and spring. No other operator of comparable size could offer such a broad range of carefully planned itineraries.

The CMV success formula remained simple: focussing on a strong niche market within the cruise sector. As the corporate cruise brands pursued ever larger vessels for their operations, CMV was single-mindedly concentrating on small to medium-sized ships, which brought significant advantages in the marketplace. Not only could CMV offer a range of cruises from conveniently situated ports right around the British Isles, but the smaller size of vessel enabled visits to ports and destinations well outside the reach of larger vessels. The formula of taking ships to passengers rather than operating from ports convenient for the cruise line had paid dividends. Further, the intimacy and personal service, which the CMV fleet could offer guests by the nature of their smaller size, was proving highly attractive to loyal repeat passengers.

The 2020 programme featured departures from London Tilbury, Portsmouth, Poole, Bristol Avonmouth and Bristol Portbury, Cobh, Ringaskiddy, Dublin, Liverpool, Belfast, Greenock, Aberdeen, Dundee, Newcastle (Tyne) and Hull. Similarly, the featured range of destinations was full of calls that could not be contemplated by bigger ships. Tobermory, Stornoway (Outer Hebrides) Kirkwall (Orkneys) and the Isles of Scilly, for example, remained highly popular CMV ports of call, bringing sustainable levels of tourism to boost the local economy.

The success of the company will come as no surprise to many thousands of Columbus Club members, as many of the membership have been cruising with CMV since its inception and will hopefully concur with the various sentiments expressed. This customer loyalty club was launched in 2013 and assumed the name Columbus, inherited when TransOcean Kreuzfahrten was acquired the following year. The

Flooding the Drydock, Damen Shipyard, Amsterdam on 2nd December 2019. *(CMV Library)*

membership throughout the tier levels has steadily increased year-on-year as can be seen from the table. It is a remarkable reflection of the loyalty and affection with which the brand is held that, for such a young company, over 450 passengers in the Diamond Tier have already notched up over 200 nights on board the various ships of the fleet. In the Purfleet office, Club members' interests were very capably looked after by Sarah Kilduff (now Partridge) as Columbus Club Manager until she took over as Passenger Sales Manager in 2019. Whilst Sarah still oversees as Columbus Club Manager, the general day to day duties are now handled by Bethany Barker; her role includes ensuring that the club register on the central computer system is always kept up to date in order that the correct level of benefits can be applied whenever members travel. Beth says:

It is very rewarding to know that I play a small part in enhancing their cruise holiday and it is a real pleasure hearing from them upon their return.

The 9th November 2019 provided an opportunity for Columbus Club members, along with some specially invited guests, to suitably celebrate the 10th Anniversary of Cruise & Maritime Voyages. *Columbus* hosted an overnight gala event on board, where almost 700 Diamond and Platinum Tier members enjoyed entertaining speeches by Chris Coates, Christian Verhounig and Simon Weeks, the premiere of a new DVD video entitled *CMV 2019 10th Anniversary Celebration*, a presentation of the shoreside heads of department, and an innovative 'Question & Answer' session with the directors. Tyler Butterworth expertly controlled proceedings and the evening continued with a splendid six-course meal in the Waterside Restaurant followed by a spectacular firework display launched from barges in the River Thames, which was closed especially for the occasion.

Diamond Tier Club members Ken and Marilyn Mealand, who have each compiled an amazing total of 1,000 nights on board, were asked what first attracted them to CMV. They stated:

The opportunity to go on a 42-night voyage to the Amazon, Orinoco, and West Indies in 2010 was our introduction to the company. After taking a Cunard 30-night QE2 cruise to the Caribbean in her final season we were looking for a more cost-effective solution for longer voyages and up popped CMV.

They added that the underlying reason that they continued their cruising with CMV was quite simple:
It's the value for money, but how CMV treat both new and returning passengers is also a major consideration.

Fellow Diamond Tier members, Neil and Pamela Edwards added that:

We continue to choose CMV's Marco Polo as she is a lovely ship and the crew are fantastic and so friendly – when you board it feels like home.

This was very much a mutual feeling, as it was echoed by Carlo Todisco, Guest Services Manager, who only joined the company in 2017 but already had a high opinion of his passengers. He commented:

CMV passengers respond so well to Columbus that it makes me feel that I am having welcome guests in my own home.

Being a good neighbour featured high on the list of corporate objectives. CMV frequently partnered with local schools around London Tilbury and the company's head office at Purfleet to set business challenges and undertake ship tours and introduce students to working life and the challenges of the world of cruises. Students of Travel and Tourism also

COLUMBUS CLUB MEMBERSHIP
Qualifying sailings from January 2010 to October 2019

Tiers:	Silver	Gold	Platinum	Diamond
Nights:	20	21-99	100-199	200
2010	33,390	2,255	2	0
2011	70,772	4,624	9	0
2012	103,764	7,708	19	2
2013	133,786	11,871	60	3
2014	162,958	15,738	93	3
2015	204,838	23,333	299	9
2016	244,039	31,038	591	36
2017	291,159	40,665	1,488	113
2018	333,013	52,300	2,732	238
2019	348,492	59,193	3,644	464

had regular opportunities to view life on board and learn about the cruise business and the CMV product offering. They reviewed career pathways in the industry and work experience opportunities with experts from CMV, before enjoying lunch on board. For the past three years, CMV has sponsored the Thurrock Education Awards, a celebration of excellence in the borough's schools.

Officers from *Marco Polo* installed the first computer ever seen in the tiny Brazilian village of Boca da Valéria, during in call in the midst of an 'Amazon, West Indies and Azores' voyage in January 2015. The village has a population of just 120 people and the donation allowed children in the village to further their education with help from a trainer in an adjacent village.

A charity fundraising day on *Magellan* saw almost £11,000 donated in support of local charity, Havens Hospices. This generosity brought the sum raised by CMV guests and passengers to over £100,000 in the first two years of dedicated support to the charity. Further events were planned to help Havens Hospices, which is local to CMV's head office in Purfleet and the home port of London Tilbury.

The increasing reputation of CMV resulted in the receipt of a growing number of awards. The company was successful from its earliest years, quickly being recognised for the quality and innovative characteristics of the brand by nomination as 'Favourite Cruise Line' in 2011, 2012, 2013 and 2015 in the Globe Travel Awards. The company enjoyed equal success with consistent

nominations in the *Cruise International Magazine* awards and the British Travel awards.

At the 2016 UK Cruise Critic 'Cruisers' Choice Awards', *Astoria* was ranked in the top five vessels in the 'Best Entertainment' category and new flagship *Magellan* featured in the top five for 'Best Shore Excursions'. Cruise Critic is the leading cruise reviews and information site hosting the largest cruise community in the world, and the Cruisers' Choice Awards were based on ratings submitted by genuine passengers whose reviews had been published on CruiseCritic.co.uk.

Then CMV took silver in the 2017 Silver Travel Advisor Awards, with second place in the 'Best Ocean Cruise Line' category. Silver Travel Advisor – a website run by mature travel industry professionals – had 44,000 members who gathered online to offer impartial advice,

Marco Polo leaves the drydock, whilst *Magellan* awaits her new livery work to be completed, Damen Shipyard, Amsterdam 2nd December 2019. *(CMV Library)*

The job complete, *Magellan* gleams at London Tilbury on 14th December 2019. *(John Bryant)*

information and trusted recommendations, and voted for their preference in the awards. The award was fitting recognition of the close fit between CMV and its customers. The awards were presented by Amanda Redman at a packed ceremony at London's Transport Museum.

Readers of *World of Cruising* magazine voted CMV as their 'Favourite Specialist Cruise Line' at the prestigious Wave Awards. The 'beast from the east' did not deter the cream of the cruise industry from enjoying an exciting evening at London's De Vere Grand Connaught Rooms on 1st March 2018. This was a clear indication that the CMV brand and product was highly considered by consumers.

CMV won the 'Best Ocean Cruise Line Operator for Groups' at the Group Travel Awards held on 1st June 2018 at The Park Plaza Riverbank Hotel in London. This prestigious event is held annually by *Group Travel Organiser*, the specialist group travel magazine. The award recognised the efforts of the growing specialist groups department at the company's head office in Purfleet, who ensure the best possible service is available for group travel organisers. Lisa Jacobs, Head of Trade Sales and Groups, noted that the most meaningful aspect of the Group Travel Awards is that the readers of the magazine voted CMV the best based upon their own experience.

Making it a hat-trick in 2018, the company was also honoured at the 2018 Group Leisure and Travel Awards at a glittering ceremony hosted by TV personality Gyles Brandreth in Birmingham on 10th October. CMV was awarded the accolade of 'Best Ocean Cruise Line' against stiff competition, a remarkable achievement for an independent cruise line. Editor Keeley Rodgers said that the winners 'continue to prove that if you get it right, you reap the rewards, receive the kudos and, most importantly, retain and attract group business.'

In October 2019, *Selling Travel Magazine* announced the winners in their Agents Choice Awards. Travel Agents across the UK had voted Cruise & Maritime Voyages as their top choice for 'Ocean Cruising – Short Haul'.

Environmental issues remain of high importance to CMV and the company is constantly looking at sustainable ways to reduce the impact of their operations. One simple way to protect the environment was to change the policy of providing plastic straws with drinks from the bars on board CMV ships. From September 2018 guests who require a straw could request one from their server. Previously the company used an estimated 1.2 million straws each year. This simple change quickly proved effective, encouraging CMV to continue the quest to reduce the amount of plastic used on board the fleet and keep the environment free of unnecessary waste.

As the brand continued to evolve, the growing popularity of the company's traditional product, its classic ship fleet and destination-focussed cruise programmes, encouraged CMV to accelerate plans to add capacity to the two top European cruise markets in the UK and Germany, which represent 85% of the company's business. Shortly after the celebratory dinner aboard *Columbus*, CMV was able to reveal dramatic expansion plans for the second decade.

The French market had long been seen as having significant potential and the establishment of a new 'Croisières Maritimes et Voyages' brand fitted perfectly with corporate ambitions to expand international business. *Astor* will be renamed *Jules Verne* at a special overnight gala event in Le Havre on 29th April 2021, followed by a second gala event in Marseille on 16th May. Her year-round new home ports of Marseille and Le Havre neatly tap into two distinct French markets, and a dedicated sales office in Marseille will replicate the success enjoyed in Germany, the USA and Mexico, and Australia. Her maiden 2021–2022 French season includes a programme of 18 sailings to Northern Europe, the Mediterranean and Black Sea, and a 'Christmas and New Year' Canaries cruise; the winter season concludes with a 123-night 'Round the World' cruise sailing from Marseille on 8th January 2022 and returning to Le Havre on 11th May.

Publicity photographs of *Astor* as *Jules Verne* depicted her in a refreshed fleet livery. Although each CMV ship is iconic and special, their liveries varied through the first decade. Like all cruise lines, the company wanted their ships to look like a common fleet and be recognisable around the world as CMV ships. The traditional nature of the ships is now reflected in using a new house-blue coloured hull right across the fleet, similar to, but suitably different from, the darker blues sported by *Marco Polo* and *Vasco Da Gama*. This look has been updated by the addition of a smart, twin, white stripe. The funnels will become blue with a stylisation of the corporate logo to add a more contemporary edge. The CMV logo appears on the sides of each ship towards the aft section, and also on the centre bow as they do currently. This smart new livery was the in-house work of Ryan Jackson, Graphic Design Manager, further demonstrating the strength of the talent within CMV.

Transferring *Astor* to serve the French market from 2021 would leave a gap in CMV's highly popular German business, and at the end of November 2019 the company revealed how this would be filled in a game-changing announcement. Not only would a sister ship partner *Vasco da Gama* in Germany, but new capacity would also be added to

Top right: ***Pacific Aria***, seen here in her P&O livery, will be deployed to the German market. *(Ferry Publications Library)*

Middle right: The larger ***Pacifc Dawn***, also from P&O Australia, will be a regular visitor at London Tilbury. *(Ferry Publications Library)*

the UK roster from 2021. In another deal with Carnival Corporation, CMV will take delivery of P&O Australia's *Pacific Dawn* and *Pacific Aria* in Singapore on 2nd March and 2nd May 2021 respectively. Both will undertake some minor upgrade work and be repainted in the new CMV corporate livery, prior to repositioning to Northern Europe for the 2021 season.

Pacific Dawn, a 70,285grt vessel, with 798 passenger cabins and capacity for around 1,400 passengers, will be deployed in the UK market from late May 2021, to bring much-needed additional capacity by cruising year-round alongside *Columbus* from London Tilbury.

Pacific Aria, a 55,819grt vessel, with 630 passenger cabins and capacity for around 1,100 passengers, will be deployed on the German market under the TransOcean Kreuzfahrten brand to bring a much-needed increase in capacity and cruise alongside her sister vessel *Vasco da Gama.*

The arrival of the two new fleet-mates will increasing CMV's lower-bed capacity to 9,000 berths and increase fleet passenger capacity by 30% in 2021.

Christian Verhounig, CEO commented:

The introduction of two more ships to the global ocean fleet is the next exciting chapter of our strategic growth objectives. This will enable us to service increasing market demand for our traditional brand of cruising generated by our expanding international network of in-house sales offices and developing source markets. We have now acquired five cruise ships in just five years and are firmly on course in carrying 200,000 passengers in 2021.

Chris Coates, Group Commercial Director added:

These two fine cruise ships perfectly complement our existing fleet providing trade partners and consumers alike with much-needed extra capacity. For 2020, we expect close to 70% of capacity to be sold by the year end, in line with expectations. This provides an ideal platform for the early introduction of new tonnage and opportunities for summer 2021 with the focus very much on higher yield business.

The second decade promises to be even brighter for CMV as the company confidently expands its international operations. With an eight-ship fleet from 2021, it is well placed to satisfy growing demand for the successful formula that it has created. Nowhere will this confidence be better exemplified than in the planned Fleet Review in Rotterdam on 21st August 2021, which will bring together all the company's vessels for the first time, with *Marco Polo* leading the fleet for a truly memorable occasion. A gathering of this scale is an outstanding achievement and demonstrates the remarkable progress CMV has made in its first decade. The next 10 years promise to be even more extraordinary. CMV is truly a brand that is going places.

With a backdrop of Table Mountain, *Astor* heads for her next port of Walvis Bay en route to the UK in April 2017. *(CMV Library)*

Celebrating a decade of success aboard *Columbus* on 9th November 2019

Top left: Captain Ilias Venetantis introduces his Heads of Department who line up in front of the CMV shoreside personnel on the Palladium Show Lounge stage. *(CMV Library)*

Top right: Tyler Butterworth poses Club members's questions to Christian Verhounig and Chris Coates in a well received Q & A session. *(CMV Library)*

Left: Proud Godmother Angela Rippon says a few words to delight the audience. *(CMV Library)*

Above: The Columbus Show Team produced a special Round the World performance for the occasion. *(CMV Library)*

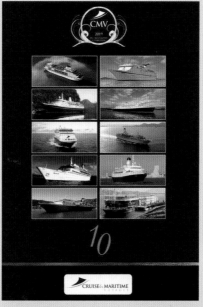

Top left: Club members enjoy the Gala Menu in the Waterfront Restaurant. *(CMV Library)*

Below left: A spectacular firework display on the River Thames was a highlight for many. *(CMV Library)*

Right: The packed programme kept everyone occupied and the reverse side featured ten different CMV vessels: one for each year of the first decade. *(CMV Library)*

Memorable nights on board

The evening of 9th November 2019 provided an opportunity for valued customers, suppliers and guests to celebrate the success of CMV's first decade *(CMV Library)*

Top left: **Magellan** Godmother Gloria Hunniford with the Reverend Phil Wright who officiated blessing proceedings at the **Magellan**, and indeed the Columbus, renaming ceremony. They are joined here by Chris Coates and Captain Psarrakis on 12th March 2015. (*CMV Library*)

Top right: Guests are welcomed to **Vasco da Gama**'s naming ceremony by Capt. Michail Smyrnaios on 9th June 2019. (*CMV Library*)

Middle left: Flanked by the senior CMV team and his officers, Capt Emmanouil Psarrakis welcomes guests to the naming ceremony of **Magellan** on 12th March 2015. (*CMV Library*)

Left: Angela Rippon admires the commemorative plaque as she names **Columbus** on 8th June 2017. (*CMV Library*)

Above: The programme of entertainment to accompany the naming of **Columbus** highlighted the diverse talents of the showteam. (*CMV Library*)

65

Chapter Nine

The Fleet – Marco Polo (January 2010 to date)

Marco Polo was built as *Alexandr Pushkin* at the VEB Mathias-Thesen-Werft in Wismar, Germany in 1965, the second of a quintet of ships named after Russian poets and writers. The Ivan Franko 'Russian poet' class ships were the fastest, largest and most prestigious Soviet liners, designed for cruising, and the possibility of reopening transatlantic voyages from Leningrad to New York when the Cold War thawed.

Alexandr Pushkin's innovative design enabled all passenger and crew accommodation to have a sea view, although not all had private facilities, so there were three bathroom blocks on the accommodation decks.

in a fully air-conditioned stabilised ship with a weatherproof heated indoor swimming pool featuring a sliding glass roof. Cabins featured taps for hot, cold and sea water. Her hull was specially strengthened for Baltic

service and the provision and storage areas were unusually large, permitting a cruising range of over 10,000 nautical miles with possible future use as a troopship in mind. The ship also featured heavy lifting-gear on deck to permit the transport of military equipment on board and side-loading ramps for vehicles. Corridors were especially wide to accommodate soldiers with kit to pass each other. *Alexandr Pushkin* had a maximum speed of 22 knots but was designed to operate at a more efficient 20.5 knots on long runs.

Alexandr Pushkin was delivered to the Baltic Steamship Company of Leningrad on 14th August 1965, to be registered and based in the city as the flagship of the fleet. She entered service later that month and operated a succession of cruises for several charter organisations around northern and western Europe and the Mediterranean. *Alexandr Pushkin*

Above: A splendid aerial shot of ***Alexandr Pushkin*** in the English Channel following her extensive refit in 1975. *(FotoFlite)*

Left: The ***Marco Polo*** at St Mary's, Isles of Scilly. *(Andrew Cooke)*

reopened the transatlantic service when she sailed from Leningrad to Helsinki and Copenhagen on 13th April 1966, before making her first call in Tilbury prior to an eight-day crossing to Québec and Montréal. Six transatlantic voyages were advertised in the first year of operation before winter ice curtailed the operation. The first season's experience led to *Alexandr Pushkin* being fitted with Denny Brown stabilisers in March 1967. On 17th April she visited Bremerhaven for the first time as the Baltic Steamship Company experimented with different intermediate ports of call. The winter programme focussed on cruising, with the first departure from Tilbury to the Canaries on 21st December 1968. Tilbury-originating cruises also called at Rotterdam in an effort to attract Continental custom, a feature of many current CMV itineraries.

An extensive refit in 1975 improved *Alexandr Pushkin* for further cruising with the addition of several inside cabins, the extension of her main lounge forward and upwards by reducing hold space to create a double-height ballroom with balcony, and an outside swimming pool was installed in what is now Scott's Bar.

As competition from airlines increased, so demand for transatlantic sailings fell and *Alexandr Pushkin* could still only offer a limited number of en-suite cabins. The Baltic Steamship Company experimented with offering cruises from Montréal and even offered a double transatlantic cruise for North Americans with a short stay in Leningrad. But the number of transatlantic passengers continued to decline and in 1979 the company chartered *Alexandr Pushkin* to TransOcean Tours of Bremen for a cruise programme. The final transatlantic sailing took place in 1980.

The Baltic Steamship Company transferred *Alexandr Pushkin* to the Far Eastern Shipping Company in August 1984 and she was re-registered in Vladivostok to work under charter to CTC Cruises Australia. Here she was employed in a very different market, including '18–30 Holidays'. The seasonal itineraries featured many sea days as *Alexandr Pushkin* ventured to the South Pacific on cruises of typically 10–14 nights duration. But her accommodation facilities were increasingly outdated and the Far Eastern Shipping Company decided to sell her. *Alexandr Pushkin* was laid up in Singapore in February 1990 to await a buyer.

She was purchased by Gerry Herrod, a British entrepreneur and

Top left: ***Alexandr Pushkin*** arriving at her adopted home port of Sydney for CTC Lines in 1987. *(Richard Bastow)*

Middle left: **Approaching the Ocean Terminal, Leith in her Orient Lines livery on 21st June 2005.** *(Iain McGeachy)*

Bottom left: **Antarctic cruising was an adventurous element of both the Orient Lines and the Transocean Tours programmes.** *(CMV Library)*

founder of Ocean Cruise Lines, in July 1991. *Alexandr Pushkin* was renamed *Marco Polo* and brought under the Bahamian flag, then taken to the Neorion Shipyard, Greece for a three-year US$60m renovation. The entire ship was gutted, her superstructure extended aft and upwards, and her funnel was heightened, enhancing her silhouette. Her interior was almost completely rebuilt under the direction of naval architect Knud E Hansen and interior designers Michael and Agni Katzourakis, with only the dining room, ship's galley, engines and lower swimming pool remaining of her original configuration. The engines were thoroughly overhauled by Sulzer Diesels. Three spiral stairwells were converted into 'square' stairways to meet new safety regulations. The original ship's bell from *Alexandr Pushkin* is now on display in the Nansen Card Room.

Marco Polo emerged in November 1993, now measuring 22,080 tons. She was now designed for expedition-destination cruising in the Far East, hence the specially commissioned Asian and Oriental artwork found aboard today. Her maiden voyage was for Orient Lines from Mombasa to Cape Town, whilst her new itineraries crossed the Indian and South Pacific Oceans and the Java Sea. The December to February period was initially spent in Antarctica with a helicopter on her heli-deck to scout for whales, wildlife and ice-free passages, but this venture could not be made to pay. In the European summer, from 1997, she headed to the Western Mediterranean.

Marco Polo proved highly popular, such that Norwegian Cruise Line absorbed both Orient Lines and *Marco Polo* into their business in 1998. Norwegian Cruise Line was, in turn, acquired by Star Cruises in 1999. Orient Lines continued to be marketed as a separate brand and the fleet was expanded, but profitability was hit by the loss of American passengers after 9/11. *Marco Polo* soldiered on but was increasingly inconsistent with the Star Cruises business and was put up for sale and purchased on 4th June 2007 by the Global Maritime Group, and chartered back to Orient Lines for a final year of operation before the brand was wound up in 2008.

Marco Polo was delivered to her new owners on 23rd March 2008 and placed on long-term charter to Transocean Tours, who had been agents for her as *Alexandr Pushkin* until 1984. *Marco Polo* was outfitted

Top right: **The popular hub of the *Marco Polo* is the enticing Captain's Club found on Magellan Deck 8.** *(CMV Library)*

Middle right: **Sparkling entertainment is offered nightly in the theatre-style Marco Polo Lounge forward on Magellan Deck 8.** *(CMV Library)*

Bottom right: **The impressive Waldorf Restaurant on Atlantic Deck 6 also offers an Indian Fusion speciality alternative dining option.** *(CMV Library)*

in Transocean livery for her inaugural cruise from Tilbury on 19th April 2008, sailing on a 'Springtime Fjordland' itinerary for Cruise & Maritime Services (CMS). She was based in Bremerhaven for her winter programme, with a predominantly German clientele, offering a voyage to Rio and four Antarctic cruises. For summer 2009 Marco Polo returned to Britain for the first half of the summer, before picking up a German programme from early August.

Sadly, this proved to be a short season, as Transocean went into administration on 1st September 2009. CMS boldly agreed to take over Marco Polo for the remainder of her charter until at least 2015, and Cruise & Maritime Voyages was born. On Saturday 2nd January 2010 Marco Polo left Tilbury on her maiden voyage for the new company on a 30-night cruise to the West Indies. She has been a stalwart of the operation ever since, covering more than half a million miles in service for the company and remaining a popular member of the expanding fleet.

Marco Polo retains the classic image of an ocean liner, with her traditional profile, teak decking and a distinctive dark-blue hull. Her passenger facilities are ranged across eight decks, with cabin accommodation available on seven of them.

The Navigator Deck 11 hosts six Deluxe cabins, two Junior Suites, and 18 Premium twin cabins. Aft on this deck can be found the Sun Terrace with three whirlpool Jacuzzis, and spectacular views across the classic tiered stern. There is a mix of cabins on Columbus Deck 10, with the two Mandarin and Dynasty De Luxe Ocean View Suites lying forward above the bridge. Both feature a king-sized bed, a walk-in wardrobe and a marble bathroom, plus a large seating area with every modern amenity. At 44.96m² there is an impressive amount of space. To the rear of this deck lies the exceptionally well appointed Jade Wellness Centre, offering a wide range of hairdressing and beauty treatments, fitness and exercise equipment as well as sauna and massage facilities. An internet café adds to the features on this deck.

Amundsen Deck 9 is primarily given over to passenger

accommodation, topped at the stern with the 141-seat Scott's Bar, a perfect home for late-night cabaret and disco.

The majority of passenger facilities can be found on Magellan Deck 9. Forward here lies the 438-seat Marco Polo Lounge, laid out in theatre style, and the venue for shows by the ship's highly acclaimed show-team, as well as the broad range of guest entertainers. The 186-seat Captain's Club brings a touch of bright modern elegance to pre-dinner cocktails, with the resident pianist providing the musical backdrop. Marco Polo's Reception and Shore Excursion desk lie midships on this deck, flanking the main lobby area, and leading through to the well-stocked boutiques and the snug 40-seat Palm Garden, which boasts panoramic views out to sea. The 60-seat nautically themed Columbus Club is another popular venue for an aperitif, whilst the Nansen Card Room and well-stocked Livingstone Library provide a haven for those seeking a different form of rest and relaxation. The 125-seat Marco's Bistro offers an informal but stylish dining experience, opening out to the main swimming pool area at the tiered stern for that al fresco experience.

Pacific Deck 7 hosts the main passenger accommodation, with a broad range of ocean-view and inside cabins. Marco Polo's impressive 446-seat Waldorf Restaurant lies midship on Atlantic Deck 6, taking advantage of natural light to provide a sumptuous dining experience on two sittings each evening. The 25-seat Indian Fusion Restaurant offers intimate speciality dining for a modest supplement. Aft on Atlantic Deck 6 lies more cabin accommodation, and the public areas on Baltic Deck 5 and Caribic Deck 4 provide more cabin options.

There is a selection of 15 cabin categories on Marco Polo, ranging from the 10.2m² of a standard twin inner cabin to the spacious 44.96m² of the De Luxe Suites with ocean view. The cabins are graded according to size and position on the ship, with standard, standard-plus, superior, superior-plus and premium categories available. All cabins feature en-suite facilities, wardrobe space, television, hair dryer, telephone, music console and personal safe.

Names	Owners/Disponent Owners	Operators
1965-1991: *Alexandr Pushkin*	1965–1985: Baltic Shipping Company	1965–1979: Baltic Shipping Company
1993 to date: *Marco Polo*	1985–1991: Far Eastern Shipping Company	1979–1984: Transocean Tours
	1991–2000: Orient Lines	1984–1985: Far Eastern Shipping Company
	2000-2004: Norwegian Cruise Line	1985–1990: CTC Cruises
	2004-2008: Ocean World Ltd	1993–2008: Orient Lines
	2008 to date: Story Cruise Lines Ltd (GMG)	2008–2009: Transocean Tours
		2010 to date: Cruise & Maritime Voyages

Technical Data

Builder:	Mathias-Thesen-Werft, Wismar, Germany
Launched:	26th April 1964
Delivered:	14th August 1965
Port of registry:	Nassau, Bahamas
Maiden CMV voyage:	2nd January 2010
Call sign:	C6JZ7
IMO number:	6417097
Length overall:	176.29m
Beam:	23.63m
Draught:	8.62m
Gross tonnage:	22,080gt
Passenger Decks:	8
Lifts:	4
Machinery:	2x 7-cylinder Sulzer 7RD-76 @ 21,000 hp each
Max/Cruising Speed:	19.5kt/17.5kt
Passengers:	800
Cabins:	425
Crew:	360

Capt. Valentyn Zhukov Master of *Magellan*, at time of publication. *(CMV Library)*

Senior Personnel

Captains	Chief Engineers	Staff Captains	Hotel Directors
Matko Antisic (2010)	Georgios Katsifarakis(2012-14, 2016-19)	Dimitrios Morfovasilis	Gernot Koschir
Valentyn Zhukov (2010-14, 2016-17)	Sergiy Karpushev (2012-13)	Panagiotis Kalaitzis	Maik Andrich
Georgios Antonelos (2011-12)	Ion Rizea (2013)	Nikolaos Michaloliakos	Marko Scavuzzo
Nektarios Rigas (2013-14)	Dimitrios Belekos (2014)	Michail Kontodios	Patrick Veysseyre
Nikolas Michaloliakos (2014-16)	Charalampos Drivas (2015)	Stamatios Kakaris	Daniel Reiter
Michail Margaritis (2015)	Petros Gazis (2015-16)	Nikolaos Giannakopoulos	Marko Scavuzzo
Antonio Manuel Marques De Morais (2015-18)	Oleksandr Aleksandrov (2016-19)	Michail Mandalenakis	Joao Luis De Sousa E Silva
Sergiy Zhygalin (2017-19)		Emmanouil Katsoudas	Jose Maria Correia
Emmanouil Psarrakis (2017-18)		Antonios Garmpidakis	De Sena Brito
Ilias Venetantis (2019			Matthew Swire
Michail Kontodios (2017, 2019)			Danilo Matrone

Ocean Countess (April 2010 to October 2012)

Originally intended as two of an eight-ship series planned by the Hollywood film company MGM, who wished to diversify their interests into the cruise business, *Cunard Countess* and her sister ship *Cunard Princess* were taken over and completed by the Cunard Line to that company's own specifications. The other six ships never materialised, but the construction was undertaken at the Burmeister and Wain shipyard in Copenhagen and *Cunard Countess* emerged on 20th September 1974. The following May she was towed around Western Europe to La Spezia to the Industrie Navali Mechaniche Affini (INMA) yard for internal fitting out and final delivery. Cunard took her over and in July she sailed on a positioning voyage to San Juan, for a christening ceremony on 8th August 1975, performed by Mrs Janet Armstrong, wife of the American astronaut, Neil Armstrong. She was purpose-built for seven-day cruises out of San Juan and for years was considered THE ship in the Caribbean prior to the era of the mega resort ships that ply the routes today. She became a firm favourite, particularly with British passengers, and, in hindsight, was undoubtedly a major player in the popularity and development of Caribbean cruising.

A change in her routine came in the autumn of 1982 when *Cunard Countess* was requisitioned by the UK Ministry of Defence for service as troop transport between Ascension and the Falkland Islands. Her duties included one particular voyage that was sponsored by HM Government as a next-of-kin pilgrimage to the graves of the service personnel killed in the Falklands War. Following this six-month charter, the ship entered Malta Dry Dock for a major reconversion back to her civilian duties and she was back in regular cruising in July 1983.

Her 20-year career in Caribbean waters came to an end in August 1996 and in the next 14 years, prior to joining the CMV fleet, she saw service with a range of different owners and operators including Awani Cruises of Indonesia and Royal Olympic Cruises in Greece before passing to Majestic International Cruises, who renamed her *Ocean Countess*. CMV felt she was an ideal vessel to resurrect their regional cruise ambitions and over the three seasons that she flew the flag, she offered sailings from London Tilbury, Hull, Newcastle Tyne, Edinburgh Leith, Greenock, Liverpool, Falmouth and Plymouth.

As her previous employment with Majestic International Cruises was on the Spanish market, with a season's charter to Quail Cruises, a little anglicising was called for. Lloyd Cross, the CMV Operations Manager, worked closely with Christian Verhounig, then Director of Hotel Operations for Global, to decide on the new names of the public rooms. Thus the Kensington Restaurant and The Boat House on Upper Deck 6 and The Holyrood Show Lounge and Hampton's on Promenade Deck 7 came into being, along with The Tower Piano Bar on Lido Deck 9. The Majestic Cinema and, with an eye to the forthcoming London Olympics, the Twenty Twelves Gym completed the set. CMV, and Lloyd in particular, were very keen to ensure that any remnants of the ship's Cunard heritage would continue to be preserved after the refurbishment, including items such as the pair of Cunard lions imprinted on the glass doors to The Boat House (ex-Satellite Café).

In addition to the necessary rebranding and new signage, a number of cabins on Reception Deck 5 and Main Deck 4 were reconfigured with the L-shaped arrangements of the beds being replaced with twin parallel beds. Externally, the most significant change was the painting of the hull from Quail white to CMV blue to match *Marco Polo*.

As she had done throughout her career, *Ocean Countess* won legions of admirers amongst the CMV clientele. She was a popular ship at her turnaround ports and it was a sad occasion on 9th October 2012 when she left on her farewell cruise from Liverpool. She arrived in Barcelona 13 nights later and whilst the passengers returned by air to the UK the ship was to be redelivered to her owners. The master, Captain Dimitrios Daoutis, set a course for Piraeus. She was to be laid up in Chalkis to await further charter business, but tragedy struck in November 2013 whilst she was being prepared to re-enter service. A fire broke out in the superstructure

Left chapter page: One of the busiest of the CMV ships, *Ocean Countess* helped pioneer the regional departure cruise programme from 2010, offering sailings from eight different UK ports. *(CMV)*

Above: The photographer provides an unusual perspective of *Ocean Countess*, with the pool prominent midships. *(FotoFlite)*

Top left: The 2012 season Main Edition brochure offered twenty-five Ocean Countess cruises from the UK regional ports of Greenock, Hull and Liverpool. *(CMV)*

and destroyed a large area between the funnel and the waterline, which ultimately proved fatal as she was declared a total loss, and in March 2014 she went under tow to shipbreakers in Aliaga, Turkey. A very sad and sudden end to a fondly remembered and much cherished ship.

Names	Owners/Disponent Owners	Operators
1975-1996: Cunard Countess	1975-1996: Cunard Cruise Ships Ltd	1975-1996: Cunard Line
1996-1998: Awani Dream 2	1996-1998: Lucky Star Nav Corp	1996-1998: Awani Cruises
1998-2002: *Olympic Countess*	1998-2002: Royal Olympic Cruises Ltd	1998-2002: Royal Olympic Cruises
2002-2004: *Olympia Countess*	2002-2004: Solar Nav Corp	2002-2004: Royal Olympia Cruises
2004-2006: *Lili Marleen*	2004 onwards: Maximus Navigation Ltd	2004-2005: Majestic International Cruise
2006-2007: *Ocean Countess*		2005-2006: Holiday Kreuzfahrten
2007-2007: *Ruby*		2007: Louis Cruise Lines
2007 onwards: *Ocean Countess*		2007: Monarch Classic Cruises
		2009: Quail Cruises
		2010-2012: Cruise & Maritime Voyages

Senior Personnel

Captains	Chief Engineers	Staff Captains	Hotel Directors
Ioannis Papangelis (2010)	Dimitrios Manolakis (2010)	Petros Poulakis	Gernot Koschir
Dimitrios Daoutis (2011-2012)	Christos Koutikas (2010)	Nektarios Kakakis	Marko Scavuzzo
	Charalambos Drivas (2010)	Konstantinos Daskalakis	Christian Shrangl
	Paraschos Manolakos 2011-2012		Patrick Veysseyre
	Volodymyr Ivanov 2012		
	Nikolaos Syrigos 2012		

Technical Data

Builder:	Burmeister and Wain, Copenhagen, Denmark	Length overall:	163.56m
Outfitted	INMA, La Spezia, Italy	Beam:	22.84m
Launched:	20th September 1974	Draught:	5.82m
Completed:	June 1976	Gross tonnage:	17,593gt
Maiden CMV voyage:	18th April 2010	Passenger Decks:	7
Port of registry:	Madeira, Portugal	Lifts:	2
Call sign:	CQRH	Machinery:	4 x B&W Diesels Type S50 HU
IMO number:	7358561	Cruising Speed:	17.5kt
		Passengers:	800
		Cabins:	400
		Crew:	350

Discovery (2013 to 2014)

The distinctive profile of **Discovery**, having slipped her berth and heading out of Portsmouth harbour on St George's Day 2011. *(Andrew Cooke)*

Discovery's two-season spell with CMV was the culmination of a colourful career spanning over 40 years for this elegant vessel. She was West German-built and launched as *Island Venture* in 1971 for Norwegian interests who operated her through Flagship Cruises on the New York to Bermuda run. She gained the name *Island Princess* in 1972 when she was initially chartered by Princess Cruises as a replacement for their *Carla C*. Ultimately P&O acquired the Princess company and the vessel was purchased outright in 1974, along with her sister ship *Pacific Princess*. For 27 years she operated on worldwide itineraries for Princess until the much larger new builds started to arrive with increasing regularity. In that time she gained an enviable reputation for being extremely spacious with high-ceilinged public rooms and wide passageways, which, with her attractive profile and exterior styling,

delivered what a contemporary commentator described as 'an excellent cruise experience in very comfortable surroundings'.

In 1977, the popular 'Love Boat' TV series commenced and, up until 1987, *Island Princess* stood in for her sister ship on a number of occasions when *Pacific Princess* was unavailable for filming. For the ABC network, having two sisters was an absolute bonus – only the sharpest-eyed viewers would be able to tell the two vessels apart as the artwork and the interior colour schemes were the only variance. However, as the commercial realities kicked in, it became apparent that the time of the smaller units in the Princess fleet was limited, and in 1999 *Island Princess* was sold to a Panamanian company that chartered her out to Hyundai Merchant Marine for the pilgrim market between South and North Korea. She served as *Hyundai Pungak* on this short-lived venture for a couple of

75

years before it failed, and she was sold again.

Her next suitor was, however, more resilient and responsible for giving the ship a welcome renaissance. Gerry Herrod, a name synonymous with the outstanding rebuilding of *Alexandr Pushkin* to create the lovely *Marco Polo* in 1993, purchased the ship in 2001. Following a refit in Turkey, she emerged as *Platinum* but, from the following year, operated as *Discovery* for Herrod's own Discovery World Cruises and during the summer service with the UK's Voyages of Discovery (VoD). Upon Herrod's retirement, Voyages of Discovery, which was acquired by the All Leisure Group in 2005, operated the ship themselves on the UK and US markets.

Trading became difficult for *Discovery* once her owners had added the newer *Voyager* to its fleet and an innovative joint venture arrangement was entered into with CMV which was, to all intents and purposes, a competitor in broadly the same market sector. As CMV had not been able to negotiate an extension to its *Ocean Countess* charter, which ended in October 2012, *Discovery* took over the former's position in 2013 and 2014 on the regional departure programme with some extra sailings from Harwich, which had always proved a popular turnaround port with VoD's clientele.

The two seasons were not without their operational challenges as there was no doubt that the vessel was ageing, and despite a lengthy pre-season dry-docking in Italy, there were a number of technical issues. However, the cruises were popular due to the attractive itineraries and the standards of service offered on board. A number of current Columbus Club members undertook their first CMV cruises aboard *Discovery* and reported that the vessel's design as a purpose-built cruise ship still held good after such a long career and that the Riviera Deck, which comprised all public rooms, was particularly becoming, especially the Discovery Lounge with its balcony, spiral staircase and double-deck windows looking out aft over the pool area. There were still plenty of reminders of the splendid Norwegian artistry that designer Robert Tillberg

introduced back in 1971, in particular the colourful glass wall panel in the reception area leading up to the Pacific Deck.

In late summer 2014, the All Leisure Group announced the sale of the ship and that, as a consequence, she would be withdrawn from service and the joint venture arrangement would cease accordingly. *Discovery* completed her final cruise with CMV in Avonmouth on Monday 6th October 2014 following a 9-night sailing to Spain, Portugal and Morocco and departed three days later for her eventual destination of the beaches of Alang, India for breaking up. Her name was changed to *Amen* during the trip and she was beached in December, where stripping out began immediately, with scrapping finally completed in August 2015.

Technical Data

Builder:	Rheinstahl Nordseewerke, Emden, W.Germany
Launched	6th March 1971
Maiden CMV voyage:	15th March 2013
Port of registry:	Hamilton, Bermuda
Call sign:	ZCDG2
IMO number:	7108514
Length overall:	168.7m
Beam:	24.06m
Draught:	7.40m
Gross tonnage:	20,216 grt
Passenger Decks:	8
Lifts:	4
Machinery:	4 x GMT-Fiat 10-cylinder Diesel Engines
Cruising Speed:	18.0 kn
Passengers:	698

Names	Owners/Disponent Owners	Operators
1971-1972: Island Venture	1971-1974: Norwegian Cruiseships	1971-1974: Flagship Cruises
1972-1999: Island Princess	1974- 1999: P&O Line	1974 -1999: Princess Cruises
1999-2001: Hyundai Pungak	1999-2001: Ringcroft Investment	1999-2001: Hyundai Merchant Marine
2001-2002: Platinum	2001- 2001: Fiducia Shipping	2001-2002 Fiducia Shipping
2002-2014: Discovery	2001-2005: Discovery Cruise Ltd	2002-2013: Voyages of Discovery
2014: Amen	2005-2014: Voyages of Discovery Ltd	2013-2014: Cruise & Maritime Voyages
	2014: Liberty Resources of Nassau	

Senior Personnel

Captains	Chief Engineers	Staff Captains	Hotel Directors
Brian Larcombe	Sergiy Menshykov	Jaska Kelez	Patrick Veysseyre
Asparuh Chorbadzhiev	Miodrag Vlacic	Asparuh Chorbadzhiev	Daniel Reiter
		Vadim Tavrovotsky	

Tendering operations are in full swing as *Discovery* lies at anchor in the Fjords. *(CMV Library)*

Funchal (October 2014)

Funchal seen here in her new Portuscale livery in September 2013. *(CMV Library)*

Although *Funchal* only served CMV for less than a month in October 2014, whilst filling in at short notice to cover the sudden withdrawal of *Discovery*, she was a ship close to the hearts of the company as, back in 1997 and detailed in chapter one, she was the first vessel brokered by Messrs Bastow and Coates at Cruise & Maritime Services. They used her again, often for the tour operator Travelsphere, on seasonal charters between 1998 and 2002. In 2004 and again in 2005 she performed a season of cruises from various regional ports in the UK for CMS under the general sales agency of Classic International Cruises, but it was to be another nine years before the company worked with her again.

Funchal had an interesting history: she was constructed in Elsinore, Denmark in 1961 as a dual-purpose mail ship and cruise liner and operated regularly until 1972 between Lisbon and the Atlantic Islands of the Azores, Madeira, and the Canaries. She had substantial cargo carrying capacity with provision for cars, mail, general cargo and, in the four refrigerated compartments in the forward holds, bananas. Early in her career she was owned by one of the wealthiest families in the Azores and one of her special passengers was the President of Portugal, Admiral Thomaz. In fact, *Funchal* went on to serve as the Presidential Yacht for state visits to the Atlantic Islands, the Portuguese African colonies, and Brazil. During the celebrations in 1972 to mark the 150th anniversary of Brazil's independence, the remains of Dom Pedro (1798–1834), the first Emperor of Brazil, were carried in an urn on board the ship on a special Lisbon to Rio de Janeiro voyage.

Mechanical problems had begun to plague the ship and, in 1972, her boilers and turbines were removed after just 11 years' service, and two diesel engines were installed at an Amsterdam shipyard. Over an eight-period the ship was effectively rebuilt. As constructed in 1961, she was a three-class vessel for her designated liner service with first-class accommodation for 80 passengers, Tourist 'A' class had 156 beds and Tourist 'B' class could accommodate 164 passengers. There was also an allowance for 100 deck passengers. The first-class passengers were kept separate from everyone else and, accordingly, there were three separate sets of public rooms. In the cabins, the first class enjoyed private facilities, and Tourist 'A' class had a shower or bath and a toilet either individually or shared with an adjoining cabin. Tourist 'B' class had communal facilities. However, by the 1970s that time had gone and she emerged as a very fine one-class cruise ship.

For the next 12 years she continued her successful cruising career, moving around various markets, and when she was acquired by Arcalia Shipping Company/Classic International Cruises in 1985, she continued to be constantly upgraded through a regular refurbishment programme. She generally wintered in Brazil where, with her Portuguese heritage and crew, she was extremely popular, and her summer business was divided between Sweden, with cruises from Gothenburg, and Belgium, where she had a regular charter partner and had also built up a regular following. However, in November 2005, *Funchal*'s winter schedule took a totally different direction when CMS persuaded CIC to position her into Western Australia for the austral summer period. CIC duly opened an office in Australia and several profitable seasons in the Antipodes followed before the Portuguese principal ceased trading in 2012, following the death of its founder and guiding light, George P. Potamianos.

So, in 2013 she changed hands and enjoyed another extensive, and this time very expensive, refit to emerge in the colours of a start-up company, Portuscale Cruises, which also had control of the rump of the former CIC fleet including *Athena*, rechristened *Azores*. Having tried its hand at operating a cruise programme under its own name with little success, Portuscale were more than happy in 2014 to step in when CMV were looking for a replacement for *Discovery*. Although she only operated the two cruises, *Funchal* undoubtedly left her passengers with some fond memories whether it was pre-dinner drinks in the Porto Bar, a floor show in the Ilha Verde Lounge or a conversation with one of the Portuguese stewards who had served in the ship for over 20 years.

Technical Data

Builder:	Helsingør Skibsværft, Copenhagen, DK
Launched	10th February 1961
Maiden CMV voyage:	18th October 2014
Port of registry:	Madeira, Portugal
Call sign:	CSBM
IMO number:	5124162
Length overall:	153. 51m
Beam:	19.05m
Draught:	6.40m
Gross tonnage:	9,563gt
Passenger Decks:	6
Lifts:	3
Machinery:	4 x BStork diesels developing 10,000bhp
Cruising Speed:	15.0kn
Passengers:	475
Crew:	155

Names	Owners/Disponent Owners	Operators
1961 onwards: *Funchal*	1961-1974: Empresa Insulana de Navegação	1961-1974: Empresa Insulana de Navegação
	1974-1985: Companhïa Portuguesa de Transportes Maritimos	1974-1985: Companhïa Portuguesa de Transportes Maritimos
	1985-2011: Great Warwick Co. Inc	1985-2011: Classic International Cruises
	2011-2013: Laid Up	2011-2013: Laid Up
	2013-2015: Pearl Cruise Transportes	2013-2014: Portuscale Cruises
		October 2014: Cruise & Maritime Voyages
		2014-2015: Portuscale Cruises

Senior Personnel

Captains	Chief Engineer	Staff Captains	Hotel Directors
Filipe Sousa	Albano Nunes	Antonio Ramos	Jose Olivera

Astor (March 2013 to date)

The stylish *Astor* has a South African background in more than one respect as highlighted in this lovely image. *(CMV Library)*

stor was ordered in 1985 by the South African Marine Corporation (Safmarine) from Howaldtswerke-Deutsche Werft of Kiel, Germany, the second of two near-sisters designed for both cruising and long-distance voyages from South Africa to the UK. She was designed to be 12 metres longer than her sister (the 1981-built Astor, later Astoria of the Transocean brand) with more powerful engines to sustain the schedules of the liner business. The interior layout and decorations of Astor were very similar to the 1981-built Astor, down to the bathroom fittings. But the 1987-built ship was designed with a larger number of suites, improved crew quarters, and a casino and conference facilities. Astor was furnished in traditional style using large amounts of dark wood, with many of the public rooms having high ceilings.

But Safmarine changed their strategy and Astor was sold in January 1986, whilst still under construction, to the Marlan Corporation of Port Louis, Mauritius. Marlan Corporation employed Morgan Leisure of Colchester and German operator Globus Cruises as their marketing agents to source charters for the vessel. Both companies had financial connections with Safmarine. Astor was launched on 30th May 1986 and delivered with a white hull, and red, white and blue funnels sporting an ML symbol.

Astor left Hamburg on her maiden cruise on 14th January 1987 heading to South America via Genoa, before cruising in the Caribbean. However, these were difficult times for a premium cruise product, and Astor was sold to the Soviet Union company Black Sea Shipping on 3rd October 1988. She was renamed Fedor Dostoevskiy and chartered by them to Transocean Tours, making her first voyage from Genoa on 23rd December 1988. From March 1990, Neckermann Seereisen took Fedor Dostoevskiy on a five-year deal, but the high charter rates demanded by her Ukrainian owners proved difficult to sustain, and in December 1995 Aquamarin Cruises became the fourth company to market the vessel in Germany. Reverting to her original name in 1995, Astor enjoyed only a short period with Aquamarin, and in April 1997 she returned to operate with Transocean Tours.

Whilst competitors were embarking on a strategy of introducing progressively larger craft, the modest capacity, premium quality, traditional style of Astor still held large appeal to the conservative German cruise market. Transocean Tours recognised this appeal in 2002 and secured the charter of her smaller sister, which remained under the Transocean flag until 2008 as Astoria. In 2005, 75% of Astor passengers were regular travellers, and the vessel had consolidated her popular position in the German market. On 28th November 2008 Somali pirates made an attempt to seize the vessel whilst she was in the Gulf of Oman

Astor reverted to her original name in 1995 but this shot shows her still in her Russian colours from her *Fedor Dostoyevsky* days. *(FotoFlite)*

en route from Sharm-al-Sheikh to Dubai, but the attack was stopped by the German frigate *Mecklenburg-Vorpommern*, without those on board *Astor* being aware of the situation.

The bankruptcy of Transocean saw Astor transfer to the ownership of Munich company Astor Premicon Hochseekreuz, and she was re-registered to the Bahamian flag with a home port of Nassau. Premicon began a long-planned €16m conversion and renovation of the vessel in 2009, deliberately retaining her small-ship feel to contrast with the behemoths of her American-owned competitors in the German market. The upgrade stayed true to Astor's unmistakable classic heritage, leaving the lounges and layout of the ship untouched to retain the large selection of public spaces on board, but focussing on cabin interiors, carpeting and the soft elements of furnishing. This was consistent with the aspirations of Transocean passengers who rebelled against large-ship cruising.

CMV chartered Astor for their Australian business in November 2013, and the following year CMV TransOcean took on the charter agreement through their Greek parent Global Cruise Line, and deployed the vessel in the German market during the summer months and Australia during the European winter.

In 2015 she was allocated to the TransOcean brand. She is the real workhorse of the CMV fleet, contributing greater mileage than any of her fleet-mates in every year since 2014 and clocking up more than

550,000 miles by the end of 2019. That is the equivalent of a trip to the moon and back, and a third of the way on her next trip.

Astor is well matched to her target guests, recreating the atmosphere of the great ocean liners of yesteryear, and it is no surprise that she built up a loyal following. Despite her winters in the Australian market, *Astor's* primary role for CMV remains in the German market for the TransOcean brand, where she is immensely popular. She was, after all, built in Germany. Each year she went through two language transitions between German and Australian English. And the on-board offer changed accordingly with Australian beers and wines coming to the fore in the winter months. The ship's interior signage and deck plans are primarily in German, although this is likely to change again with her move to the French market in 2021, but her small size makes it difficult to get lost aboard.

Astor's facilities are mainly found on the upper four decks. The Sun Deck has an active role, in addition to catering for those who enjoy outdoor seating. The deck has a jogging and walking track around the perimeter, and there is a large sports court with opportunities for basketball, volleyball, table tennis, big board chess, half-court tennis, golf, and yoga. Sun seekers will be attracted to the Sun Terrace aft on the Bridge Deck, with drinks service from the intimate Hanse Bar, which lies adjacent to the Fitness Centre. There's even shuffleboard for the mildly energetic.

At the forward end of the boat deck lie the largest and most luxurious suites aboard. The two Senator Suites and the Astor Suite include a bedroom, dining room, lounge area, balcony and a large bathroom. All rooms have been fully upgraded to modern standards, whilst the passenger corridors are notably wide. Aft of the passenger cabins is a promenade area, which leads to the outdoor alfresco area and the Übersee Club Bistro for an informal dining experience. Much of the teak deck space is given over to sun lounges, but there is also an outdoor pool and two whirlpools.

The main ship facilities can be found on the Promenade Deck. The 443-seat Astor Show Lounge occupies a large space at the forward end, in classic cabaret lounge style with grouped seating, a bar and small

Top left: Sailing off into the sunset after another successful day ashore in October 2008. *(CMV Library)*

.Middle left: One of the two spacious Senator Suites located in a premium forward position on Boat Deck. *(CMV Library)*

Bottom left: The pool and lido area viewed from the Sun Terrace outside the popular Hanse Bar on Bridge Deck. *(CMV Library)*

stage. The quality of entertainment matches the high standards for which CMV is renowned, with production shows, musicians and guest artists providing a lively focus each evening. Outside the Show Lounge lies a well-stocked library to port and a card room to starboard, always a popular venue. From here guests can promenade round the tempting boutique, take advantage of the expansive views to sea from the large floor-to-ceiling windows, visit the internet café, book a shore excursion, or be tempted by the jewellers or the Photo Shop. Here are also large portraits of the Russian poets Alexander Pushkin and Leo Tolstoy — relics from the time when *Astor* sailed as *Fedor Dostoevskiy*.

Admiral's Restaurant offers an Asian Fusion menu and the Commodore's Restaurant features Mediterranean dishes, both available for that special occasion for a modest supplement.

The Atlantic Deck is primarily given over to cabin and suite accommodation, but also houses the vessel's concierge and reception area, whilst lower down the Baltic Deck has 144 cabins and an Ironing Room. On the Caribic Deck, the lowest passenger deck, is the Astor's medical centre and the well-equipped Oasis Spa and Wellness Centre with its indoor pool, sauna area, heated seating, deck chairs, massage area and beauty salon, recreating the classic spa environment of the great

A totally relaxing experience in the Oasis Spa and Wellness Centre on Caribic Deck. *(CMV Library)*

The heated indoor pool in the Spa area is a rare feature for a ship of this size but has proved universally popular with Astor passengers. *(CMV Library)*

The hub of the midships area is the 79-seat Captain's Club, a centrally located, immensely popular bar and lounge. This is home to morning coffee rendezvous, afternoon cocktails, and pre-dinner drinks, and hosts evening entertainment including live bands and karaoke. The resident pianist ensures the ambience encourages friendliness and warmth, and officers can frequently be seen engaging with guests.

The main dining facilities lie aft on the Promenade Deck. The main restaurant, the 278-seat Waldorf, decorated in brown and beige tones, spans the full width of the far aft end of the vessel, offering breakfast and lunch, and two sittings for dinner, to accommodate busy sailings. There is a wide choice of menus prepared by the Executive Chef, and typically a five-course dinner each evening. There are also two 36-seat restaurants forward of the Waldorf, offering a more select dining experience. The

ocean liners.

Astor provides an excellent selection of modern cabin accommodation in a total of 289 cabins (of which 42 are suites, three have balconies, 198 are ocean-view, and 91 are inside) in a choice of 16 grades from Standard to De Luxe with 70% of cabins having an ocean view. All cabins have baths and individually controlled air-conditioning. They vary in size from the 13m2 twin berth inside cabin to the dramatic 48m2 of the Senator Suites and the magnificent 59m2 of the Astor Suites for the ultimate in on-board opulence. These have three flat-screen televisions with DVD player, a separate living and seating area, an outdoor terrace with seating, and luxury bathrooms with underfloor heating, bath and shower, and a separate guest toilet.

Names	**Owners/Disponent Owners**	**Operators**
1987-88: Astor	1987-88: Marlan Corporation	1987-88: Morgan Leisure (Astor Cruises)
1988-91: *Fedor Dostoyevskiy*	1988-91: Black Sea Steamship Company	1988-90: Transocean Tours
1991-95: *Fedor Dostoyevsky*	1991-96: Fedor Dostoyevskiy Shipping Co	1990-95: Neckermann Seereisen
1995 to date: *Astor*	1996-2010: Astor Shipping Co	1995-96: Aquamarin
	2010-14: Premicon	1996-2013 Transocean Tours
	2014 to date: Passion Shipping Ltd (GMG)	2010-2013: Premicon
		2013 to date: Cruise & Maritime Voyages

Senior Personnel

Captains	**Chief Engineer**	**Staff Captains**	**Hotel Directors**
Emmanouil Psarrakis (2013-16)	Georgios Katsifarakis (2013)	Igor Smerichynsky	Laurence (Larry) Jackson
Filipe Jorge Pestana Camolino E Sousa (2015)	Oleksandr Lysenko (2014-19)	Viacheslav Kolesnykov	Christian Shrangl
Nikolas Michaloliakos (2016)	Sergiy Taranenko (2014-19)	Andrey Lesnichiy	Marko Scavuzzo
Sergiy Strusevych (2014-19)		Adrian David	Daniel Reiter
Andrey Lesnichiy (2016-19)		Christos Karatsalis	Joao Luis De Sousa E Silva
Michail Smyrnaios (2018)		Igor Popyenko	Maximilian Klassen
			Mathias Schmidt

Technical Data

Builder:	Howaldtswerke-Deutsche Werft, Kiel, Germany
Launched:	24th June 1986
Delivered:	14th January 1987
Port of registry:	Nassau, Bahamas
Maiden CMV voyage:	29th March 2013
Call sign:	C6JR3
IMO number:	8506373
Length overall:	176.5m
Beam:	22.6m
Draught:	6.1m
Gross tonnage:	20,606gt
Passenger Decks:	7
Lifts:	2
Machinery:	4 x Sulzer-Wartsila Diesels
Max/Cruising Speed:	18.0kt/16.5kt
Passengers:	600
Cabins:	289
Crew:	260

Astoria (January 2015 to date)

Astoria leaves Poole heading for the River Seine on 31st August 2018. *(Kevin Mitchell)*

Towards the end of the Second World War, Swedish America Line needed a new transatlantic liner for their Gothenburg to New York service. An order was placed with the Götaverken-Hisingen shipyard of Gothenburg in October 1944 and the keel was laid down April 1945, but delivery was delayed, and *Stockholm* was not launched until 9th September 1946. She was the fourth company vessel to bear the name. *Stockholm* was finally delivered to Swedish America Line on 7th February 1948, then the largest ship ever built in Sweden. With a raked bow and cruiser stern, *Stockholm* was one of the smallest liners on the North Atlantic run at 11,650grt. She could carry 395 passengers, 113

First Class and 282 Tourist Class, although there were some interchangeable cabins between First and Tourist, and she had a crew of 220. All cabins had a porthole or a window, a unique feature for the time. *Stockholm* retained the tasteful design and décor standards for which the company was noted, but in a more intimate environment than other vessels in the fleet. She was outfitted in Swedish America Line's distinctive white hull, with a yellow funnel with a round blue shield containing three golden crowns.

Stockholm departed from Gothenburg on her maiden voyage on 21st February 1948 and immediately encountered some of the worst winter

storms on the North Atlantic. Her slender hull design and lack of stabilisers made this a memorable trip for all the wrong reasons. She acquired a reputation for being 'The Worst Roller on the North Atlantic', but although unsuited for the North Atlantic, her yacht-like appearance made her a natural for the cruise market and she proved both popular and successful on cruises from New York to the Caribbean.

In 1952 *Stockholm* underwent a major refit, with her superstructure enlarged forward to include passenger cabins for an additional 178 passengers, making a total of 568 in 215 cabins, as well as a small cinema. Her tonnage was now registered as being 12,644grt. Further accommodation was added forward on the Promenade Deck in early 1956 when Denny Brown stabilisers were fitted.

Stockholm left New York for Gothenburg on her 103rd eastbound crossing on 25th July 1956. As she approached Nantucket at 18 knots on a foggy night she encountered the much larger liner *Andrea Doria* inbound from Genoa at 22.5 knots. The two vessels were on parallel courses, with *Andrea Doria* in fog and *Stockholm* in clearer conditions, but the master of *Andrea Doria* turned his ship to port in contravention of Maritime Law, and the two vessels collided at around 23:10. *Stockholm's* bow was wrenched off as she struck the starboard side of *Andrea Doria*, but the majority of passengers and crew survived the collision and three ships responded to provide assistance. *Stockholm* was partially crippled for some time when one of her anchor cables sank to the seabed, but as soon as it could be raised she went to the rescue and was able to take on board 327 passengers, as well as 245 crew members from *Andrea Doria*. *Andrea Doria* capsized and sank the next morning. *Stockholm* returned slowly to New York with a badly twisted and crumbled bow, and 1,319 people on board – her lifeboat capacity was for 846 persons. Sadly 47 people from *Andrea Doria* and five crew of *Stockholm* lost their lives in the collision.

The subsequent inquiry judged the Captain of *Andrea Doria* should take the major share of the blame.

Stockholm's bow was repaired for $1m at the Bethlehem Steel Company Shipbuilding Division in Brooklyn, and just over three months later *Stockholm* returned to her regular services. She was, however, a

Top left: **The spacious seating areas and classic promenade deck at the stern of** *Astoria. (Andrew Cooke)*

Middle left: **Sirens Lounge wraps round the atrium and the double stairway to Mediterranean Deck 4.** *(CMV Library)*

Bottom left: **Stained glass provides a backdrop to the Chapel.** *(Andrew Cooke)*

small ship in relation to others operated by Swedish America Line, and on 15th May 1959 she was purchased by the East German Freier Deutscher Gewerkschaftsbund, a Trade Union seeking a full-time cruise ship for workers.

After a comprehensive refit she was renamed *Völkerfreundschaft* (the Peoples' Friend Ship) on 3rd January 1960, operating as a Soviet cruise ship, primarily visiting Eastern bloc countries as well as Cuba. She was registered in Rostock, under the management of the VEB Deutsche Seereederei. She was occasionally chartered to Stena Line for Swedish winter cruises to the Caribbean. Mounting losses forced her sale in 1985 to Neptunus Rex Enterprises, who shortened her name to *Völker* and she was laid up at Holmestrand, then from December 1985 in Southampton. *Völker* was chartered to Norwegian interests in December 1986 to become an accommodation ship for refugees in Oslo as the renamed *Fridtjof Nansen*.

In May 1989, she was sold to Italian Star Lauro Lines for conversion into a luxury cruise ship, but she remained under charter as *Fridtjof Nansen* in Oslo until 1993, when she was towed to Genoa, home port of *Andrea Doria*. Star Lauro quickly renamed her *Italia I*. The following year she was renamed *Italia Prima* and completely stripped down to her hull for a radical rebuild as a luxury cruise ship. She emerged with new diesel engines and a new streamlined superstructure with a modern, stylised funnel and a large sponson added to her stern to improve stability. Her interior was elegant and spacious, with elegant décor featuring Italian marble, art and touches of brass and chrome designed by Italian interior designer Giuseppe de Jorio. Unusually all cabins were fitted with a full bath with an overhead shower, with the floor and basin tops covered in Italian marble; every bathroom was given a bidet. The full rebuild cost over US$150m.

Italia Prima was managed by Nina Cia. di Navigazione from 1995 to 2002, including charters to other travel and cruise companies. She made her first 'Round the World' voyage for Neckermann Seereisen in 1997, which included inaugural visits to Australian ports including Sydney. In 1998 *Italia Prima* was chartered to the Valtur Tourist Organisation and renamed *Valtur Prima,* but this proved to be a short-lived venture, and the vessel was laid up in Cuba from 2001 until 2002. *Valtur Prima* was purchased by Festival Cruise Line and renamed *Caribe* to operate voyages to Cuba from 2002, but again the Line struggled financially and in 2004 she was laid up again. This time she returned to the Italian ownership of Nina Cia. di Navigazione to be renamed *Athena* and chartered to Arcalia Shipping for their Classic International Cruises (CIC) fleet.

After an extensive refit *Athena* entered a successful period of service in Europe, with several winter visits to Australia. She was purchased outright by Arcalia Shipping in 2008 and re-registered in Madeira under the Portuguese flag but continued to sail for the CIC fleet, often under charter to tour operators. The company went into liquidation at the end of 2012 and *Athena* was acquired at auction by Portuscale Cruises of Lisbon early in 2013 and renamed *Azores*. A period of lay-up followed, before *Azores* was chartered to Ambiente Kreuzfahrten from 10th March 2014. *Azores* found herself laid up and again on the market at the end of 2014, but her style and condition made her well-suited to the CMV philosophy of traditional country-house-style cruising and she was long-term chartered as a replacement for *Discovery.* She left Portland on 26th January 2015 on her 30-night CMV maiden voyage to the West Indies. *Azores* was renamed *Astoria* after her first season of operation.

In a poignant moment during the maiden voyage in February 2015, Rosalea Ryan presented the ship's bell from *Stockholm,* on loan to CMV, for display in a cabinet outside the boutique on Calypso Deck 4a. The bell was lost during the collision with *Andrea Doria* but recovered by divers from the seabed. It is a poignant reminder of the five crew members of *Stockholm* who lost their lives.

Following a short 2017 spring season for CMV from London Tilbury, *Astoria* was chartered by Rivages du Monde to operate a programme of cruises from France to Northern Europe. The pattern was repeated in 2018. From winter 2019 *Astoria* will operate itineraries to Baja California and Mexican Riviera ports leaving from her new home port of Puerto Peñasco, Mexico, whilst returning to sail from St Nazaire, Dunkirk and Zeebrugge for Rivages du Mode during summer 2020.

Astoria is the second-oldest ocean-going passenger vessel in the world, reflecting the quality of her original build and the care with which successive owners have maintained her in more than seven decades of operation. She still retains the capacity to enchant guests with her sophisticated internal décor, inviting lounges and homely retreats.

Astoria offers a traditional maritime experience in extremely comfortable surroundings. Her facilities are spread across eight decks, numbered one to seven, with the Calypso Deck labelled 4a as a consequence of being added during the 1994 rebuilding.

Aft on Observation Deck 7 lies the sauna, beauty salon and fitness centre, with panoramic views out to sea from the spacious classic open decks. The Navigators Deck 6 is given over to suite and cabin accommodation, with the Calypso Bar serving the outside deck at the stern. The forward end of Promenade Deck 5 is also an accommodation area, but aft lies the large auditorium conference room and the intimate

Astoria is dressed overall as she leaves Portsmouth with a Captain's overnight Gala cruise on 15th September 2018. *(Andrew Cooke)*

night club, where night owls can dance the night away. There is further outdoor deck space to the stern.

Calypso Deck 4a hosts the main passenger facilities for *Astoria*. The forward end is dedicated to the Calypso Show Lounge, home for cabaret performances, production shows and guest entertainers. There's a dedicated bar, and the adjacent Captain's Club offers a smaller, more intimate environment for live music. On the starboard side lies the Library and Internet Room, and the ever-popular Card Room, whilst to port there is the Photo Shop. Midships on Calypso Deck 4a can be found the boutique shops, the Astoria Lounge, and Circe's Casino. The central walkway opens out to the Sirenes Bar, where guests can enjoy more of their favourite melodies from the ship's entertainment team, and the atrium that takes guests down to the reception on Mediterranean Deck 4. The Lotus Buffet offers a wide choice of informal al fresco dining opportunities for breakfast, lunch, afternoon tea, and dinner, and opens out at the stern to the main swimming pool with a large outdoor seating area.

Mediterranean Deck 4 is primarily an accommodation deck, but as well as being home to *Astoria's* reception also hosts the small ship's chapel.

The Olissipo Restaurant on Atlantic Deck 3 offers sumptuous meals served by *Astoria's* attentive restaurant staff. Dining is always a special event on board and passengers will experience high levels of gastronomic delight. Breakfast, lunch and dinner are served in the Olissipo or alternatively in the Lotus Buffet, which also provides the choice to eat 'al fresco' on the Pool Deck.

Astoria offers 277 cabins (9 suites, 43 balcony, 229 ocean-view, and 49 inside) with 17 choices of interior and ocean-view cabins in standard, standard-plus, superior, superior-plus, premium, deluxe, junior suite, and junior suite deluxe categories. There are eight De Luxe Balcony Suite two-room cabins with private balcony and one two-roomed Owners Presidential Suite, which lies behind the bridge in the officers' mess area. 85% of cabins have an ocean view and almost 20% are of a deluxe standard. All cabins are air-conditioned with private en-suite facilities in marble-floored bathrooms with a bath and shower over, coupled with ample wardrobe and storage space. Each features music channels, a hairdryer, fridge, television with in-house movies, news and information channels, and a personal safe. The suite accommodation also has the benefit of a jacuzzi bath and a seating area. Cabin sizes vary from the 10.92m² of the Premium Twin Inner cabins to the expansive 30.35m² of the De Luxe Balcony Suites.

Senior Personnel

Captains
Michail Smyrnaios (2015, 2018)
Filipe Jorge Pestana Camolino E Sousa
(2016-2017)
Antonio Manuel Marques De Morais (2017-19)
Christos Ntaoutis (2017)
Valentyn Zhukov (2018)
Emmanouil Psarrakis (2019)
Andrian Medina Gonzalez (2019)

Chief Engineer
Vasileos Stavridis (2015)
Joao Manuel Severino Mauricio (2015-18)
Emmanouil Bouzounierakis (2016)
Charalampos Drivas (2016-19)
Petros Gazis (2017, 2019)
Enrique Estrada Bueno (2019)

Staff Captains
Andrian Medina Gonzalez
Stamatios Kakaris
Christos Karatsalis
Michail Smyrnaios

Hotel Directors
Patrick Veysseyre
Joao Luis De Sousa E Silva

Names	Owners/Disponent Owners	Operators
1948-60: Stockholm	1948-59: Swedish America Line	1948-60: Swedish America Line
1960-65: Völkerfreundschaft	1959-85: Freier Deutscher Gewerkschaftsbund	1960-66: VEB Deutsche Seereederei
1985-86: Völker	1985-89: Neptunus Rex Enterprises	1966-85: VEB Deutsche Seereederei/Stena Line
1986-89: Fridtjof Nansen	1989-94: StarLauro	1985-94: Laid up and extensively rebuilt
1993-94: Italia 1	1994-2002: Nina Cia. Di Navigazione	1994-95: Nina Cia. Di Navigazione
1994-98: Italia Prima	2002-04: Festival Cruises	1995-98: Neckermann Seereisen
1998-2002: Valtur Prima	2005-2008 Classic International Cruises SA	1998: Laid up
2002-05: Caribe	2008 to date: Islands Cruises Transportes	1998-2001: Valtur Tourist
2005-13: Athena	Maritimos, Unipessoal Lda	2001-02: Laid up
2013-16: Azores		2002-04: Festival Cruises
2016 to date: Astoria		2004-05: Laid up
		2005-13: Classic International Cruises
		2013-14: Portuscale Cruises
		2015 to date: Cruise & Maritime Voyages

Technical Data

Builder:	Götaverken-Hisingen, Gothenburg, Sweden (Yard No 611)	Gross tonnage:	16,144gt
		Passenger Decks:	8
Launched:	9th September 1946	Lifts:	2
Delivered:	21st February 1948	Machinery:	2 x Wartsila 16V32, 10,700kW (14,300hp)
Port of registry:	Madeira	Max/Cruising Speed:	16.5kt/15.0kt
Maiden CMV voyage:	26th January 2015	Passengers:	550
Call sign:	CQRV	Cabins:	277
IMO number:	5383304	Crew:	300
Length overall:	160.07m		
Beam:	21.03m		
Draught:	7.6m		

Magellan (March 2015 to date)

Magellan at Honfleur on 1st September 2018. *(Andrew Cooke)*

Magellan is a Holiday-class vessel built originally for Carnival Cruise Line as *Holiday* by Aalborg Værft in Denmark and completed in 1985. *Holiday* was fitted with the characteristic Carnival 'fins' astride her funnel to carry engine exhaust up and away from the ship, based on the earlier designs of the famous SS *France*. She was the largest ship in the Carnival fleet until her sister *Jubilee* was delivered in 1986. In her earliest form *Holiday* was noted as an unstable ship, but the issue was corrected by the addition of a supplementary pontoon welded across the bottom of her transom stern. She was the last vessel built at the yard, as shortly after delivery Aalborg Værft went out of business.

The $170m *Holiday* was described by Carnival as a 'SuperLiner', but her only 'Liner' voyage was on delivery to Miami. A contemporary report described *Holiday* as 'a mindboggling array of gathering palaces – from glittering Broadway and Times Square to the tropical Tahiti Lounge and a multi-tiered theatre. Mix that with a sedate library, an ear-popping disco, a bar from Bogie's Casablanca and a beehive-busy casino, and you get the picture.' The interior design by architect Joe Farcus featured a restored 1934-built 18-passenger Danish bus – the Bette Astrup – at the Bus Stop Café on the Promenade Deck, with an inauthentic Coney Island destination blind. Carnival's newest ship quickly proved immensely popular, sailing 100% full for the first couple of seasons. How many were attracted to the 'Grandmas and Honeymooners' parties on board is not recorded. Her schedules were based in Miami, offering 7-night cruises to St Maarten, St Thomas and Nassau year-round every Saturday, but the slow speed requirement was not best-suited for her diesel engines. *Holiday* was flagged in Nassau, Bahamas.

The Caribbean schedules continued but it was not until 2003 that *Holiday* went for her first major dry dock renovation. By then she was beginning to appear particularly tired in appearance.

Holiday was one of three ships taken out of service by Carnival in late 2005 for charter to the Federal Emergency Management Authority (FEMA) to act as emergency accommodation for victims of Hurricane Katrina. She was docked in Mobile, Alabama and lay empty for weeks whilst the agency determined what to do with her. *Holiday* initially housed 150 people who had been sheltering in Pascagoula, Mississippi, before transferring to that port as facilities were restored. In early 2006 *Holiday* underwent an extensive three-week refit when her FEMA contract finished. She received new carpeting and tiling across the ship, and a redesigned lobby with new seating. A nine-hole mini-golf course was added to the Verandah Deck, and the Spa Carnival was refreshed with an updated salon and new exercise equipment. The Four Winds and

Holiday, dressed overall in the plain Carnival livery with her distinctive red funnel prominent. *(Ferry Publications Library)*

Seven Seas, *Holiday's* main dining rooms, had their ceilings replaced, and the ship's galleys received new and updated equipment. Meanwhile her propellers were repaired and engines refurbished.

Holiday returned to her normal cycle of sailings around the western Caribbean, home-porting at Mobile, Alabama, which continued until November 2009 when she was retired from the Carnival fleet. She was laid up for a short while before undergoing a comprehensive €55m dry dock refit prior to transfer to the Iberocruceros brand within the Carnival Group in April 2010. She emerged purged of all traces of her Carnival history and tailored to meet Spanish tastes as *Grand Holiday*, retaining her distinctive funnel now painted in dark blue, with her white hull adorned with coloured graphics of people in holiday mode. Decks were renamed after Spanish places – Valencia, Sevilla, Pamplona etc, and all shipboard facilities became Spanish in style and name. *Grand Holiday* made her maiden voyage for Iberocruceros on 18th May 2010, now registered in Madeira, Portugal and based in the Western Mediterranean.

During the 2014 winter Olympics *Grand Holiday* served as a floating 4-star hotel, moored at Port Sochi Imeretinsky from 5th to 24th February. One further season for *Grand Holiday* followed with Iberocruceros but in November 2014 the company was absorbed by Costa Crociere, also within the Carnival Group. CMV announced on 3rd November 2014 that *Grand Holiday* would be joining the British fleet as *Magellan* in Spring 2015. Her first season's programme was released the following day.

Ferdinand Magellan was a Portuguese explorer who organised a Spanish expedition to find a westward route to the Spice Islands. His fleet of five vessels left Spain on 20th September 1519 and headed across the Atlantic, reaching Rio de Janeiro in December. Magellan faced mutiny during a five-month winter lay-up but overcame this to lead his dwindling fleet through the Straits of Magellan and out into the Pacific. He finally reached the Philippines on 6th March 1521 but was killed in a battle with indigenous islanders on 21st April. The remaining party finally located the Spice Islands in November 1521 and were able to trade for spices, but only one vessel was able to make it back to Spain on 6th September 1522. Less than 20 of the original crew of 270 men survived.

Magellan was formally renamed by Gloria Hunniford on 12th March 2015 at London Tilbury and immediately became the flagship of the CMV fleet. She left London Tilbury bound for Iceland and the Faroe Islands on 15th March on her maiden 'Solar Eclipse and Northern Lights' voyage for CMV.

The introduction of *Holiday* had been a big step forward in design for Carnival Cruises and her wide corridors, spacious interiors and extensive wooden deck areas still make a big impression on passengers. Her nine passenger decks are Caribbean Deck 4, Baltic Reception Deck 5, Atlantic Main Deck 6, Pacific Upper Deck 7, Amundsen Deck 8, Magellan Deck 9, Columbus Deck 10, Navigator Deck 11, and Sun Deck 12. Passenger facilities are found on the upper decks from Amundsen Deck 8 to Sun Deck 12, whilst accommodation is predominantly on the lower decks from Caribbean Deck 4 to Pacific Upper Deck 7.

Sun Deck 12 offers a Sun Terrace and large whirlpool, affording the finest views from above the bridge. Suite accommodation is located forward on the Navigator Deck 11, where six Royal Suites, four Deluxe Suites and four Junior Suites offer the finest accommodation on the vessel. All these suites offer balconies. This deck also hosts the well-equipped gym, and makes the most of the elevated position with spectacular views from the Neptune Observation Bar outdoors at the stern. This area also has a small stage for outdoor performances.

Magellan's bridge lies on Columbus Deck 10, with the main lido pool located midships where bathers and sunbathers are supported by the 224-seat Eros Bar. The Indian Fusion Restaurant on the port side offers

Top left: **Magellan's restaurant is ready to receive another sitting of satisfied guests** *(CMV Library)*

Middle left: **The cool ambience of Sinatra's.** *(CMV Library)*

Bottom left: **The sumptuously-appointed Spa is an outstanding feature.** *(CMV Library)*

Magellan's spectacular Reception area on Deck 5. *(CMV Library)*

drinks, whilst Sinatra's Lounge Bar brings a touch of themed elegance to a more intimate music venue. The new Taverner's Pub is a taste of home for guests, with a classic British environment featuring a tempting selection of bottled and draught beers and a trained bar team ready to mix the most exotic cocktail. A dartboard completes this home from home. Aft on Magellan Deck 9 can be found the popular Nansen Card and Bridge Room and the pampered paradise of the superbly equipped opulent Jade Spa. Here guests can enjoy hairdressing and beauty treatments and visit the sauna and massage facilities. There's still room to fit in an attractively 'grassed' Sun Terrace at the stern.

Guests descend by stairway or lift from Magellan Deck 9 to the main 514-seat Waldorf and 344-seat Kensington dining rooms on Amundsen Deck 8, which lie aft and forward of the main galley. These restaurants serve full English breakfast, a five-course lunch and a sumptuous dinner with two-sitting dining.

The lower tier of the Magellan Main Show Lounge lies forward on this deck, which also hosts the Shackleton Conference Room and *Magellan's* main shopping galleria, with a tempting array of well-priced boutique goods on offer. Hampton's Lounge Bar sits astride the walkway from the Kensington Restaurant to the Magellan Main Show Lounge: the perfect rendezvous for a pre-dinner cocktail or that postprandial aperitif.

The lower decks host the majority of *Magellan's* 726 cabins in 15 different categories including standard, superior, premium, and premium-plus accommodation. All air-conditioned cabins offer private en-suite facilities, ample wardrobe and storage space, flat-screen television, mirrored dressing table, hairdryer, and personal safe. Specially designed ocean-view cabins feature windows allowing natural light, whereas the inner cabins have artificial light only. Cabin sizes vary from the 12.28m² of a superior single inner cabin to the 27.42m² of the Royal Suites, with the majority offering around 13m². *Magellan* offers five categories of inside cabin and seven types of outside cabin, including two categories for single occupancy as part of CMV's commitment to the solo traveller. All the inside and ocean-view cabins are found on Pacific Upper Deck 7, Atlantic Main Deck 6, Baltic Reception Deck 5 and Caribbean Deck 4. Baltic Reception Deck 5 also hosts the Reception and Shore Excursion Desks.

the best in Asian cuisine for a modest supplement. The delightfully informal Raffles Bistro offers space for 230 casual diners to eat indoors and space for a further 210 to enjoy outdoor dining. At the stern lies the Lido Bar and pool, with two whirlpools tempting guests from the extensive sunbathing area, a popular place to enjoy the open sea in sunny weather.

The magnificent, tiered, Magellan Main Show Lounge spans the forward area of both Magellan Deck 9 and Amundsen Deck 8 offering the opportunity for 793 guests to enjoy the splendid array of production shows and guest artists on offer. The upper level of the Show Lounge on Magellan Deck 9 is reached through the Photo Gallery to port and starboard, which lies forward of the Captain's Club, a bright and popular convivial space for a pre-show drink. Moving astern, the Casino Royale combines blackjack tables with gaming machines and flanks the entrance to the more peaceful environment of the Livingstone Library. Cappuccino's coffee shop fulfils the modern needs for speciality hot

Names	Owners/Disponent Owners	Operators
1985-*2009: Holiday*	1985-2015: Carnival Corporation	1985-2009: Carnival Cruise Lines
2010-14: *Grand Holiday*	2015 to date: Epic Cruise Ltd (GMG)	2010-14: Iberocruceros
2015 to date: *Magellan*		2015 to date: Cruise & Maritime Voyages

Senior Personnel

Captains	Chief Engineer	Staff Captains	Hotel Directors
Nikolas Michaloliakos (2015-16)	Venizelos Vardiampasis (2015-16)	Nikolaos Giannakopoulos	Daniel Reiter
Efstathios Gkoumas (2016)	Emmanouil Bouzounierakis (2015-16)	Michail Smyrnaios	Patrick Veysseyre
Emmanouil Psarrakis (2016)	Christos Koutikas (2015)	Igor Smerichynsky	Marko Scavuzzo
Panagiotis Mantzavinos (2016-17)	Christos Chouchoulis (2015-16)	Nicolai Andre Back	Joao Luis De Sousa E Silva
Filipe Jorge Pestana Camolino E Sousa (2017)	Dimitrios Dramitinos (2017, 2019)	Michail Mandalenakis	Jose Maria Correia de Sena
Ilias Venetantis (2017-18)	Periklis Papazafeiropoulos (2017)	Emmanouil Katsoudas	Brito
Oleksandr Dudov (2017)	Dimitrios Daillidis (2017-19)	Dimitrios Moschonas	Allwyn Furtado
Andrey Lesnichiy (2018)	Oleksandr Aleksandrov (2018-19)		
Michail Margaritis (2019)	Ioannis Korres (2017,2019)		
Valentyn Zhukov (2017-19)			

Technical Data

Builder:	Aalborg Værft, Aalborg, Denmark
Launched:	10th December 1983
Maiden voyage:	21st June 1985
Port of registry:	Nassau, Bahamas
Maiden CMV voyage:	15th March 2015
Call sign:	CQNH
IMO number:	8217881
Length overall:	221.30m
Beam:	28m
Draught:	7.45m
Gross tonnage:	46,052gt
Passenger Decks:	9
Lifts:	8
Machinery:	2 x 11,200kW Sulzer type engines, 3 x 3,750kW Wartsila generators
Max/Cruising Speed:	15.5kt
Passengers:	1,250
Cabins:	726
Crew:	660

A feeling of spaciousness is evident in the Mall on *Magellan*. *(Andrew Cooke)*

Columbus (June 2017 to date)

Columbus heads gracefully through the Bay of Biscay en route for Gibraltar during her 'Canary Islands & Madeira' cruise in October 2019. *(Kevin Mitchell)*

Columbus was built for Sitmar Cruises by Chantiers de L'Atlantique as *Sitmar FairMajesty* in 1988 The Italian Societa Italiana Transporti Marittimi SpA (Sitmar) was a family managed cruise operator established in 1938 serving the Mexican, Alaskan and Caribbean markets from the USA, and the Australian market from Sydney. The company was put up for sale in early 1988 and purchased by P&O for £125m. Amongst the assets acquired by P&O was *Sitmar FairMajesty*, which had been launched on 28th May 1988 but was still under construction at the Chantiers de L'Atlantique yard in Saint-Nazaire, France. She was fitted out in pastel shades and shiny finished interior designs to a design by Welton Becket Associates of California and emerged as *Star Princess* for P&O subsidiary Princess Cruises on 15th March 1989. She was christened by Audrey Hepburn on 23rd March 1989 in Fort Lauderdale, Florida, who also joined her maiden cruise.

On delivery *Star Princess* was the world's fourth-largest cruise ship, the largest in the P&O fleet (until 1990) and amongst the first large cruise ships to have her lifeboats nested lower down in the hull. She was the first large passenger ship to be built with diesel-electric propulsion, now

Star Princess was one of the largest cruise ships in the world when she entered service with Princess Cruises in 1989. *(Ferry Publications Library)*

the industry standard. Her design included the domed ceilinged 'Windows of the World' 270° observation lounge on Deck 14, affectionately known as 'Le Camembert' by her French builders.

Star Princess was deployed on alternate eastern and western Caribbean itineraries from Fort Lauderdale during the winter months and Alaskan cruises from Vancouver during the summer, with a 16-day positioning voyage through the Panama Canal at the start of each season.

Star Princess was chosen as the replacement for P&O's *Canberra* when she sailed for the breaker's yard in October 1997. The following month *Star Princess* arrived at Harland & Wolff, Belfast, for a £14m conversion into *Arcadia*, work which included adding more lounges and bars, reducing the size of her casino by half to make way for a bridge room, and installing a full-size half-section replica of a Polynesian war canoe from *Canberra* in her main dining room.

Arcadia made her maiden voyage for P&O Cruises on 23rd December 1997 and followed this with her inaugural world cruise between 5th January and 6th April 1998. She established a pattern of sailing in Northern Europe, the Atlantic Isles and the Mediterranean during the summer and repeating a world cruise each winter.

In 2003 P&O Cruises created a new sister brand 'Ocean Village', offering an alternative cruise experience 'for people who don't do cruises' and seeking to emulate the success which sister brand Aida had

achieved in Germany in attracting a new generation of cruise passengers. The brand targeted families and the 30–50-year-old market who were looking for a less formal experience, with a focus on freedom and flexibility in dining, dress standards, and entertainment. *Arcadia* was transferred from P&O Cruises to spearhead the new brand and renamed *Ocean Village* to sail in the Mediterranean in the summer and the Caribbean and Mexico in the winter. *Ocean Village* appeared in a bold colourful livery with red, orange and mauve motifs, breaking from the image of her sister company and was renamed by Ulrika Jonsson on 28th April 2003. She was joined by *Ocean Village Two,* the former *AidaBlu*, in 2007. This expansion coincided with the global downturn following the financial crash of 2008, and on 30th October 2008 Ocean Village announced that the brand would cease operations at the end of the 2010 season, with both vessels transferring to the P&O Cruises Australia fleet. There were too many 'people who don't do cruises' in the sector the company wished to attract. *Ocean Village Two* left the fleet in October 2009, whilst *Ocean Village* completed her final cruise a year later.

After completion of pre-fabrication works in July 2010 at Mivan's manufacturing facility in Northern Ireland, the *Ocean Village* underwent installation work in Singapore at Sembawang Shipyard, a subsidiary of Sembcorp Marine. This work was carried out over a 36-day period from November 2010, with over 1,800 people engaged to deliver the ship in the week before Christmas. The scope of work involved creation of new restaurants and bars including the Salt Grill and Waterfront restaurants, Connexions and Oasis Bars and the Choc Café. The vessel was given a complete change-over by overhauling all areas of the 11 passenger decks. Her hull was also given a new look through repainting with the latest high-tech and eco-friendly silicone paint. The Pool Deck received a new, 7m x 4m television screen and the atrium was refitted into a multipurpose entertainment, café, bar and retail space.

Ocean Village was renamed *Pacific Pearl* by New Zealand's board-sailing Olympic champion Barbara Kendall at Waitemata Harbour, Auckland on 21st December 2010 and left Auckland on her maiden voyage for P&O Cruises Australia the following day. Her new owners pitched *Pacific Pearl* at young couples, singles of all ages and families under the banner 'Your Choice Cruising', sailing from Sydney and Auckland and visiting destinations in Australia, New Zealand and the Pacific Islands. *Pacific Pearl* also featured a reverse osmosis (RO) plant and digital propulsion system.

She underwent an extensive refit in August 2015.

On 3rd March 2016 P&O Cruises Australia announced that *Pacific Pearl* would transfer out of the fleet in March 2017. She had completed

294 cruises and carried more than 500,000 passengers during her five years with the line. Shortly afterwards it was revealed that CMV would be her new operator. *Pacific Pearl* left Auckland on her final voyage for P&O Cruises Australia on 27th March 2017, reaching Singapore on 12th April, where she was handed over to CMV. She sailed on to the Damen Shiprepair Schiedam at Rotterdam for dry-docking and an upgrade in facilities before emerging as *Columbus*.

Columbus was officially named by Angela Rippon in the Palladium Show Lounge whilst berthed at London Tilbury on 8th June 2017. The naming ceremony was followed by a spectacular firework display which lit up the Thames. *Columbus* sailed on her maiden 3-night cruise to Amsterdam and Antwerp on 11th June 2017.

It is easy to see in the innovative design of *Columbus* how she helped set the standard of design of cruise vessels for generations to come, establishing an internal layout that has been much copied. Her passenger flows were designed so that passengers are never far from the main public rooms on the Promenade Deck: two passenger decks lie below the promenade whilst four are above. The lower decks are linked via a three-deck-high atrium.

Her passenger facilities are concentrated on three main decks.

At the forward end, above the bridge on the Sun Deck 14, is one of the most impressive lounges on *Columbus*, the 176-seater Dome Observatory and Nightclub. This beautifully decorated lounge has large windows that offer panoramic views on three sides of the ship by day, but is transformed in the evening into a modern nightclub with a large wooden dance floor. The Sun Deck provides areas to relax and take in the views, together with a jogging track. At the after end of the Sun Deck is a second observation lounge overlooking the stern of the vessel.

The Sun Deck overlooks the well-sheltered Lido Deck 12, which has two substantial heated swimming pools and a plethora of traditional teak decking, a strong feature of much of the open space on *Columbus*. At night the pool area comes alive with subtle lighting creating an appropriate mood. Informal dining is offered by the Alfresco Grill when weather permits, Gelato's is perfect for the poolside ice cream, and Cappuccino's brings a coffee-shop facility to those lounging round the pool. For those seeking the supreme formal dining experience, the 25-seat Grill is an exclusive environment offering the highest standards of

Top right: **The Chef's Table features an outstanding wine cellar.** *(CMV Library)*

Middle right: **Taverner's recreates the atmosphere of a typical English pub.** *(Andrew Cooke)*

Bottom right: **A well-appointed double balcony cabin.** *(CMV Library)*

Columbus lies alongside during a visit to Antwerp. *(Andrew Cooke)*

cuisine for a modest supplement, whilst the 40-seat Asian-themed Fusion restaurant lies next to the Plantation Bistro and is open to all passengers for dinner service. Al fresco dining can be found at the 125-seat Plantation Bistro, the main buffet restaurant on *Columbus*, situated at the after end of the Lido Deck and featuring a rich mix of tropical displays including shells and plants. At the aft end of Lido Deck 12 lies one of a series of small-tiered teak-deck terraced areas looking out over the stern.

Navigator's Deck 11 is primarily given over to passenger cabin accommodation, but also hosts the Crafter's Studio at the forward end of the vessel, the library, where it is possible to spend all day reading in comfortable surroundings, and Trumps & Aces Card and Bridge Room both of which lie towards the stern

The impressive Palladium Show Lounge, where *Columbus* was officially named by Angela Rippon, spans the Columbus Deck 8 and Promenade Deck 7 at the bow of the vessel. With seating for 690 passengers it hosts a wide variety of entertainment from production spectaculars by *Columbus's* in-house theatre company to speciality acts: with two shows each evening there are opportunities for all passengers to enjoy the show. It has perfect sight lines and a retractable stage that can be converted to a large floor to facilitate ballroom dancing. The Upper Deck 8 level is served by Hampton's Bar, whilst the Palladium Bar provides drinks to passengers on the Lower Deck 7 level.

Moving aft from the Palladium Show Lounge, passengers reach the

three-deck-high atrium situated just forward of amidships. This colourful, stylish area with sweeping staircases is the heart of *Columbus* and allows access down to Main Deck 6 and Reception Deck 5. There are shops and a photo gallery by the atrium on Promenade Deck 7 and the civilised seating environment is a sophisticated place to relax and unwind. The public rooms on the Promenade Deck are linked by corridors that run from either side, from the theatre along to the main restaurant. Overlooking the promenade and lit by natural light, these rooms include Connexions, for a smaller light entertainment venue with patterned carpets and numerous decorative features, and the Taverner's Pub, a throwback to *Columbus'* previous career with P&O Cruises. The lounges give access to the traditional wide teak-decked promenade that recreates the experience of old-fashioned sea travel.

The 812-seater Waterfront Restaurant can be found at the after end of the Promenade Deck. It cleverly offers a strong feeling of intimacy by using small partition screens to break up the space, and the muted decoration is stylish and attractive under a partly coffered ceiling. Two sittings are offered each evening. The 12-seater Chef's Table is a private dining area in the Waterfront Restaurant's impressive wine cellar.

More shopping can be found on Main Deck 6, adjacent to the atrium, with Raffles Bar convenient for the cabins on this primarily accommodation deck. Hemingway's on Reception Deck 5 – the lowest level of the atrium – serves speciality teas and coffees as well as a wide range of cakes and pastries. Here is another mini-hub for *Columbus*, with Reception, Guest Services, Future Cruise Sales and the Shore Excursions Desk all within easy reach. Pacific Deck 4 hosts the ship's fully equipped medical centre, whilst the Jade Spa lies on Caribbean Deck 2, with a thermal suite, hair and beauty salon and gym in close proximity.

Columbus has three sets of lifts, and there are a pair of striking staircases aft which descend through eight decks. Three quarters of the 775 cabins on *Columbus* have ocean views. All state rooms on board *Columbus* are carpeted, include twin beds that can be converted into a queen-sized bed, an en-suite bathroom, safety deposit box, TV, wardrobe, desk and hairdryer, and are serviced daily. There are 36 Junior Balcony Suites offering 34.5m² of space and 28 deluxe balcony cabins at an average size of 23.5m², all on Navigator's Deck 11. Other cabins on *Columbus* are a spacious 17.5m², with 13 categories of twin-occupancy cabins, with twin beds that can normally be converted into a queen-sized bed, and a choice of five single-occupancy cabin types.

Names

1988: *Sitmar Fairmajesty*

1989-97: *Star Princess*

1997-2003: *Arcadia*

2003-10: *Ocean Village*

2010-17: *Pacific Pearl*

2017 to date: *Columbus*

Owners/Disponent Owners

1988: Sitmar Cruises

1989-97: Princess Cruises

1997-2002: P&O

2002-17: Carnival Corporation

2017 to date: Lyric Cruise Ltd (GMG)

Operators

1989-97: Princess Cruises

1997-2002: P&O Cruises

2003-10: Ocean Village

2010-17: P&O Cruises Australia

2017 to date: Cruise & Maritime Voyages

Senior Personnel

Captains

Panagiotis Mantzavinos (2017)

Carlo Servillo (2017-18)

Michail Smyrnaios (2018)

Nektarios Rigas (2019)

Ilias Venetantis (2017-19)

Chief Engineer

Emmanouil Bouzounierakis (2017-18)

Dimitrios Daillidis (2017, 2019)

Konstantinos Svolimis (2018)

Lazaros Kritikopoulos (2019)

Staff Captains

Michail Smyrnaios

Adrian David

Dimitrios Kardasilaris

Dimitrios Moschonas

Vyacheslav Kolesnykov

Taras Kompaniyets

Pantelis Ampatzis

Hotel Directors

Daniel Reiter

Maximilian Klassen

Danilo Matrone

Joao Luis De Sousa e Silva

Allwyn Furtado

Vincent Jean Paul Richard Chabrier

Technical Data

Builder:	Chantiers de l'Atlantique, Saint-Nazaire, France
Launched:	28th May 1988
Maiden voyage:	15th March 1989
Port of registry:	Nassau, Bahamas
Maiden CMV voyage:	11th June 2016
Call sign:	C6CP4
IMO number:	8611398
Length overall:	247m
Beam:	28m
Draught:	8.12m
Gross tonnage:	63,786gt
Passenger Decks:	11
Lifts:	9
Machinery:	4 x Diesels
Max/Cruising Speed:	22.0/16.5kt
Passengers:	1,400
Cabins:	775
Crew:	625

The Jade Wellness Centre provides plenty of pampering opportunities on *Columbus*. *(CMV Library)*

Vasco da Gama (June 2019 to date)

Vasco da Gama makes a fine sight as she heads up the River Thames in June 2019. *(CMV Library)*

Vasco da Gama joined the CMV fleet in April 2019, but began life as *Statendam*, built for Holland America Line in 1993. When Carnival Corporation purchased Holland America Line in January 1989, they inherited a four-ship fleet together with an order for two new 600-passenger cruise ships. These were deemed inappropriate for Carnival's planned expansion of the line, so a new order was placed with Fincantieri in late 1989. The plans for three c55,000 ton vessels with capacity for 1,200 passengers were designed to double Holland America Line's capacity and allow for expansion into new markets. The engineering and overall architectural design was entrusted to London-based Technical Marine Planning, with Dutch firm VFD Architects given the task of designing every aspect of the interior. The ship design was based on the hull form of *Costa Classica* of 1991, with modifications to reflect the lowered Schat-Harding lifeboats inset into the ship's side.

Statendam, the fifth vessel to carry the name for the company, was a game changer for Holland America Line. The original design encompassed a Dutch theme, with the two-storey Van Gogh Show Lounge boasting an interior of blue, green and gold, based on the classic *Irises* and *Starry Night* paintings. The innovative Crow's Nest placed a 360° observation lounge with floor-to-ceiling windows atop the fully enclosed wheelhouse – a first for Holland America Line. Bucking the trend of placing restaurants low down in the hull, *Statendam* featured the Rotterdam Dining Room, spanning decks 7 and 8, at the stern of the vessel, with panoramic windows enhancing diners' experience by offering full 180° visibility for scenic cruises. *Statendam* boasted an exceptional art collection, topped by the centrepiece of the three-storey atrium, the 26ft *Fountain of the Sirens* sculpture depicting tales of Greek mythology associated with the sea and the gods Aphrodite, Poseidon and Triton. Staterooms were designed to be 30% larger than those on cruise ships of similar size, and two decks featured accommodation with private balconies.

A top cruising speed of 22 knots was achieved from the power generated by two Sulzer 12ZAV40S diesels coupled with three Sulzer 8ZA40S power plants. *Statendam* was designed to be manoeuvrable from the outset, with twin bow thrusters at the bow and a single thruster near the stern. On test she demonstrated that she could undertake a crash stop in as little as 171 seconds in a distance of 1,000 yards.

Delivery of the US$180m *Statendam* was heavily delayed by construction issues, and her christening by Mrs Lin Arison did not take place until January 1993, a year later than anticipated. Her maiden passenger voyage, on a 16-night cruise from Fort Lauderdale to Los Angeles, sailed on 25th January 1993. On 7th May she left New York for

Vasco da Gama's elegant profile is shown to good effect in this aerial shot. Reverend Norman 'Paddy' Mallon, a passenger onboard with his wife Jacqueline, kindly officiated an onboard blessing ceremony prior to the ship sailing from Singapore on her CMV maiden voyage on 24th April 2019. *(FotoFlite)*

Bermuda and returned across the Atlantic to circuit the Mediterranean and Baltic, before reaching London Tilbury for the first time on 11th June.

The design proved immensely popular and resulted in the building of three identical S-class sister ships and a further four near-sister designs for Holland America Line. *Statendam* spent much of her subsequent career deployed on Alaskan cruises from Vancouver during the summer months, with winters spent variously in the Caribbean and South Pacific.

2015 proved to be *Statendam's* final summer in Alaska before her transfer within the Carnival Group to sister company P&O Cruises Australia. She was dry-docked in Sembcorp Marine Admiralty Yard, Singapore, for an extensive refit which saw her transformed to bring a more modern Australian look and feel to her interior. The team fitted 20,000m2 of carpet, 2,500m2 of wall coverings, and added more than 300 pieces of art, 2,500 pieces of furniture and 2,500 signs, as well as applying 500 litres of paint to the vessel. *Statendam* was renamed *Pacific Eden* for her maiden cruise from Fremantle on 15th November 2015, with a formal christening ceremony via twitter by Kate Ritchie on 25th November during a five-ship fleet gathering in Sydney. After three seasons cruising around Australia *Pacific Eden* was sold to CMV, an announcement trailed in March 2018. *Pacific Eden* concluded her 2018–2019 programme of sailings for P&O Cruises Australia and was handed over to CMV in Singapore on the evening of 8th April 2019, sharing the quay with her fleet-mate *Columbus* in the midst of her world cruise. She had carried 290,000 passengers during her time with P&O Cruises Australia, contributing an estimated AU$156m to the economy.

Following her extensive refit in 2015 when *Pacific Eden* had been

extensively renovated and modernised, her stylish interior presented a very different look and feel to her original design. She was in excellent condition and only required a short docking period for a livery change, rebranding and some technical work before she left Singapore on her maiden voyage as *Vasco da Gama* for CMV to London Tilbury on Wednesday, 24th April 2019.

It was quickly clear why the acquisition of *Vasco da Gama* was such a prize for CMV. Her small to mid-sized characteristics fit perfectly with CMV's core market proposition, enabling cruise programmes that could visit smaller ports, contrasting with the trend for larger mega-ships amongst the large conglomerates. She combined the style of a classic cruise ship with a beautiful, contemporary internal décor.

The impressive on-board facilities are spread across four decks.

On Sports Deck 12 The Dome provides a maritime-styled viewing lounge with panoramic vistas of the sea from high above the bridge during the day, and is transformed into the perfect location to dance the night away as the sun sets. A jogging and walking track passes round the retractable roof for the main pool, and there are tennis and basketball courts for the energetic.

Lido Deck 11 also benefits from spectacular views from the Fitness Centre, a fully equipped gym with high-quality equipment located above the bridge, with panoramic windows looking forward. Behind this lies the Jade Spa, a well-appointed wellbeing centre with beautiful modern spa amenities, and hair and beauty facilities, all available at modest prices. Midships on this deck is the main pool, which benefits from a retractable roof to cater for all weather conditions. Guests can enjoy drinks service from the Lido Bar or Cappuccino's coffee shop, and the Alfresco Grill provides classic fast food in an informal environment for those enjoying the sunshine. Further aft on the Lido Deck lies the 280-seat Club Bistro, a buffet-style restaurant for breakfast, lunch and dinner. The Club Bistro leads out onto a terrace area, which gives access to the Oasis Pool on the Navigator's Deck, Deck 10, which has its own bar.

For the German market, the Kinderland stretches over the Lido and Sports decks, offering fun-filled activity for different age groups, including indoor and outdoor areas. It offers childcare, various play areas

Top left: **The stylish Ocean Bar takes advantage of picture windows to create a bright airy venue.** *(CMV Library)*

Middle left: **Sophia Loren adds a touch of Italian elegance to the Waterfront Mediterranean restaurant.** *(CMV Library)*

Bottom left: **The catering team gets ready to tempt guests with more culinary delights in the Club Bistro.** *(CMV Library)*

and age-appropriate activities, making *Vasco da Gama* particularly attractive for families with children.

Upper Deck 8 and Boat Deck 7 contain the main passenger facilities, including the two-tiered 'Hollywood's' show lounge forward on the ship, which spans both decks and forms the main on board entertainment venue, capable of showcasing everything from speciality acts to full-cast production performances. Moving aft on Upper Deck 8 the impressive three-deck atrium is the focal point of the ship, linking Decks 6 to 8 and offering access to a delightful shopping galleria, cinema, casino, the Trumps & Aces Card and Bridge Room, arts and crafts area, coffee shop and a well-stocked library. Passengers can enjoy a range of lounge bars and entertainment venues, with cleverly designed seating areas allowing groups of all sizes to congregate, whilst providing quiet areas for those who just wish to chill out and relax. The stylish musical themed Blue Room offers an intimate venue in which to enjoy entertainment, whilst the bright sophisticated Ocean Bar makes the most of large windows.

Aft of the Library and The Study on Upper Deck 8 lie the main dining areas of *Vasco da Gama*. Passengers have a choice of three Waterfront Restaurants. On the starboard side of the vessel lies the 140-seat Waterfront Mediterranean Restaurant, themed to provide a range of dishes with a special Mediterranean twist in a classic Italian environment. To port lies the 130-seat Waterfront Eurasia Restaurant, bringing an authentic Asian dining experience in an appropriate ambience. Or passengers can descend to the main Waterfront Restaurant which seats 350 guests on Deck 7. This dining choice is available to all and, in a first for CMV, all dining in these restaurants is flexible, with no fixed sittings except on formal dining nights.

There are also two speciality restaurants – The Grill (which seats 66 guests) and the Chef's Table (providing a 9-course culinary experience for just 14 guests) – which are available at a supplement for an exclusive on-board dining experience. These can be found forward of the Waterfront Restaurants on Upper Deck 8.

Boat Deck 7 hosts the lower tier of 'Hollywood's', from which passengers can walk aft past the Photo Gallery to the atrium, where the ship's Reception, Shore Excursions Desk, and Future Cruise Sales facilities can be found. Aft of the atrium lies The Auditorium cinema and the Cellar Door, for a unique wine tasting experience. There are even two conference rooms, the Bondi and the Noosa, which pay homage to *Vasco da Gama's* winter deployment.

Vasco da Gama offers extensive deck areas and port and starboard promenades with traditional timber-style decking on Promenade Deck 6.

The choice of comfortable accommodation is wide and can be found

The double height Waterfront Restaurant gives a strong feeling of spaciousness (*CMV Library*)

across five different decks. *Vasco da Gama* was noted for offering larger-than-normal cabins when built. She now offers 630 cabins in 21 different categories capable of accommodating a maximum of 1,220 passengers, ranging from 29 spacious balcony suites to 120 balcony cabins, 501 cabins with an ocean view and 129 interior cabins. Thus 80% of cabins have an ocean view and there is an impressive passenger lower-bed space ratio of 48. There are 100 cabins available for single occupancy. All accommodation is en suite and makes the most of mirrors to create a feeling of space. Cabin sizes range from 176ft² (16.32m²) in standard inside cabins to 1,095ft² (101.73m²) in the Royal Penthouse Suite. The majority of twin-bedded cabins convert to doubles, and some are interconnected so that family groups can easily be accommodated. All cabins are air-conditioned and come equipped with television, radio, telephone, hair dryer and personal safe.

Navigator's Deck 10 boasts the Royal Penthouse Suite, the Deluxe Suites and Premium Balcony cabins, plus Premium Inner cabins. Verandah Deck 9 hosts the Superior-Plus and Superior Balcony cabins, and a small number of Superior twin cabins. The bulk of the ocean-view and inner cabins can be found on Promenade Deck 6, Main Deck 5 and Atlantic Deck 4.

When *Vasco da Gama* is deployed by TransOcean during the summer months the on-board language is German, reverting to English for the winter Australian programme. Likewise, there is a change of currency from Euros to Australian dollars.

Names	Owners/Disponent Owners	Operators
1992-2015: *Statendam*	1993-2019: Carnival Corporation	1993-2015: Holland America Line
2015-19: *Pacific Eden*	2019 to date: Mythic Cruise Ltd (GMG)	2015-19: P&O Cruises Australia
2019 to date: *Vasco da Gama*		2019 to date: Cruise & Maritime Voyages

Senior Personnel

Captains	Chief Engineer	Staff Captains	Hotel Directors
Michail Smyrnaios (2019)	Viacheslav Kolesnykov (2017-18)	Artemios Kontizas	Maximilian Klassen
Andrey Lesnichiy (2019)	Igor Popyenko (2019)	Dimitrios Daillidis	

Technical Data

Builder:	Fincantieri, Monfalcone, Italy
Launched:	3rd April 1992
Port of registry:	Nassau, Bahamas
Maiden CMV voyage:	22nd April 2019
Call sign:	C6EG8
IMO number:	8919245
Classification:	Lloyd's Register
Length overall:	219.4m
Beam:	30.8m
Draught:	7.6m
Gross tonnage:	55,877gt
Passenger Decks:	10
Lifts:	8
Machinery:	2 x ABB 12,000kW
Max/Cruising Speed:	22.0/16.5kt
Passengers:	1,220
Cabins:	630
Crew:	557

An inviting balcony cabin on *Vasco da Gama.* (*CMV Library*)

Pacific Aria (to be renamed)

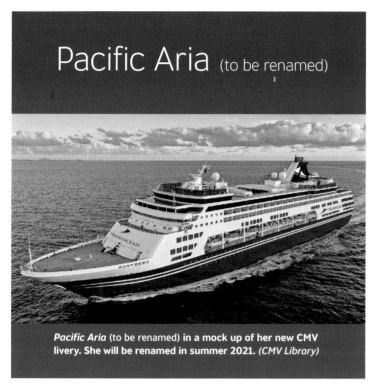

Pacific Aria (to be renamed) **in a mock up of her new CMV livery. She will be renamed in summer 2021.** *(CMV Library)*

When *Vasco da Gama* joined the CMV fleet in April 2019 she quickly proved immensely popular. CMV looked to capitalise on this success and expand further in the German market, and in December 2019 announced the acquisition of *Pacific Aria*, one of *Vasco da Gama's* three sisters. *Pacific Aria* was built as *Ryndam* for Holland America line, the third of four Statendam-class vessels constructed by Fincantieri for the company. The order was placed with Fincantieri in late 1989 and *Ryndam* was christened in New York in October 1994 by Madeleine Arison, wife of Carnival Corporation CEO Micky Arison.

At 55,819grt, *Ryndam* was 219m in length, with a beam of 31m, and a draft of 8.20m. She boasted passenger facilities spread across 10 decks, with 630 passenger cabins (501 ocean view with 129 balcony cabins) and 1,260 lower beds. The vessel was designed with longer-duration cruising in mind, with an emphasis on a familiar cultural environment on board and strong use of specially commissioned art pieces. Holland America's house design company was employed to undertake the design, with Frans Dingemans in the lead. On completion the Statendam-class vessels were described as 'the last word in cruise

ship design, technology and interior appointment' (Cudahy (2001)). The vessels were significant in turning around the fortunes of Holland America Line by repositioning the company at the forefront of modern cruising.

Ryndam emerged from drydock in October 2004 as the first Holland America Line vessel to incorporate the line's new Signature of Excellence features and was rededicated by Madeleine Arison.

Ryndam was deployed on North American itineraries in the Caribbean and Alaska for the bulk of her Holland America career, but latterly spent some summers in Europe, including a final season cruising from Harwich in 2015. Her final cruise for the company left Venice for Singapore via the Suez Canal on 3rd October 2015

On arrival in Singapore she received an extensive makeover by Sembcorp Marine alongside *Statendam* (*Vasco da Gama*) before both vessels transferred within the Carnival Corporation group to join the P&O Australia fleet. *Ryndam* emerged as *Pacific Aria*, significantly adapted to match stylish but relaxed Australian tastes. Swedish designer Petra Ryberg-Bid from Tillberg Designers took inspiration from Australia's fresh, modern, confident outlook tinged with humour. This manifested itself in light fixtures made of trumpets, duck feet lanterns in the Ocean Bar, stairwells with numbered stairs for those who like to count, and elevators painted in trompe-l'oeil 3D style, to give the appearance of stepping into a spacious meadow or an expansive patio. *Pacific Aria* was renamed by entertainer Jessica Mauboy in Sydney on 25th November 2015, prior to year-round deployment in the Austral market in which she was to spend the next six and a half years.

CMV will take delivery of *Pacific Aria* (to be renamed) in Singapore on 2nd May 2021 and, following dry-docking to undertake minor upgrade work and be repainted in the new CMV corporate livery, she will embark on her maiden positioning voyage for CMV via the Suez Canal to Northern Europe. The new CMV ship name for *Pacific Aria* will be announced in January 2020.

Pacific Aria (to be renamed) will be deployed on the German market under the TransOcean Kreuzfahrten brand bringing a much-needed increase in capacity, whilst cruising alongside the familiar *Vasco da Gama*. With nine bars and nightclubs, *Pacific Aria* (to be renamed) offers seven dining options, and two pools including one with an all-weather retractable roof. She will replace the 580 passenger *Astor,* which is to be renamed *Jules Verne* and redeployed to the French market from May 2021. The two sister vessels will bring a degree of homogeneity and consistency to the TransOcean product, which will help satisfy growing demand in the German market.

Pacific Dawn (to be renamed)

Pacific Dawn (to be renamed) in a mock up of her new CMV livery. She will be renamed in summer 2021. *(CMV Library)*

Pacific Dawn (to be renamed) was one of a trio of ships that included *Columbus*, under order for Sitmar Cruises when the company was purchased by P&O Princess Cruises in 1988. She was built alongside a sister vessel by Fincantieri at the Monfalcone yard in Italy to a design by Renzo Piano – a brave move, as the yard had not built a cruise ship for 20 years and the designer had never designed a ship. The result was a highly distinctive vessel with a dolphin's head-shaped dome atop the forward end of the superstructure, built from aluminium alloy to save weight. Her cylindrical funnel was designed for practical purposes and became a standard on many future cruise ship designs. Outwardly she presented a very sleek appearance, with lifeboats recessed into the superstructure. Like *Columbus*, she featured a three-deck atrium and was amongst the first Princess ships to feature a double-height show lounge.

The design of the three Sitmar vessels became the standard for the next generation of large passenger vessels, although Renzo Piano did no further cruise work. Fincantieri, however, became the yard of choice for cruise ship construction.

The vessel was launched on 29th March 1991 and, following successful sea trials was delivered on 20th July 1991 to Astamar, a subsidiary of the P&O Group. She sailed to New York City to be officially named *Regal Princess* at Pier 8, Brooklyn on 8th August 1991 by Margaret Thatcher. At 70,285grt, *Regal Princess* was 245m long as built, with a beam of 31m and a draft of 8.2m. Her passenger facilities were spread across 11 decks and she boasted 798 passenger cabins (of which 498 were ocean view and 148 balcony cabins) with 1,596 lower beds. She had an outstanding passenger to space ratio of 44, making her one of the most spacious ships afloat.

Regal Princess entered service with sister ship *Crown Princess* cruising from Fort Lauderdale to the Caribbean during the northern hemisphere winter, transferring to the Alaska in the summer. Her ownership transferred to Princess Cruises in 1992 and she was transferred to the Liberian flag

From 2003 she spent northern summers in the Mediterranean and Baltic Seas before transferring to become a permanent member of the P&O Cruises Australia fleet in late 2007. *Regal Princess* was renamed *Pacific Dawn* by Olympic gold medallist Cathy Freeman on 8th November 2007, coinciding with P&O's 75th anniversary in Australia, following an extensive refurbishment in Singapore. She moved to her new home port in Hamilton, Brisbane in December 2009.

Pacific Dawn (to be renamed) was refurbished in 2010 and again in November 2014, when a number of facilities including a zipline, 'crow's nest experience' and rock-climbing wall were added.

CMV will take delivery of *Pacific Dawn* in Singapore on 2nd March 2021 and the vessel will undertake dry-docking, minor upgrade works and repainting in the new corporate livery before embarking on her maiden positioning voyage for CMV via the Suez Canal to Northern Europe. The new CMV ship name for *Pacific Dawn* will be announced in January 2020.

On arrival in the UK *Pacific Dawn* (to be renamed) will home port alongside *Columbus* at London Tilbury from late May 2021. With 798 passenger cabins and typically carrying around 1,400 passengers, she will provide much-needed year-round additional capacity to satisfy the growing UK market.

The skies above London Tilbury are lit up by a spectacular firework display to mark the christening of *Magellan* on 12th March 2015. *(CMV Library)*

Cruise programme summary 2010-2019

2010
Launch programme of Britain's newest cruise line

Programme highlights include: -

- **46 no fly cruising holidays** from Tilbury, Hull, Newcastle, Leith, Greenock, Liverpool and Plymouth

- **CMV's maiden *Marco Polo* cruise** – The West Indies – 30 nights, 2 January 2010

- **42-night Amazon & Orinoco Discovery cruise** – *Marco Polo*, 1 February 2010

Total Ports visited: **117** (all maiden calls)

Total mileage: **118,267** nautical miles

Market Deployment/Vessels:
UK – **Marco Polo** & **Ocean Countess**

Maiden Calls

Being the first season of CMV's own operation, all 117 ports of call visited in 2010 would have to be considered as maiden calls! The Amazon itinerary became a staple ingredient of the company's winter programmes and here is the famous Manaus Opera House.

Title picture: *Marco Polo* called at Manaus, the furthest point on her Amazon river navigation, on 20th February 2010.

Marco Polo

Code	Cruise	Nights	Departure date
P001	**Caribbean** London Tilbury - Amsterdam - Ponta Delgada - Antigua - St. Maarten - St. Barts - St. Kitts - Barbados - St. Vincent - Bequia - Castries - Funchal - Lisbon - London Tilbury	30	02 Jan 2010
P002	**Amazon & Orinoco Discovery** London Tilbury - Amsterdam - Lisbon - Tenerife - Mindelo - Belém - Almeirim - Alter do Chao - Parintins - Manaus - Boca da Valéria - Santarém - Paraíso - Macapá - Îles du Salut - Puerto Ordaz - Scarborough - Barbados - Ponta Delgada - London Tilbury	42	01 Feb 2010
P003	**Land of the Northern Lights** London Tilbury - Amsterdam - Molde - Svartisen - Svolvær - Narvik - Tromsø - Alta - Ålesund - Bergen - London Tilbury	14	15 Mar 2010
P004	**Easter Canary Islands** London Tilbury - Vigo - Agadir - Arrecife - Tenerife - La Gomera - Funchal - Leixoes - London Tilbury	14	29 Mar 2010
P005	**Iberian Highlights** London Tilbury - Cherbourg - Vigo - Lisbon - Cadiz - Gibraltar - Tangier - Portimão - Gijón - London Tilbury	11	12 Apr 2010
P006	**Gallic Discovery** London Tilbury - Rouen - St. Peter Port - St. Mary's - London Tilbury	6	23 Apr 2010
P007	**Bulbfields Weekend** London Tilbury - Amsterdam - Antwerp - London Tilbury	3	29 Apr 2010
P008	**Springtime Fjordland** London Tilbury - Ulvik - Eidfjord - Vik - Flåm - Bergen - London Tilbury	6	02 May 2010
P009	**British Isles Discovery** London Tilbury - Invergordon - Stornoway - Tobermory - Dublin - St. Mary's - St. Peter Port - Honfleur - London Tilbury	9	08 May 2010
P010	**Majestic Fjordland** London Tilbury - Ulvik - Eidfjord - Skjolden - Hellesylt - Geiranger - Bergen - London Tilbury	7	17 May 2010

Marco Polo

Code	Cruise	Nights	Departure date
P011	**Fjordland Splendour** London Tilbury - Bergen - Molde - Åndalsnes - Geiranger - Flåm - Vik - Eidfjord - London Tilbury	8	24 May 2010
P012	**British Isles Discovery** London Tilbury - Invergordon - Stornoway - Tobermory - Dublin - St. Mary's - St. Peter Port - Honfleur - London Tilbury	9	01 Jun 2010
P013	**North Cape & Land of the Northern Lights** London Tilbury - Ulvik - Eidfjord - Olden - Leknes - Hammerfest - Honningsvåg - Tromsø - Svartisen - Ålesund - Bergen - London Tilbury	12	10 Jun 2010
P014	**Iceland & Northern Isles** London Tilbury - Kirkwall - Heimaey - Surtsey - Reykjavik - Ísafjörður - Akureyri - Seyðisfjörður - Tórshavn - Lerwick - London Tilbury	12	22 Jun 2010
P015	**Grand British Isles** London Tilbury - Invergordon - Kirkwall - Stornoway - Tobermory - Dublin - Holyhead - St. Mary's - St. Peter Port - Honfleur - London Tilbury	11	04 Jul 2010
P016	**Spitzbergen & North Cape** London Tilbury - Lerwick - Geiranger - Svartisen - Honningsvåg - Longyearbyen - Magdalenafjord – Ny-Ålesund - Tórshavn - Stornoway - London Tilbury	15	15 Jul 2010
P017	**Baltic Treasures & St. Petersburg** London Tilbury - Kiel Canal - Warnemünde - Tallinn - St. Petersburg - Helsinki - Stockholm - Kalundborg - Kiel Canal - London Tilbury	12	30 Jul 2010
P018	**Fjordland Splendour** London Tilbury - Bergen - Molde - Åndalsnes - Geiranger - Flåm - Vik - Eidfjord - London Tilbury	8	11 Aug 2010
P019	**Norway & Scottish Highlights** London Tilbury - Edinburgh Leith - Bergen - Hellesylt - Geiranger - Nordfjordeid - Olden - Flåm - Vik - Lerwick - London Tilbury	10	19 Aug 2010

Marco Polo

Code	Cruise	Nights	Departure date
P020	**Celtic Explorer** London Tilbury - Cherbourg - St. Mary's - Glengariff - Killybegs - Belfast - Douglas - Portree - Invergordon - London Tilbury	10	29 Aug 2010
P021	**Baltic Cities & St. Petersburg** London Tilbury - Oslo - Kalundborg - Tallinn - St. Petersburg - Helsinki - Stockholm - Kiel Canal - London Tilbury	12	08 Sep 2010
P022	**Mediterranean Odyssey** London Tilbury - Gijón - Portimão - Gibraltar - Tangier - Port Mahon - Palma - Ibiza - Lisbon - London Tilbury	14	20 Sep 2010
P023	**Baltic Cities & St. Petersburg** London Tilbury - Copenhagen - Warnemünde - Tallinn - St. Petersburg - Helsinki - Nynäshamn - Kiel Canal - London Tilbury	12	04 Oct 2010
P024	**Canary Island & Madeira** London Tilbury - Vigo - Agadir - Arrecife - Tenerife - La Gomera - Funchal - Leixoes - London Tilbury	14	16 Oct 2010

Botanical Gardens, Funchal

Ocean Countess

Code	Cruise	Nights	Departure date
C001	**Amsterdam Weekend** London Tilbury - Amsterdam - Hull	2	18 Apr 2010
C002	**Springtime Fjordland** Hull - Ulvik - Eidfjord - Vik - Flåm - Bergen - Hull	6	20 Apr 2010
C003	**Springtime Fjordland** Hull - Ulvik - Eidfjord - Vik - Flåm - Bergen - Hull	6	26 Apr 2010
C004	**Springtime Fjordland** Hull - Bergen - Ulvik - Eidfjord - Vik - Flåm - Hull	6	02 May 2010
C005	**British Isles Discovery** Hull - St. Helier - Falmouth - St. Mary's - Dublin - Portree - Kirkwall - Edinburgh Leith - Hull	9	08 May 2010
XC006	**Charter** Hull - Dunkirk - Newcastle	6	17 May 2010
C007	**Springtime Fjordland** Newcastle Tyne - Geiranger - Flåm - Gudvangen - Bergen - Lerwick – Newcastle Tyne	6	23 May 2010
C008	**Baltic Treasures & St. Petersburg** Newcastle Tyne - Kiel Canal - Warnemünde - Helsinki - St. Petersburg - Tallinn - Stockholm - Copenhagen – Newcastle Tyne	12	29 May 2010
C009	**North Cape & Land of the Midnight Sun** Newcastle Tyne- Hellesylt - Geiranger - Leknes - Honningsvåg - Tromsø - Molde - Åndalsnes - Bergen - Rosendal - Kirkwall - Edinburgh Leith	12	10 Jun 2010
C010	**Fjordland Splendour** Edinburgh Leith - Ulvik - Eidfjord - Vik - Flåm - Olden - Geiranger - Bergen - Edinburgh Leith	8	22 Jun 2010
C011	**Baltic Cities & St. Petersburg** Edinburgh Leith - Oslo - Copenhagen - Helsinki - St. Petersburg - Tallinn - Stockholm - Kiel Canal - Edinburgh Leith	12	30 Jun 2010
C012	**Iceland & Northern Isles** Edinburgh Leith - Kirkwall - Heimaey - Surtsey - Reykjavik - Ísafjörður - Akureyri - Húsavík - Tórshavn - Lerwick - Edinburgh Leith	12	12 Jul 2010
C013	**British Isles Discovery** Edinburgh Leith - Honfleur - Portland - St. Mary's - St. Peter Port - Milford Haven - Cobh - Douglas - Greenock	9	24 Jul 2010

Ocean Countess

Code	Cruise	Nights	Departure date
C014	**Iberian Discovery** Greenock - Leixoes - Lisbon - Cadiz - Gibraltar - Tangier - Malaga - Praia da Rocha - Cobh - Greenock	12	02 Aug 2010
C095	**Fjordland Splendour** Greenock - Bergen - Molde - Åndalsnes - Geiranger - Flåm - Vik - Lerwick - Greenock	8	14 Aug 2010
C096	**Islands Mini Cruise** Greenock - Stornoway - Tórshavn - Portree - Greenock	4	22 Aug 2010
C097	**Overnight Party Cruise** Greenock - Liverpool	1	26 Aug 2010
CO98	**Fjordland Splendour** Liverpool - Lerwick - Bergen - Ulvik - Eidfjord - Vik - Flåm - Oban - Liverpool	8	27 Aug 2010
C099	**British Isles Discovery** Liverpool - Oban - Kirkwall - Invergordon - Honfleur - St. Peter Port - St. Mary's - Cobh - Liverpool	9	04 Sep 2010
C018	**Iberian Discovery** Liverpool - Lisbon - Cadiz - Casablanca - Gibraltar - Malaga - Praia da Rocha - Gijón - Liverpool	12	13 Sep 2010
C019	**Mini Cruise to Cork** Liverpool - Cobh - Plymouth	2	25 Sep 2010
C020	**Iberian Highlights** Plymouth - Leixoes - Lisbon - Cadiz - Casablanca - Gibraltar - Malaga - Praia da Rocha - Plymouth	11	27 Sep 2010
C021	**Iberian Highlights** Plymouth - Dublin - Lisbon - Praia da Rocha - Gibraltar - Tangier - La Coruña - Dublin - Plymouth	11	08 Oct 2010
C022	**Canary Island & Madeira** Plymouth - Vigo - Agadir - Arrecife - Santa Cruz de Tenerife - San Sebastián de La Gomera - Funchal - Leixoes - Plymouth	12	19 Oct 2010

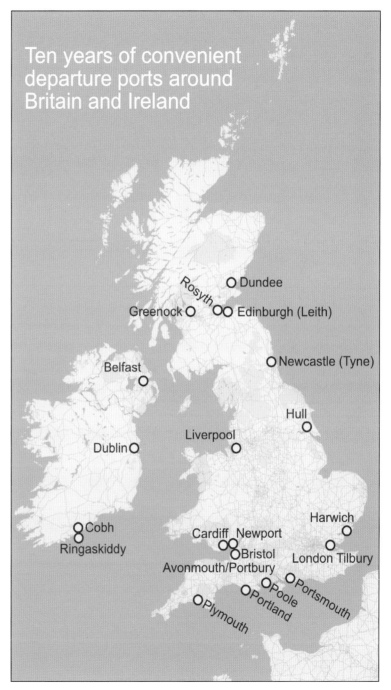

Ten years of convenient departure ports around Britain and Ireland

Cruise programme summary 2010-2019

2010-2011
Over 80,000 passengers carried in two years

Programme highlights include: -

- A total of **four cruises** to Norway and the **Land of the Northern Lights**

- A choice of **17 summer cruises** to the Norwegian fjords from five UK departure ports

- New Mediterranean Odyssey cruises aboard *Marco Polo* and *Ocean Countess*

Total Ports visited: **111** (24 maiden calls)

Total mileage: **134,651** nautical miles

Market Deployment/Vessels:
UK – *Marco Polo* & *Ocean Countess*

Maiden Calls

During 2011, *Marco Polo* and *Ocean Countess* made 24 maiden visits to new ports of call, which included such diverse locations as Helsingborg, Sweden; Livorno, the gateway to Pisa and Florence in Italy; Scrabster in the far north of Scotland and the picturesque town of Villefranche on the French Riviera.

Title picture: **The Northern Lights were a popular feature of *Marco Polo*'s February/March programme.**

Marco Polo

Code	Cruise	Nights	Departure date
P101	**Christmas Markets** London Tilbury - Amsterdam - Zeebrugge - London Tilbury	3	03 Dec 2010
P102	**Christmas Caribbean** London Tilbury - Amsterdam - Ponta Delgada - Antigua - St. Kitts - Castries - Soufriere - Bonaire - Curaçao - Aruba - Grenada - St. Vincent - Bequia - Bridgetown - Funchal - Lisbon - London Tilbury	35	06 Dec 2010
P103	**Amazon Discovery** London Tilbury - Amsterdam - Lisbon - Tenerife - Mindelo- Belém - Almeirim - Alto do Chão - Santarém – Parintins - Manaus - Boca da Valéria - Macapá - Îles du Salut - Scarborough - Castries - Bridgetown - Ponta Delgada - London Tilbury	42	10 Jan 2011
P104	**Land of the Northern Lights** London Tilbury - Amsterdam - Molde - Svartisen - Bodo- Narvik - Tromsø - Alta - London Tilbury	14	21 Feb 2011
P105	**Land of the Northern Lights** London Tilbury - Amsterdam - Ålesund - Svartisen - Svolvær - Narvik - Tromsø - Alta - Molde - Bergen - London Tilbury	14	07 Mar 2011
P106	**Land of the Northern Lights** London Tilbury - Amsterdam - Molde - Svartisen - Svolvær - Narvik - Tromsø - Alta - Ålesund - Bergen - London Tilbury	14	21 Mar 2011
P107	**Amsterdam City Break** London Tilbury - Amsterdam - London Tilbury	2	04 Apr 2011
P1R8	**British Isles Discovery** London Tilbury - Invergordon - Stornoway - Tobermory - Dublin - St. Mary's - St. Peter Port - Honfleur - London Tilbury	9	06 Apr 2011
P109	**Nordic Cities** London Tilbury - Oslo - Helsingborg - Copenhagen - Warnemünde – Kiel Canal - Amsterdam - London Tilbury	8	15 Apr 2011
P110	**Spring Gardens & Charms** London Tilbury - St. Mary's - St. Peter Port - Rouen - London Tilbury	6	23 Apr 2011
P111	**Bulbfields Weekend** London Tilbury - Amsterdam - Antwerp - London Tilbury	3	29 Apr 2011

Marco Polo

Code	Cruise	Nights	Departure date
P112	**Springtime Fjordland** London Tilbury - Ulvik - Eidfjord - Flåm - Gudvangen - Bergen - London Tilbury	6	02 May 2011
P113	**Springtime Fjordland** London Tilbury - Ulvik - Eidfjord - Flåm - Gudvangen - Bergen - London Tilbury	6	08 May 2011
P114	**British Isles Discovery** London Tilbury - Invergordon - Kirkwall - Stornoway - Tobermory - Dublin - St. Mary's - St. Peter Port - Portland - London Tilbury	10	14 May 2011
P115	**Fjordland Splendour** London Tilbury - Bergen - Molde - Åndalsnes - Geiranger - Flåm - Vik - Eidfjord - London Tilbury	8	24 May 2011
P116	**Baltic Treasures & St. Petersburg** London Tilbury - Copenhagen - Warnemünde - Tallinn - St. Petersburg- Helsinki - Stockholm – Kiel Canal - London Tilbury	12	01 Jun 2011
P117	**North Cape** London Tilbury - Florø - Leknes - Honningsvåg - Alta - Tromsø - Svartisen - Molde - Åndalsnes - Bergen - London Tilbury	12	13 Jun 2011
P118	**Iceland & Northern Isles** London Tilbury - Kirkwall - Heimaey - Surtsey - Reykjavik - Ísafjörður - Akureyri - Seyðisfjörður - Tórshavn - Lerwick - London Tilbury	12	25 Jun 2011
P119	**Grand British Isles** London Tilbury - Invergordon - Kirkwall - Stornoway - Tobermory - Dublin - St. Mary's - St. Peter Port - Honfleur - London Tilbury	10	07 Jul 2011
P120	**Spitzbergen & North Cape** London Tilbury - Lerwick - Geiranger - Svartisen - Bodo - Honningsvåg - Longyearbyen - Magdalenafjord - Ny-Ålesund - Tórshavn - Kirkwall - London Tilbury	15	17 Jul 2011
P121	**Baltic Treasures & St. Petersburg** London Tilbury - Copenhagen - Warnemünde - Tallinn - St. Petersburg- Helsinki - Stockholm – Kiel Canal - London Tilbury	12	01 Aug 2011
P122	**Majestic Fjordland** London Tilbury - Ulvik - Eidfjord - Flåm - Hellesylt - Geiranger - Bergen - London Tilbury	7	13 Aug 2011

Marco Polo

Code	Cruise	Nights	Departure date
P123	**Majestic Fjordland** London Tilbury - Ulvik - Eidfjord - Flåm - Hellesylt - Geiranger - Bergen - London Tilbury	7	20 Aug 2011
P124	**Bank Holiday Break** London Tilbury - Amsterdam - Antwerp - London Tilbury	3	27 Aug 2011
P125	**British Isles Discovery** London Tilbury - Invergordon - Stornoway - Tobermory - Dublin - St. Mary's - St. Peter Port - Honfleur - London Tilbury	9	30 Aug 2011
P126	**Fjords & Fairytales** London Tilbury - Ulvik - Eidfjord - Flåm - Vik - Oslo - Helsingborg - Copenhagen - Kiel Canal - Amsterdam - London Tilbury	10	08 Sep 2011
P127	**Baltic Cities & St. Petersburg** London Tilbury - Copenhagen - Warnemünde - Tallinn - St. Petersburg - Helsinki - Stockholm - Kiel Canal - London Tilbury	11	18 Sep 2011
P128	**Baltic Cities & St. Petersburg** London Tilbury - Copenhagen - Warnemünde - Tallinn - St. Petersburg - Helsinki - Stockholm - Kiel Canal - London Tilbury	11	29 Sep 2011
P129	**Mediterranean Odyssey** London Tilbury - Lisbon - Tangier - Mahon - Ajaccio - Livorno - Villefrance - Barcelona - Gibraltar - La Coruña - London Tilbury	16	10 Oct 2011
P130	**Beautiful Rouen & Bruges** London Tilbury - Rouen - Zeebrugge - London Tilbury	11	26 Oct 2011
P131	**Canary Islands & Madeira** London Tilbury - Lisbon - Funchal - Santa Cruz de la Palma - Santa Cruz de Tenerife Arrecife - La Coruña - London Tilbury	13	30 Oct 2011

> **❝We continue to choose the *Marco Polo* as it is a lovely ship and the crew are fantastic and so friendly - when you board it feels like home. ❞**
>
> Neil & Pamela Edwards

City Hall Copenhagen

Ocean Countess

Code	Cruise	Nights	Departure date
CT04	**Weekend Party Cruise** London Tilbury - Hull	1	19 Mar 2011
C1R5	**Land of the Northern Lights** Hull - Molde - Svolvær - Narvik - Tromsø - Alta - Ålesund - Bergen - Hull	13	20 Mar 2011
C1R6	**Nordic Cities** Hull - Helsingborg - Copenhagen - Oslo - Hull	6	02 Apr 2011
C107	**Wartime Memories** Hull - Honfleur - St. Peter Port - Dunkirk - Amsterdam - Hull	6	08 Apr 2011
C108	**British Isles in Bloom** Hull - St. Peter Port - Falmouth - St. Mary's - Dublin - Oban - Scrabster - Edinburgh Leith - Hull	9	14 Apr 2011
C109	**Springtime Fjordland** Hull - Ulvik - Eidfjord - Vik - Flåm - Bergen - Hull	6	23 Apr 2011
C110	**Springtime Fjordland** Hull - Ulvik - Eidfjord - Vik - Flåm - Bergen - Hull	6	29 Apr 2011
C111	**Springtime Fjordland** Hull - Ulvik - Eidfjord - Vik - Flåm - Bergen - Hull	6	05 May 2011
C112	**Springtime Fjordland** Hull - Ulvik - Eidfjord - Vik - Flåm - Bergen - Hull	6	11 May 2011
C113	**British Isles Discovery** Hull - St. Peter Port - St. Mary's - Falmouth - Dublin - Tobermory - Scrabster - Edinburgh Leith - Hull	9	17 May 2011

Ocean Countess

Code	Cruise	Nights	Departure date
C114	**Fjordland Splendour** Hull - Bergen - Molde - Åndalsnes - Geiranger - Flåm - Vik - Ulvik - Eidfjord - Hull	8	26 May 2011
C115	**Baltic Cities & St. Petersburg** Hull - Oslo - Copenhagen - Helsinki - St. Petersburg - Tallinn - Stockholm – Kiel Canal - Hull	12	03 Jun 2011
C116	**Swinging Sixties Party Cruise** Hull – Newcastle Tyne	1	15 Jun 2011
C117	**Fjordland** Newcastle Tyne - Geiranger - Flåm - Gudvangen - Bergen - Lerwick - Newcastle Tyne	6	16 Jun 2011
C118	**Fjordland** Newcastle Tyne - Geiranger - Flåm - Gudvangen - Bergen - Lerwick - Newcastle Tyne	6	22 Jun 2011
C119	**Fjordland Splendour** Newcastle Tyne - Ulvik - Eidfjord - Vik - Flåm - Olden - Geiranger - Bergen - Lerwick - Newcastle Tyne	8	28 Jun 2011
C120	**Baltic Cities & St. Petersburg** Newcastle Tyne - Oslo - Copenhagen - Helsinki - St. Petersburg - Tallinn - Stockholm - Kiel Canal - Newcastle Tyne	12	06 Jul 2011
C121	**Summertime Fjordland** Newcastle Tyne - Hellesylt - Geiranger - Bergen - Kirkwall - Edinburgh Leith	5	18 Jul 2011
C122	**Baltic Cities & St. Petersburg** Edinburgh Leith - Copenhagen - Helsinki - St. Petersburg - Tallinn - Stockholm - Oslo - Edinburgh Leith	12	23 Jul 2011
C123	**Baltic Cities & St. Petersburg** Edinburgh Leith - Copenhagen - Helsinki - St. Petersburg - Tallinn - Stockholm - Oslo - Edinburgh Leith	12	04 Aug 2011
C124	**Fjordland Splendour** Edinburgh Leith - Bergen - Molde - Åndalsnes - Geiranger - Flåm - Vik - Eidfjord - Edinburgh Leith	8	16 Aug 2011
C125	**Scottish Isles & Faroes** Edinburgh Leith - Lerwick - Tórshavn - Stornoway - Rothesay - Liverpool	5	24 Aug 2011
C126	**Fjordland Splendour** Liverpool - Kirkwall - Florø - Flåm - Gudvangen - Bergen - Lerwick - Liverpool	8	29 Aug 2011
C127	**British Isles Discovery** Liverpool - Oban - Kirkwall - Invergordon - Honfleur - St. Peter Port - St. Mary's - Cobh - Liverpool	9	06 Sep 2011
CL27	**Ireland Mini-Cruise** Liverpool - Cobh - St. Mary's - Waterford - Liverpool	4	15 Sep 2011
C128	**Spain, Portugal & North Africa** Liverpool - Lisbon - Cadiz - Casablanca - Gibraltar - Malaga - Praia da Rocha - Gijón - Liverpool	12	19 Sep 2011
C129	**Overnight Mini-Cruise** Liverpool - Dublin	1	01 Oct 2011
CD30	**France, Spain & Portugal** Dublin - Falmouth - Leixoes - Lisbon - Gibraltar - Casablanca - Vigo - Dublin	10	02 Oct 2011
CD31	**Canary Islands & Madeira** Dublin - Falmouth - Leixoes - Agadir - Arrecife - Las Palmas - Funchal - Lisbon - Vigo - Dublin	13	12 Oct 2011
CD32	**Mediterranean Odyssey** Dublin - Falmouth - Leixoes - Lisbon - Cartagena - Palma - Mahon - Nice	10	25 Oct 2011

"We continue cruising with CMV because of the cleanliness of all the ships we have sailed on, the friendliness and helpfulness of staff, the great onboard atmosphere, good food, great entertainment and great medical service if needed. All giving great value for money."

David & Jacqueline Russell

Cruise programme summary 2010-2019

2011-2012
Launch of CMV TV, a dedicated video channel of our cruise programme

Programme highlights include: -

· Britain's Maritime Heritage
   – **Titanic centenary and celebration of great liners**, *Marco Polo*, 10 April 2012

· **No less than 17 short breaks** and party cruises – an ideal introduction to the CMV cruise experience

· **Emerald Isle Discovery** – *Marco Polo's* unique itinerary around the coast of Ireland – 8 July 2012

Total Ports visited: **119** (20 maiden calls)

Total mileage: **110,067** nautical miles

Market Deployment/Vessels:
UK – **Marco Polo** & **Ocean Countess**

Maiden Calls

During 2012, *Marco Polo* and *Ocean Countess* notched up a further 20 maiden calls to new ports of call, which included such cities and towns as varied as Fort William and Ullapool in Scotland; Galway, Hamburg and a trio of Spanish ports Barcelona, Cartagena and Valencia.

Title picture: *Hamburg* visited by Ocean Countess on 6th May 2012 during a Bank Holiday Break cruise from Hull.

Marco Polo

Code	Cruise	Nights	Departure date
P201	**Christmas Markets** London Tilbury - Amsterdam - Zeebrugge - Antwerp - London Tilbury	4	03 Dec 2011
P202	**Christmas Markets** London Tilbury - Antwerp - Amsterdam - London Tilbury	3	08 Dec 2011
P203	**Christmas Markets** London Tilbury - Antwerp - London Tilbury	2	11 Dec 2011
P204	**Christmas Markets** London Tilbury - Antwerp - Amsterdam - London Tilbury	3	17 Dec 2011
P205	**Christmas & New Year Canaries** London Tilbury - Vigo - Lisbon - Santa Cruz de la Palma - Tenerife - Arrecife - Funchal - Leixoes - London Tilbury	14	20 Dec 2011
P206	**Amazon, West Indies & the Azores** London Tilbury - Amsterdam - Lisbon - Funchal - Mindelo - Belém - Macapá - Almeirim - Alto do Chão - Parintins - Manaus - Boca do Valeria - Santarem - Îles du Salut - St. George's - Mayreau - St. John's - Castries - Bridgetown - Horta - Ponta Delgada - London Tilbury	45	03 Jan 2012
P207	**Land of the Northern Lights** London Tilbury - Amsterdam - Svolvær - Narvik - Tromsø - Alta - Bergen - London Tilbury	14	17 Feb 2012
P208	**Land of the Northern Lights** London Tilbury - Amsterdam - Molde - Narvik - Leknes - Tromsø - Alta - Bergen - London Tilbury	14	02 Mar 2012
P209	**Land of the Northern Lights** London Tilbury - Amsterdam - Molde - Harstad - Narvik - Tromsø - Alta - Ålesund - Bergen - London Tilbury	14	16 Mar 2012
P210	**Spring Weekend Cruise** London Tilbury - Amsterdam - Antwerp - London Tilbury	3	30 Mar 2012
P211	**Easter Cruise** London Tilbury - Honfleur - St. Jean de Luz - Le Verdon - Brest - St. Peter Port - London Tilbury	8	02 Apr 2012

Marco Polo

Code	Cruise	Nights	Departure date
P212	**Ocean Liner Heritage** London Tilbury - Cherbourg - Kinsale - Cobh - Belfast - Liverpool - London Tilbury	7	10 Apr 2012
P213	**Majestic Fjordland** London Tilbury - Ulvik - Eidfjord - Flåm - Bergen - London Tilbury	6	17 Apr 2012
P214	**British Isles Discovery** London Tilbury - Invergordon - Tobermory - Dublin - Cobh - Honfleur - London Tilbury	9	23 Apr 2012
P215	**May Break** London Tilbury - Antwerp- London Tilbury - Newcastle Tyne	4	02 May 2012
P216	**Majestic Fjordland** Newcastle Tyne- Ulvik - Eidfjord - Bergen - Flåm - Stavanger - Newcastle Tyne	7	06 May 2012
P217	**British Isles Discovery** Newcastle Tyne - Honfleur - St. Helier - St. Mary's - Milford Haven - Belfast - Tobermory - Kirkwall - Invergordon - Newcastle Tyne	10	13 May 2012
P218	**Scottish Highlights** Newcastle Tyne- Kirkwall - Stornoway - Ullapool - Invergordon - Edinburgh Leith	5	23 May 2012
P219	**Diamond Jubilee British Isles** Edinburgh Leith - London Tilbury - Portsmouth - St. Mary's - Cardiff - Belfast - Douglas - Edinburgh Leith	9	28 May 2012
P220	**Baltic Capitals & St Petersburg** Edinburgh Leith - Copenhagen - Warnemünde - Tallinn - St. Petersburg - Helsinki - Stockholm - Kiel Canal - Edinburgh Leith	12	06 Jun 2012
P221	**Fjordland Splendour** Edinburgh Leith - Hellesylt - Åndalsnes - Olden - Skjolden - Bergen - Kirkwall - Edinburgh Leith	8	18 Jun 2012
P222	**North Cape & Land of the Midnight Sun** Edinburgh Leith - Molde - Åndalsnes - Leknes - Honningsvåg - Tromsø - Hellesylt - Rosyth - London Tilbury	12	26 Jun 2012
P223	**Emerald Isle Discovery** London Tilbury - Cobh - Glengariff - Galway - Killybegs - Greencastle - Douglas - Belfast - Edinburgh Leith - London Tilbury	12	08 Jul 2012

Marco Polo

Code	Cruise	Nights	Departure date
P224	**Grand British Isles** London Tilbury - Invergordon - Kirkwall - Tobermory - Dublin - St. Mary's - St. Peter Port - Honfleur - London Tilbury	10	20 Jul 2012
P225	**Baltic Capitals & St. Petersburg** London Tilbury - Kiel Canal - Tallinn - St. Petersburg - Helsinki - Stockholm - Copenhagen - Oslo - London Tilbury	12	30 Jul 2012
P226	**Azores & Madeira** London Tilbury - La Coruna - Horta - Praia - Funchal - Leixoes - London Tilbury	15	11 Aug 2012
P227	**Fjordland Splendour** London Tilbury - Ulvik - Eidfjord - Flåm - Hellesylt - Bergen - London Tilbury	7	26 Aug 2012
P228	**British Isles Discovery** London Tilbury - Invergordon - Ullapool - Tobermory - Dublin - St. Mary's - St. Helier - Honfleur - London Tilbury	9	02 Sep 2012
P229	**French Leave** London Tilbury - Gijón - Le Verdon - Brest - St. Mary's - St. Peter Port - Honfleur - London Tilbury	9	11 Sep 2012
P230	**Amsterdam /Antwerp Weekend** London Tilbury - Antwerp - Amsterdam - London Tilbury	3	20 Sep 2012
P231	**Baltic Capitals & St. Petersburg** London Tilbury - Warnemünde - Tallinn - St. Petersburg - Helsinki - Nynäshamn - Kiel Canal - London Tilbury	12	23 Sep 2012
P232	**Great European Waterways** London Tilbury - Amsterdam - Honfleur - Rouen - Antwerp - London Tilbury	5	05 Oct 2012
P233	**Mediterranean Gold** London Tilbury - Lisbon - Tangier - Malaga - Cartagena - Palma de Mallorca - Valencia - Gibraltar - La Coruna - London Tilbury	14	10 Oct 2012
P235	**Amsterdam Weekender** London Tilbury - Amsterdam - London Tilbury	2	27 Oct 2012

Ocean Countess

Code	Cruise	Nights	Departure date
C201	**Springtime Fjordland** Hull - Ulvik - Eidfjord - Flåm - Stavanger - Hull	6	21 Apr 2012
C202	**Majestic Fjordland** Hull - Ulvik - Eidfjord - Bergen - Flåm - Stavanger - Hull	7	27 Apr 2012
C203	**Bank Holiday Break** Hull - Amsterdam - Hamburg - Hull	4	04 May 2012
C204	**Majestic Fjordland** Hull - Ulvik - Eidfjord - Bergen - Flåm - Stavanger - Hull	7	08 May 2012

Helsinki

Code	Cruise	Nights	Departure date
C205	**Fjordland Splendour** Hull - Bergen - Åndalsnes - Geiranger - Flåm - Ulvik - Eidfjord - Hull	8	15 May 2012
C206	**Springtime Gardens** Hull - Honfleur - Cherbourg - Fowey - Holyhead - Liverpool	6	23 May 2012
C207	**Diamond Jubilee Highland Experience** Liverpool - Holyhead - Invergordon - Scrabster - Fort William - Rothesay - Liverpool	8	29 May 2012

Hassan II Mosque in Casablanca

Ocean Countess

Code	Cruise	Nights	Departure date
C208	**Fjordland Splendour** Liverpool - Stavanger - Ulvik - Eidfjord - Flåm - Oban - Liverpool	8	06 Jun 2012
C209	**Celtic Explorer** Liverpool - Cobh - Dublin - Liverpool	4	14 Jun 2012
C210	**Spain, Portugal & Morocco** Liverpool - Lisbon - Portimão - Casablanca - Cadiz - Gibraltar - La Coruna - Cobh - Liverpool	12	18 Jun 2012
C211	**Party Cruise** Liverpool - Greenock	1	30 Jun 2012
C212	**Majestic Fjordland** Greenock - Bergen - Åndalsnes - Geiranger - Lerwick - Greenock	7	01 Jul 2012
C213	**Iceland & Northern Isles** Greenock - Reykjavik - Ísafjörður - Akureyri - Seyðisfjörður - Tórshavn - Lerwick - Greenock	10	08 Jul 2012

Ocean Countess

Code	Cruise	Nights	Departure date
C214	**Canary Islands & Madeira** Greenock - Leixoes - Funchal - Santa Cruz de la Palma - Tenerife - Vigo - Greenock	13	18 Jul 2012
C215	**Scottish Islands & Faroes** Greenock - Stornoway - Kollafjørður - Portree - Greenock	4	31 Jul 2012
C216	**Party Cruise** Greenock - Liverpool	1	04 Aug 2012
C217	**Fjordland Splendour** Liverpool - Lerwick - Stavanger - Ulvik - Eidfjord - Flåm - Oban - Liverpool	8	05 Aug 2012
C218	**Baltic Capitals & St. Petersburg** Liverpool - Oslo - Copenhagen - Helsinki - St. Petersburg - Tallinn - Stockholm - Kiel Canal - Hull	12	13 Aug 2012
C219	**Majestic Fjordland** Hull - Skjolden - Olden - Åndalsnes - Bergen - Hull	7	25 Aug 2012
C220	**Scandinavian Cities** Hull - Oslo - Helsingborg - Copenhagen - Aalborg - Hull	7	01 Sep 2012
C221	**Autumn Gardens** Hull - Zeebrugge - Honfleur - St. Peter Port - Cobh - Liverpool	6	08 Sep 2012
C222	**British Isles Discovery** Liverpool - Killybegs - Cobh - St. Mary's - St. Peter Port - Falmouth - Milford Haven - Liverpool	9	14 Sep 2012
C223	**Celtic Explorer** Liverpool - Cobh - Dublin - Belfast - Liverpool	4	23 Sep 2012
C224	**Spain, Portugal & Morocco** Liverpool - Lisbon - Huelva - Casablanca - Cadiz - Gibraltar - La Coruna - Dublin - Liverpool	12	27 Sep 2012
C225	**Canary Islands & Madeira** Liverpool - Lisbon - Funchal - Santa Cruz de la Palma - Tenerife - Arrecife - Agadir - Malaga - Barcelona		09 Oct 2012

Cruise programme summary 2010-2019

2012-2013
Discovery replaces *Ocean Countess* and *Astor* joins the fleet

Programme highlights include: -

- **New Additions Programme of enrichment and entertainment** on board *Marco Polo* and *Discovery*

- ***Discovery* cruises to Russia's White Sea** and **fly-cruise programme** to the Mediterranean and Black Sea

- ***Astor's* 46-night voyage** to Iceland, Greenland and Canada - 25 July 2013

Total Ports visited: **194** (95 maiden calls)

Total mileage: **182,663** nautical miles

Market Deployment/Vessels:
UK – *Marco Polo* & *Discovery*
Germany – *Astor*
Australia – *Astor*

Maiden Calls

With the introduction of *Discovery*, the number of maiden calls increased to 95 in 2013 due to the diversity of her itineraries that brought in Northern Russia, the Eastern Mediterranean and the Black Sea for the first time. *Astor* meanwhile, whilst enroute to Canada, was making landfall in the spectacular scenery of Greenland.

Title picture: **Stunning scenery seen during an** *Astor* **call to Illulissat, which was first visited on 7th August 2013**

Astor

Code	Cruise	Nights	Departure date
TO-17355	**Springtime Voyage** Lisbon - Porto - Bordeaux - St. Malo - Plymouth - Honfleur - Oostende - Amsterdam - Bremerhaven	11	29 Mar 2013
TO-17360	**Springtime Discovery Cruise** Bremerhaven- Amsterdam – Harwich - Stavanger - Oslo - Esbjer- Bremerhaven	9	09 Apr 2013
TO-17361	**Baltic Sea Mini-Cruise** Bremerhaven – List - Kiel Canal - Copenhagen - Kiel	5	18 Apr 2013
TO-17362	**Baltic & St. Petersburg** Kiel - Karlskrona - Kappelshamn - Stockholm – Helsinki - St. Petersburg - Tallinn - Sassnitz - Kiel Canal - Bremerhaven	11	23 Apr 2013
TO-17363	**British Isles** Bremerhaven - Dover – Portsmouth - Plymouth – Falmouth - Portland - Hamburg	7	04 May 2013
TO-17364	**Overnight Cruise to Nowhere** Hamburg - Hamburg	1	11 May 2013
TO-17365	**Norwegian Fjords** Hamburg - Flåm – Hellesylt - Geiranger - Bergen - Bremerhaven	6	12 May 2013
TO-17366	**North Cape** Bremerhaven – Flåm – Vik – Åndalsnes - Honningsvag – Tromsø - Leknes - Geiranger - Hellesylt - Bergen - Bremerhaven	12	18 May 2013
TO-17367	**Iceland & Spitzbergen** Bremerhaven - Kirkwall - Hafnarfjörður - Akureyri - Longyearbyen – Ny-Ålesund - Magdalenafjord- Honningsvåg – Tromsø - Bergen - Bremerhaven	16	30 May 2013
TO-17368	**British Isles** Bremerhaven - Falmouth – Cobh - Dublin - Liverpool - Belfast - Londonderry - Stornoway - Rosyth - Harwich - Kiel	14	15 Jun 2013
TO-17369	**Hidden Baltic** Kiel - Gdansk - Baltiysk - Klaipėda - Riga - Tallinn - St. Petersburg - Helsinki - Stockholm - Visby - Copenhagen - Kiel	14	29 Jun 2013

Astor

Code	Cruise	Nights	Departure date
TO-17370	**Land of the Midnight Sun** Kiel – Flåm - Trondheim – Honningsvåg - Tromsø - Leknes – Geiranger – Hellesylt - Bergen - Bremerhaven	12	13 Jul 2013
TO-17371/2	**Voyage to Greenland & Canada** Bremerhaven – Kirkwall – Tórshavn - Hafnarfjörður - Ísafjörður- Qaqortoq – Nuuk - Kangerlussuaq –Ilulissat - St. Anthony - Red Bay - Sept Îles - Montréal	24	25 Jul 2013
TO-17373	**Canadian Adventure** Montréal - Québec – Saguenay – Gaspé – Charlottetown - Cap-aux-Meules - Corner Brook – Sydney – Halifax - Saint John - St. Pierre & Miquelon - St. John's - Cobh - Plymouth - Bremerhaven	22	18 Aug 2013
TO-17374	**Amsterdam Short Break** Bremerhaven - Amsterdam - Bremerhaven	3	09 Sep 2013
TO-17375	**Antwerp Short Break** Bremerhaven - Antwerp - Bremerhaven	3	12 Sep 2013
TO-17376	**South to Lisbon** Bremerhaven – Ijmuiden - Dover - Le Havre – Villagarcia - Lisbon	7	16 Sep 2013
TO-17377	**Mediterranean** Lisbon – Almeria - Palma de Mallorca – Messina – Kotor - Dubrovnik – Hvar – Zadar – Katakolon - Piraeus	13	23 Sep 2013
TO-17378	**The Black Sea** Piraeus - Istanbul - Sinop - Trabzon – Sochi – Sevastopol - Odessa - Constanta - Çanakkale - Thessaloniki - Naxos - Piraeus	14	06 Oct 2013

Spitzbergen

"We were attracted by the opportunity to sail on a small traditional ship to a destination we really wanted to visit."

Robert & Jean Stephenson

Tobermory

Godafoss Waterfall Iceland

Discovery

Code	Cruise	Nights	Departure date
D302	**Land of the Northern Lights** Bristol Avonmouth - Ålesund - Narvik - Alta - Tromsø - Åndalsnes - Bergen - Bristol Avonmouth	15	15 Mar 2013
D303	**Easter Cruise to Spain & Portugal** Bristol Avonmouth - La Coruna - Leixoes - Lisbon - Aviles - Bristol Avonmouth	8	30 Mar 2013
D304	**Springtime Gardens & Charms** Bristol Avonmouth - Dublin - Tresco - Cherbourg - Falmouth - Bristol Avonmouth	5	07 Apr 2013
D305	**Celtic Landscapes** Bristol Avonmouth - Dublin - Oban - Tobermory - Cobh - Bristol Avonmouth	7	12 Apr 2013
D306	**Fjordland Spectacular** Bristol Avonmouth - Stavanger - Flåm - Bergen - Bristol Avonmouth	8	19 Apr 2013
D307	**Weekend Mini-Cruise** Bristol Avonmouth - Liverpool	1	27 Apr 2013
D308	**British Isles Discovery** Liverpool - Kirkwall - Invergordon - Honfleur - St. Helier - St. Mary's - Falmouth - Liverpool	9	28 Apr 2013
D309	**Fjordland Spectacular** Liverpool - Kirkwall - Stavanger - Ulvik - Eidfjord - Flåm - Bergen - Oban - Liverpool	9	07 May 2013
D310	**Celtic Explorer** Liverpool - Cobh - St. Mary's - St. Peter Port - Falmouth - Portland - Harwich	6	16 May 2013
D311	**Baltic Symphony** Harwich - Copenhagen - Turku - Tallinn - St. Petersburg - Gdynia - Warnemünde - Kiel Canal - Harwich	13	22 May 2013
D312	**Natural Wonders & Wildlife** Harwich - Lerwick - Tórshavn - Seyðisfjörður - Húsavík - Ísafjörður - Reykjavik - Heimaey - Kirkwall - Harwich	12	04 Jun 2013
D313	**Summer Solstice & The White Sea** Harwich - Bergen - Leknes - Honningsvåg - Kirkenes - Archangel - Solovetsky Islands - Murmansk - Tromsø - Florø - Harwich	18	16 Jun 2013
D314	**Mini-Cruise** Harwich - Hull	1	04 Jul 2013

Discovery

Code	Cruise	Nights	Departure date
D315	**Baltic Capitals & Russia** Hull - Kiel Canal - Warnemünde - Helsinki - St. Petersburg - Tallinn - Stockholm - Copenhagen - Hull	12	05 Jul 2013
D316	**Summertime Fjords** Hull - Bergen - Flåm - Eidfjord - Hull	6	17 Jul 2013
D317	**Mini-Cruise** Hull – Newcastle Tyne	1	23 Jul 2013
D318	**North Cape & Land of Midnight Sun** Newcastle Tyne - Olden - Leknes - Hammerfest - Honningsvåg - Tromsø - Åndalsnes - Bergen - Newcastle Tyne	11	24 Jul 2013
D319	**Iceland & the Northern Isles** Newcastle Tyne - Kirkwall - Heimaey - Reykjavik - Ísafjörður - Akureyri - Eskifjörður - Tórshavn - Lerwick - Newcastle Tyne	11	04 Aug 2013
D320	**Majestic Fjordland** Newcastle Tyne - Flåm - Gudvangen - Geiranger - Olden - Bergen - Newcastle Tyne	7	15 Aug 2013
D321	**British Isles Discovery** Newcastle Tyne - Honfleur - St. Peter Port - St. Mary's - Dublin - Tobermory - Stornoway - Invergordon - Newcastle Tyne	9	22 Aug 2013
D322	**St. Petersburg & Baltic Capitals** Newcastle Tyne - Oslo - Copenhagen - Stockholm - Helsinki - St. Petersburg - Tallinn - Warnemünde – Kiel Canal - Newcastle Tyne	15	31 Aug 2013
D383	**Mini-Cruise** Newcastle Tyne - Harwich	1	14 Sep 2013
D323	**Iconic Iberia** Harwich - Cherbourg - La Coruna - Leixoes - Gibraltar - Almeria - Valencia - Barcelona	10	15 Sep 2013
D324	**Mediterranean Odyssey** Barcelona - Monte Carlo - Bastia - Portoferraio - Civitavecchia - Trapani - Valletta - Syracuse - Argostoli - Nauplion - Piraeus	12	25 Sep 2013
D325	**Black Sea Discovery** Piraeus - Volos - Çanakkale - Nesebar - Odessa - Sevastopol - Yalta - Istanbul	10	07 Oct 2013
D326	**Treasures of the Black Sea** Istanbul - Trabzon - Sochi - Novorossiysk - Yalta - Sevastopol - Odessa - Çanakkale - Bodrum	11	17 Oct 2013
D327	**School Cruise** Bodrum - Haifa - Ashdod - Rhodes - Kusadasi - Piraeus	7	28 Oct 2013

Tallinn

Midnight Sun North Cape

Marco Polo

Code	Cruise	Nights	Departure date
P301	**Christmas Markets** London Tilbury - Antwerp - Amsterdam - London Tilbury	3	16-Dec-2012
P302	**Christmas & New Year Canaries** London Tilbury - Vigo - Lisbon - Puerto Rosario - Las Palmas - Santa Cruz de la Palma - Funchal - Leixoes - London Tilbury	14	20-Dec-2012
P303	**Amazon, W. Indies & The Azores** London Tilbury - Amsterdam - Lisbon - Funchal - Mindelo - Macapá - Santarém - Boca da Valéria - Manaus - Parintins - Alto do Chão - Santana/Macapa- Îles du Salut - St. George's - Kingstown - Castries - Bridgetown - Horta - Ponta Delgada - London Tilbury	42	03-Jan-2013
P304	**Land of the Northern Lights** London Tilbury - Amsterdam - Ålesund - Narvik - Alta - Tromsø - Sortland - Åndalsnes - Bergen - London Tilbury	14	14-Feb-2013
P305	**Land of the Northern Lights** London Tilbury - Amsterdam - Ålesund - Narvik - Alta - Tromsø - Sortland - Antwerp	14	28-Feb-2013
P307	**Bulbfields & Gardens** London Tilbury - Amsterdam - Antwerp - Cherbourg - St. Mary's - Honfleur - London Tilbury	7	31-Mar-2013
P308	**British Isles Discovery** London Tilbury - Invergordon -Stornoway - Tobermory - Dublin - Fowey - St. Helier - Honfleur - London Tilbury	9	07-Apr-2013
P309	**Springtime Fjordland** London Tilbury - Ulvik - Eidfjord - Flåm - Bergen - London Tilbury	6	16-Apr-2013
P310	**Springtime Fjordland** London Tilbury - Ulvik - Eidfjord - Flåm - Bergen - London Tilbury	6	22-Apr-2013
P311	**Majestic Fjordland** London Tilbury - Eidfjord - Flåm - Skjolden - Bergen - London Tilbury	7	28-Apr-2013
P312	**Baltic Cities & St. Petersburg** London Tilbury - Copenhagen - Warnemünde - Tallinn - St. Petersburg - Helsinki - Stockholm - Kiel Canal - London Tilbury	12	05-May-2013

Marco Polo

Code	Cruise	Nights	Departure date
P313	**Fjordland Splendour - Hardanger Music Festival** London Tilbury - Eidfjord - Odda - Geiranger - Flåm - Bergen - London Tilbury	8	17-May-2013
P314	**Overnight Party Cruise** London Tilbury - Edinburgh Leith	1	25 May 2013
P315	**Scottish Islands & Faroes** Edinburgh Leith - Tórshavn - Stornoway - Kirkwall - Edinburgh Leith	5	26 May 2013
P316	**Baltic Cities & St. Petersburg** Edinburgh Leith - Copenhagen - Warnemünde - Tallinn - St. Petersburg - Helsinki - Stockholm- Kiel Canal - Edinburgh Leith	12	31 May 2013
P317	**Majestic Fjordland** Edinburgh Leith - Flåm - Olden - Geiranger - Bergen - Kirkwall - Edinburgh Leith	7	12 Jun 2013
P318	**Iceland & the Faroe Islands** Edinburgh Leith - Kirkwall - Heimaey - Reykjavik - Ísafjörður - Akureyri - Seyðisfjörður - Klaksvik - Kollafjordur - Lerwick - Edinburgh Leith	11	19 Jun 2013
P319	**North Cape & Spitzbergen** Edinburgh Leith - Molde - Åndalsnes - Tromsø - Honningsvåg - Longyearbyen - Ny Alesund - Tórshavn - Kirkwall - Edinburgh Leith	13	30 Jun 2013
P320	**Overnight Party Cruise** Edinburgh Leith - London Tilbury	1	13 Jul 2013
P321	**North Cape & Land of the Midnight Sun** London Tilbury - Bergen - Olden - Leknes - Honningsvåg - Tromsø - Åndalsnes - Stavanger - London Tilbury	12	14 Jul 2013

> **The stand-out CMV cruise for me was a Round the World itinerary, with 186 nights on *Astor's* Line Voyages**
>
> Hendrik Mulder

Amsterdam Bulbfields

Marco Polo

Code	Cruise	Nights	Departure date
P322	**British Isles Discovery**	9	26 Jul 2013
	London Tilbury - Invergordon - Stornoway		
	- Tobermory - Dublin - St. Mary's		
	- St. Peter Port - Honfleur - London Tilbury		
P323	**Iceland & Northern Isles**	12	04 Aug 2013
	London Tilbury - Kirkwall - Reykjavik		
	- Ísafjörður - Akureyri - Seyðisfjörður		
	- Tórshavn - Lerwick - London Tilbury		
P324	**Fjordland & Edinburgh Festival**	8	16 Aug 2013
	London Tilbury - Eidfjord - Flåm - Fjærland		
	- Balestrand - Olden - Bergen - London Tilbury		
P325	**Baltic Cities & St. Petersburg**	12	24 Aug 2013
	London Tilbury - Copenhagen - Warnemünde		
	- Tallinn - St. Petersburg - Helsinki - Stockholm		
	- Kiel Canal - London Tilbury		
P326	**Treasures of the British Isles**	10	05 Sep 2013
	London Tilbury - Invergordon - Kirkwall		
	- Stornoway - Tobermory - Dublin - St. Mary's		
	- St. Peter Port - Honfleur - London Tilbury		
P327	**Autumn Fjordland**	6	15 Sep 2013
	London Tilbury - Eidfjord - Flåm - Bergen -		
	London Tilbury		
P328	**Baltic Cities & St. Petersburg**	12	21 Sep 2013
	London Tilbury - Copenhagen - Warnemünde		
	- Tallinn - St. Petersburg - Helsinki		
	- Nynäshamn - Kiel Canal - London Tilbury		
P329	**Amsterdam & Ghent Break**	3	03 Oct 2013
	London Tilbury - Ghent - Amsterdam		
	- London Tilbury		
P330	**Land of the Northern Lights**	14	06 Oct 2013
	London Tilbury - Eidfjord - Olden - Leknes		
	- Alta - Honningsvåg - Tromsø - Narvik		
	- Åndalsnes - Bergen - London Tilbury		
P331	**Baltic Cities & St. Petersburg**	12	20 Oct 2013
	London Tilbury - Copenhagen - Warnemünde		
	- Tallinn - St. Petersburg - Helsinki - London Tilbury		
P400	**The West Indies**	30	03 Nov 2013
	London Tilbury - Ponta Delgada - St. John's		
	- Gustavia - St. Maarten - Basseterre - Castries		
	- Kingstown - Bequia - Mayreau - Bridgetown		
	- Horta - London Tilbury		

Tórshavn, Faroe Islands

Mayreau

Cruise programme summary 2010-2019

2013-2014
CMV Australia office opens in Sydney and joint venture with All Leisure Group announced

Programme highlights include: -

- *Astor's* voyages to **South Africa** and **Australia**
- Inaugural **Signature River Cruise** programme
- **Largest ever Scottish programme** with 13 sailings from Edinburgh Leith and Rosyth and Glasgow Greenock

Total Ports visited: **183** (45 maiden calls)

Total mileage: **216,660** nautical miles

Market Deployment/Vessels:
UK – ***Marco Polo, Discovery*** & ***Funchal***
Australia – ***Astor***
Germany – ***Astor***

Maiden Calls

Astor's first season in Australia brought a spate of new destinations with the two line voyages and the cruise season from Fremantle pushing the number of maiden calls in 2014 up by another 45. One significant visit was made by *Marco Polo* to Wismar in Germany for the first time since she was constructed at the Mathias Thesen yard there in 1965.

Astor

Code	Cruise	Nights	Departure date
A401	**Southbound Voyage to Australia** Civitavecchia – Livorno – Messina – Valletta – Piraeus – transit Suez Canal – Aqaba – Salalah – Colombo – Phuket – Singapore – Benoa – Fremantle	36	05 Nov 2013
A404	**Pre-Christmas Party Weekend** Fremantle – Fremantle	3	13 Dec 2013
A405	**Wine, Food & Fitness Cruise** Fremantle – Albany – Bunbury – Fremantle	4	16 Dec 2013
A406	**Christmas Bali Cruise** Fremantle – Benoa- Fremantle	10	20 Dec 2013

The Western Australian port of Broome received its first call from Astor on 28th February 2014

Code	Cruise	Nights	Departure date
A407	**New Year Cruise** Fremantle – Fremantle	3	30 Dec 2013
A408	**Bali** Fremantle – Benoa – Lombok – Fremantle	11	02 Jan 2014
A409	**Explore the Coast** Fremantle – Esperance – Albany – Fremantle	5	13 Jan 2014
A410	**Short Break** Fremantle – Fremantle	2	18 Jan 2014
A411	**Coastal Escape** Fremantle – Esperance – Albany – Fremantle	5	20 Jan 2014

Astor

Code	Cruise	Nights	Departure date
A412	**Australia Day Cruise** Fremantle - Fremantle	3	25 Jan 2014
A413	**Cruise Round Australia** Fremantle – Penneshaw – Adelaide – Hobart - Port Arthur – Melbourne – Eden – Sydney - Brisbane - Cairns - Darwin - Benoa- Lombok - Komodo Island – Broome - Fremantle	35	28 Jan 2014
A414	**Far East Delights** Fremantle - Port Klang – Langkawi – Phuket - Phi Phi Island – Penang – Singapore – Benoa - Fremantle	24	04 Mar 2014
A415	**Weekend Escape** Fremantle - Fremantle	3	28 Mar 2014
A416	**Astor Farewell Party**	1	31 Mar 2014
A417	**Northbound Voyage to Europe** Fremantle - Port Louis - Pointe des Galets - Durban - Mossel Bay - Cape Town - Walvis Bay - Jamestown - Porto Grande – Tenerife - Lisbon - Le Havre – Harwich - Bremerhaven	40	01 Apr 2014
A425	**Scandinavian Cities** Bremerhaven – Gothenburg – Oslo – Stavanger - Bergen - Bremerhaven	8	12 May 2014
A426	**Fjordland** Bremerhaven – Flåm – Hellesylt - Geiranger - Bergen - Bremerhaven	6	20 May 2014
A427	**British Isles** Bremerhaven - Falmouth - Dublin – Holyhead – Belfast – Oban – Stornoway - Invergordon - Rosyth- Harwich- Bremerhaven	13	26 May 2014
A428	**North Cape** Bremerhaven – Flåm – Trondheim - Honningsvåg – Tromsø - Leknes – Svartisen - Hellesylt - Geiranger- Bergen - Bremerhaven	13	08 Jun 2014
A429	**European Cities / UK** Bremerhaven - London Tilbury - Zeebrugge - Ijmuiden - Bremerhaven	6	21 Jun 2014
A430	**Canada & Greenland** Bremerhaven – Kirkwall – Tórshavn – Tasiilaq - St. John's – Sydney NS – Charlottetown – Gaspé – Québec - Montréal	18	27 Jun 2014

Astor

Code	Cruise	Nights	Departure date
A476	**Canada & Greenland** Montréal – Saguenay - Sept Îles - Havre St. Pierre - Cap-aux-Meules - Corner Brook - L'Anse aux Meadows – Cobh - Portland – Helgoland - Bremerhaven	19	15 Jul 2014
A431	**Iceland & Spitzbergen** Bremerhaven – Kirkwall – Hafnarfjörður – Ny-Ålesund – Honningsvåg - Tromsø - Bergen - Kiel	15	03 Aug 2014
A432	**Baltic Cities & Russia** Kiel – Flensburg – Gdansk – Riga – Tallinn - St. Petersburg – Helsinki – Stockholm – Visby - Karlskrona - Kiel Canal - Bremerhaven	13	18 Aug 2014
A433	**British Isles** Bremerhaven - Falmouth - Milford Haven - St. Peter Port – Southampton - Bremerhaven	8	31 Aug 2014
A434	**North Cape** Bremerhaven - Bergen – Åndalsnes – Honningsvåg – Tromsø - Leknes – Geiranger - Kristiansand - Copenhagen - Kiel	14	08 Sep 2014
A435	**Baltic Cities & Russia** Kiel – Baltiysk – Tallinn - St. Petersburg - Helsinki- Stockholm – Visby – Klaipėda – Gdansk- Kiel	14	22 Sep 2014
A436	**Beauties of the North** Kiel – Flensburg – Rönne - Copenhagen – Gothenburg – Oslo – Stavanger - Bremerhaven	9	06 Oct 2014

❝ We have been cruising for many years and decided to have a complete change of cruise line and, after looking at the itineraries and competitive pricing, we booked our first cruise with CMV some four years ago – we haven't looked back. ❞

Gordon & Beryl Williams

Northern lights

Copenhagen Little Mermaid

Iceland Blue Lagoon Spa

Flåm

Discovery

Code	Cruise	Nights	Departure date
D440	**Land of the Northern Lights** Bristol Avonmouth - Ålesund - Alta - Tromsø - Narvik - Bergen - Stavanger - Kirkwall - Liverpool	15	24 Feb 2014
D442	**Land of the Northern Lights** Liverpool - Ålesund - Alta - Honningsvåg - Tromsø - Narvik - Bodo - Åndalsnes - Bergen - Hull	15	11 Mar 2014
D443	**Grand British Isles** Hull - Rosyth - Lerwick - Scrabster - Tobermory - Belfast - Dublin - St. Mary's - St. Peter Port - Dover - Hull	10	26 Mar 2014
D444	**Majestic Fjordland** Hull - Rosyth - Ulvik - Eidfjord - Flåm - Bergen - Hull	7	05 Apr 2014
D445	**Easter Fjordland** Hull - Rosyth - Lerwick - Bergen - Skjolden - Flåm - Odda - Hull	8	12 Apr 2014
D446	**Baltic Cities & St. Petersburg** Hull - Rosyth - Copenhagen - Helsinki - St. Petersburg - Tallinn - Stockholm - Oslo - Hull	13	20 Apr 2014
D447	**Scottish Isles & Faroes** Hull - Rosyth - Kirkwall - Tórshavn - Portree - Tobermory - Bristol Avonmouth	7	03 May 2014
D401	**Scottish Highlands & Islands** Bristol Avonmouth - Dublin - Kirkwall - Lerwick - Ullapool - Bristol Avonmouth	8	10 May 2014
D402	**Springtime Gardens** Bristol Avonmouth - Cork - St. Mary's - St. Helier - Honfleur - Bristol Avonmouth	6	18 May 2014
D403	**Whitsun Fjordland Splendour** Bristol Avonmouth - Ulvik - Eidfjord - Flåm - Bergen - Bristol Avonmouth	8	24 May 2014
D448	**D-Day Anniversary Cruise** Bristol Avonmouth - Honfleur - St. Peter Port - Cherbourg - Plymouth	6	01 Jun 2014
D404	**Overnight to Liverpool** Plymouth - Liverpool	1	07 Jun 2014
D405	**Iceland & Northern Isles** Liverpool - Stornoway - Kollafjørður - Eskifjörður - Akureyri - Ísafjörður - Reykjavik - Liverpool	10	08 Jun 2014

Discovery

Code	Cruise	Nights	Departure date
D406	**Fjordland Spectacular** Liverpool - Lerwick - Ålesund - Åndalsnes - Geiranger - Flåm - Bergen - Tobermory - Liverpool	10	18 Jun 2014
D408	**Overnight to Greenock** Liverpool - Greenock	1	28 Jun 2014
D409	**Scottish Isles & Faroes** Greenock - Ullapool - Kirkwall - Kollafjørður - Stornoway - Greenock	5	29 Jun 2014
D410	**Majestic Fjordland** Greenock - Lerwick - Geiranger - Åndalsnes - Bergen - Greenock	7	04 Jul 2014
D411	**Iceland & Northern Isles** Greenock - Kollafjørður - Eskifjörður - Akureyri - Ísafjörður - Reykjavik - Heimaey - Kirkwall - Edinburgh Leith	10	11 Jul 2014
D412	**Baltic Cities & St. Petersburg** Edinburgh Leith - Copenhagen - Helsinki - St. Petersburg - Tallinn - Stockholm - Oslo - Edinburgh Leith	12	21 Jul 2014
D413	**North Cape/Land of Midnight Sun** Edinburgh Leith - Geiranger - Leknes - Hammerfest - Honningsvåg - Tromsø - Ålesund - Edinburgh Leith	10	02 Aug 2014
D414	**Majestic Fjordland** Edinburgh Leith - Åndalsnes - Olden - Flåm - Eidfjord - Edinburgh Leith	7	12 Aug 2014
D415	**Scottish Isles & Faroes** Edinburgh Leith - Kirkwall - Kollafjørður - Portree - Greenock	4	19 Aug 2014
D416	**Overnight to Liverpool** Greenock - Liverpool	1	23 Aug 2014
D417	**Fjordland Spectacular** Liverpool - Lerwick - Ålesund - Geiranger - Flåm - Bergen - Tobermory - Liverpool	9	24 Aug 2014
D418	**Celtic Explorer** Liverpool - Cork - St. Mary's - Milford Haven - Bristol Avonmouth	4	02 Sep 2014

Discovery

Code	Cruise	Nights	Departure date
D420	**Azores & Madeira** Bristol Avonmouth - La Coruna - Leixoes - Ponta Delgada - Praia - Porto Santo - Funchal - Lisbon - Bristol Avonmouth	14	07 Sep 2014
D421	**Autumn Gardens** Bristol Avonmouth - Falmouth - Honfleur - Antwerp - Amsterdam - Bristol Avonmouth	6	21 Sep 2014
D422	**Spain & Portugal Autumn Sun** Bristol Avonmouth - Lisbon - Tangier - Portimão - La Coruna - Bristol Avonmouth	9	27 Sep 2014

Funchal

Code	Cruise	Nights	Departure date
F400	**Land of the Northern Lights** Bristol Avonmouth - Stavanger - Ålesund - Narvik - Alta - Honningsvåg - Tromsø - Åndalsnes - Bergen - Douglas - Liverpool	16	06 Oct 2014
N401	**Madeira & Lisbon** Liverpool - Funchal - Portimão - Lisbon	8	22 Oct 2014

Funchal

Marco Polo

Code	Cruise	Nights	Departure date
P401	**Christmas Shopping** London Tilbury - Ghent - Amsterdam - London Tilbury	3	15 Dec 2013
P402	**Belgium's Christmas Market** London Tilbury - Antwerp - London Tilbury	2	18 Dec 2013
P403	**Christmas & New Year Cruise** London Tilbury – La Coruna - Santa Cruz de Tenerife - Santa Cruz de la Palma - Funchal – Le Havre - London Tilbury	14	22 Dec 2013
P404	**The Annual Marco Polo Amazon Cruise** London Tilbury - Amsterdam - Lisbon - Funchal - Mindelo - Santarém - Boca da Valéria - Manaus - Parintins - Alto do Chão - Santana- Îles du Salut - St. George's - Kingstown - Castries - Bridgetown - Horta - Ponta Delgada - London Tilbury	42	05 Jan 2014
P405	**Land of the Northern Lights** London Tilbury - Amsterdam - Ålesund - Narvik - Alta - Tromsø - Sortland - Åndalsnes - Bergen - London Tilbury	14	16 Feb 2014
P406	**Land of the Northern Lights** London Tilbury - Amsterdam - Ålesund - Narvik - Alta - Tromsø - Åndalsnes - Bergen - London Tilbury	14	02 Mar 2014
P407	**Land of the Northern Lights** London Tilbury - Amsterdam - Ålesund - Narvik - Alta - Tromso- Narvik - Åndalsnes - Bergen - London Tilbury	14	16 Mar 2014
P408	**Welcome to Spring** London Tilbury - Amsterdam - Rouen - Zeebrugge - London Tilbury	5	30 Mar 2014
P409	**British Isles Discovery** London Tilbury - Invergordon - Stornoway - Tobermory - Dublin - St. Mary's - St. Peter Port - Honfleur - London Tilbury	9	04 Apr 2014
P410	**Springtime Fjordland** London Tilbury - Eidfjord - Flåm - Bergen - London Tilbury	6	13 Apr 2014
P411	**Easter Fjordland** London Tilbury - Ulvik - Eidfjord - Flåm - Bergen - London Tilbury	6	19 Apr 2014

Marco Polo

Code	Cruise	Nights	Departure date
P412	**Majestic Fjordland** London Tilbury - Eidfjord - Flåm - Skjolden - Bergen - London Tilbury	7	25 Apr 2014
P413	**Bank Holiday Treat** London Tilbury - Amsterdam - Zeebrugge - Honfleur - London Tilbury	4	02 May 2014
P414	**Baltic Cities & St. Petersburg** London Tilbury - Copenhagen - Warnemünde - Tallinn - St. Petersburg - Helsinki - Stockholm - Kiel Canal - London Tilbury	12	06 May 2014
P415	**Springtime Fjordland** London Tilbury - Ulvik - Eidfjord - Flåm - Bergen - London Tilbury	6	18 May 2014
P416	**British Isles Discovery** London Tilbury - Invergordon - Stornoway - Tobermory - Dublin - St. Mary's - St. Peter Port - Honfleur - London Tilbury	9	24 May 2014
P417	**D-Day 70th Anniversary Cruise** London Tilbury - Zeebrugge - Portsmouth - Honfleur - Cherbourg - London Tilbury	6	02 Jun 2014
P418	**Overnight to Tyne** London Tilbury - Newcastle Tyne	1	08 Jun 2014
P419	**Scottish Isles & Faroes** Newcastle Tyne - Tórshavn - Ullapool - Lerwick - Kirkwall – Newcastle Tyne	6	09 Jun 2014
P420	**Baltic Cities & St. Petersburg** Newcastle Tyne - Kiel Canal - Warnemünde - Tallinn - St. Petersburg - Helsinki - Stockholm - Copenhagen – Newcastle Tyne	12	15 Jun 2014
P421	**Majestic Fjordland** Newcastle Tyne - Geiranger - Åndalsnes - Olden - Skjolden – Newcastle Tyne	7	27 Jun 2014
P422	**North Cape & Murmansk** Newcastle Tyne - Geiranger - Gravdal - Kirkenes - Murmansk - Honningsvåg - Tromsø - Åndalsnes - Bergen – Newcastle Tyne	14	04 Jul 2014
P423	**Overnight to Tilbury** Newcastle Tyne - London Tilbury	1	18 Jul 2014
P424	**British Isles Discovery** London Tilbury - Invergordon - Kirkwall - Stornoway - Tobermory - Dublin - St. Mary's - St. Peter Port - Honfleur - London Tilbury	10	19 Jul 2014

Marco Polo

Code	Cruise	Nights	Departure date
P425	**Fjordland Splendour** London Tilbury - Eidfjord - Flåm - Fjærland - Balestrand - Olden - Bergen - London Tilbury	8	29 Jul 2014
P445	**Antwerp & Amsterdam** London Tilbury - Antwerp - Amsterdam - London Tilbury	3	06 Aug 2014
P426	**Iceland & Northern Isles** London Tilbury - Tórshavn - Eskifjörður - Akureyri - Ísafjörður - Reykjavik - Heimaey - Kirkwall - London Tilbury	12	09 Aug 2014
P427	**Baltic Cities & St. Petersburg** London Tilbury - Copenhagen - Sassnitz - Tallinn - St. Petersburg - Helsinki - Stockholm - London Tilbury	12	21 Aug-2014
P428	**British Isles Discovery** London Tilbury - Invergordon - Stornoway - Tobermory - Dublin - St. Mary's - St. Peter Port - Honfleur - London Tilbury	9	02 Sep 2014
P429	**Majestic Fjordland** London Tilbury - Ulvik - Eidfjord - Flåm - Geiranger - Bergen - London Tilbury	7	11 Sep 2014
P430	**Amsterdam & Antwerp** London Tilbury - Antwerp - Amsterdam - London Tilbury	3	18 Sep 2014
P431	**Baltic Cities & St. Petersburg** London Tilbury - Copenhagen - Warnemünde - Tallinn - St. Petersburg - Helsinki - Nynäshamn - Kiel Canal - London Tilbury	12	21 Sep 2014
P432	**Amsterdam Mini-Cruise** London Tilbury - Amsterdam - London Tilbury	2	05 Oct 2014
P433	**Scandinavian Cities** London Tilbury - Amsterdam - Kiel Canal - Wismar - Helsingborg - Copenhagen - Oslo - London Tilbury	8	07 Oct 2014
P434	**Baltic Cities & St. Petersburg** London Tilbury - Copenhagen - Warnemünde - Tallinn - St. Petersburg - Helsinki - Klaipeda - Kiel Canal - London Tilbury	12	15 Oct 2014
P435	**Land of the Northern Lights** London Tilbury - Eidfjord - Olden - Leknes - Alta - Honningsvåg - Tromsø - Narvik - Åndalsnes - Bergen - London Tilbury	14	27 Oct 2014

Cruise programme summary 2010-2019

2014-2015
Azores and *Magellan* join the CMV fleet

Programme highlights include: -

- *Magellan* **Maiden Voyage** and **Solar Eclipse rendezvous** with *Marco Polo* and *Azores*

- *Marco Polo* **50th Anniversary Voyage** to Greenland and Canada

- *Azores* **sailings** from **Bristol** Avonmouth, **Hull** and **Liverpool** plus **new Mediterranean Fly-Cruises**

Total Ports visited: **175** (23 maiden calls)

Total mileage: **273,766** nautical miles

Market Deployment/Vessels:
UK – *Marco Polo, Magellan, Astoria* & *Astor*
Australia – *Astor*
Germany – *Astor*

Maiden Calls

A further 23 maiden visits were made during 2015 as *Magellan* joined the programme and *Astoria* explored the Caribbean and the Mediterranean. New ports included Corfu, Esbjerg, Mykonos, Rostock, Santorini and Tobago.

Title page: *Astoria* made her first visit to Santorini on 21st September 2015 during a Mediterranean Classics and Treasures cruise.

Astor

Code	Cruise	Nights	Departure date
A501	**Southbound Voyage to Australia** London Tilbury - Le Havre – Lisbon – Tenerife - Porto Grande – Jamestown - Cape Town – Durban - Pointe des Galets - Port Louis - Fremantle	38	05 Nov 2014
A504	**Southern Explorer** Fremantle - Esperance - Albany - Fremantle	5	15 Dec 2014
A505	**Merry Christmas Bali** Fremantle - Benoa- Fremantle	10	20 Dec 2014
A506	**Happy New Year** Fremantle - Fremantle	3	30 Dec 2014
A507	**Summer Short Break** Fremantle - Fremantle	3	02 Jan 2015
A508	**Summer in Bali** Fremantle - Benoa - Fremantle	10	05 Jan 2015
A510	**Summer Sailaway** Fremantle - Fremantle	3	16 Jan 2015
A511	**Coastal Explorer** Fremantle - Esperance - Albany - Fremantle	5	19 Jan 2015
A512	**Australia Day Celebration** Fremantle - Fremantle	3	24 Jan 2015
A513	**Grand Round Australia Voyage** Fremantle - Esperance - Penneshaw - Adelaide - Burnie - Melbourne - Sydney - Brisbane - Cairns - Darwin - Benoa - Exmouth - Fremantle	33	27 Jan 2015
A514	**Cruise the Coast** Fremantle - Esperance - Albany - Fremantle	5	01 Mar 2015
A516	**Summer Escape** Fremantle - Esperance - Albany - Fremantle	5	07 Mar 2015
A518	**Weekend Celebration** Fremantle - Fremantle	3	13 Mar 2015
A519	**Northbound Voyage via Africa** Fremantle - Port Louis - Pointe des Galets - Durban - Mossel Bay - Cape Town - Walvis Bay - Jamestown - Casablanca - Lisbon - London Tilbury	38	16 Mar 2015
A520	**British Isles Discovery** London Tilbury - Invergordon - Portree - Tobermory - Dublin - St. Mary's - Honfleur - London Tilbury	8	23 Apr 2015

Astor

Code	Cruise	Nights	Departure date
A525	**Season Opening / "Welcome Europe"** London Tilbury - Bremerhaven	1	01 May 2015
A526	**City Lights / Western Europe / River Thames & Seine** Bremerhaven - London Tilbury - Rouen - Antwerp - Bremerhaven	7	02 May 2015
A527	**North Sea Islands** Bremerhaven - Esbjerg - List - Helgoland - Bremerhaven	4	09 May 2015
A528	**Great Britain & Ireland** Bremerhaven - Portsmouth - Falmouth - Dublin - Belfast - Stornoway - Invergordon – Rosyth - Newcastle Tyne - Bremerhaven	11	13 May 2015
A529	**Norway, Sweden & Denmark** Bremerhaven - Stavanger - Kristiansund - Oslo - Gothenburg - Esbjerg - Bremerhaven	7	24 May 2015
A530	**Britain's East Coast** Bremerhaven – Harwich - Newcastle Tyne - Rosyth - Invergordon - Bremerhaven	8	31 May 2015
A531	**Baltic Sea** Bremerhaven - Kiel Canal - Gdansk - Baltiysk - Klaipėda - Riga - Tallinn - St. Petersburg - Helsinki - Stockholm - Kiel	12	08 Jun 2015
A533	**Southern Norway Beautiful Fjords** Kiel - Stavanger - Flåm - Vik - Hellesylt - Geiranger - Bergen - Kiel	7	21 Jun 2015
A534	**Party Night (Kiel Week Closing Fireworks)** Kiel - Kiel Canal - Bremerhaven	1	28 Jun 2015
A535	**Iceland & North Cape** Bremerhaven - Tórshavn - Reykjavik - Akureyri - Barentsburg - Pyramiden - Longyearbyen - Honningsvåg - Tromsø - Hellesylt - Geiranger - Bergen - Bremerhaven	16	29 Jun 2015
A536	**North Cape** Bremerhaven - Vik - Flåm - Åndalsnes - Leknes - Honningsvåg - Tromsø - Geiranger - Bergen - Bremerhaven	12	15 Jul 2015
A537	**Great Britain & Ireland** Bremerhaven - Portsmouth - Falmouth - Dublin - Stornoway - Invergordon - Rosyth - Bremerhaven	11	27 Jul 2015

Astor

Code	Cruise	Nights	Departure date
A538	**Iceland** Bremerhaven - Invergordon - Tórshavn - Hafnarfjörður - Ísafjörður - Akureyri - Seyðisfjörður - Bergen - Bremerhaven	12	07 Aug 2015
A539	**North Cape** Bremerhaven - Flåm - Molde - Honningsvåg - Leknes - Ålesund - Geiranger - Bergen - Kiel	11	19 Aug 2015
A540	**Baltic Sea** Kiel - Klaipéda - Riga - Tallinn - St. Petersburg - Helsinki - Stockholm - Kiel	10	30 Aug 2015
A541	**North Sea Islands** Kiel - Kiel Canal - Esbjerg - List - Helgoland - Bremerhaven	4	09 Sep 2015
A542	**England, Ireland, Scotland** Bremerhaven - Portsmouth - Falmouth - Dublin - Londonderry - Stornoway - Invergordon - Rosyth - Bremerhaven	10	13 Sep 2015
A543	**English Channel** Bremerhaven - Ijmuiden - St. Peter Port - Honfleur - Oostende - Rotterdam - Bremerhaven	6	23 Sep 2015
A544	**City Lights / Western Europe / River Thames & Seine** Bremerhaven - London Tilbury - Rouen - Antwerp - Bremerhaven	7	29 Sep 2015
A545	**End of Season / "Goodbye Europe"** Bremerhaven - Antwerp	1	06 Oct 2015

> **"Our favourite was very much the *Astor* as we had 22 wonderful cruises on her. But, after doing 46 nights on *Vasco Da Gama* we got to love her equally, and look forward to our next seven booked cruises in 2020/21."**
>
> Uwe & Patricia Voigt

Antwerp

Azores

Code	Cruise	Nights	Departure date
R500	**Voyage to the West Indies** Plymouth - Lisbon - Funchal - St. John's - Gustavia- St. Maarten - Basseterre - Castries - Kingstown - Bequia - Tobago - St. George''s - Bridgetown - Ponta Delgada - Lisbon - Portland	30	26 Jan 2015
R501	**Land of the Northern Lights** Portland - Ålesund - Narvik - Tromsø - Alta - Honningsvåg - Kristiansund - Bristol Avonmouth	15	27 Feb 2015
R502	**Solar Eclipse & Northern Lights** Bristol Avonmouth - Dublin - Reykjavik - Kollafjørður - Kirkwall - Stornoway - Bristol Avonmouth	12	14 Mar 2015
R503	**Springtime in the Sub Tropical Azores** Bristol Avonmouth - La Coruna - Leixoes - Horta - Praia da Vitória - Ponta Delgada - Funchal - Lisbon – Bristol Avonmouth	16	26 Mar 2015
R504	**British Isles Discovery** Bristol Avonmouth - Tobermory - Kirkwall - Honfleur - St. Peter Port - Bristol Avonmouth	8	11 Apr 2015
R505	**Portugal & Seville Fiesta** Bristol Avonmouth - Lisbon - Portimão - Gibraltar - Cadiz - Leixoes - La Coruña - Bristol Avonmouth	11	19 Apr 2015
R506	**Fjordland Splendour** Bristol Avonmouth - Eidfjord - Flåm - Bergen - Bristol Avonmouth	8	30 Apr 2015
R507	**British Isles Discovery** Bristol Avonmouth - Kirkwall - Invergordon - Honfleur - St. Peter Port - St. Mary's - Bristol Avonmouth	9	08 May 2015
R508	**Scottish Highlands, Islands & Faroes** Bristol Avonmouth - Portree - Lerwick - Tórshavn - Kirkwall - Ullapool - Tobermory - Bristol Avonmouth	9	17 May 2015
R509	**Iceland's Land of Ice & Fire** Bristol Avonmouth - Stornoway - Tórshavn - Eskifjörður - Akureyri - Ísafjörður - Reykjavik - Heimaey - Dublin - Bristol Avonmouth	12	26 May 2015
R510	**Summertime Gardens & Medieval Cities** Bristol Avonmouth - St. Mary's - Cherbourg - Rouen - Honfleur - Amsterdam - Hull	8	07 Jun 2015

Barbados

Azores

Code	Cruise	Nights	Departure date
R511	**Iceland & Northern Isles** Hull - Tórshavn – Seydisfjordur - Akureyri - Ísafjörður - Reykjavik - Heimaey - Lerwick - Kirkwall - Hull	12	15 Jun 2015
R512	**Fjordland Splendour** Hull - Eidfjord - Flåm - Olden - Geiranger - Bergen - Hull	8	27 Jun 2015
R513	**Baltic Cities & St. Petersburg** Hull - Copenhagen - Warnemünde - Tallinn - St. Petersburg - Helsinki - Nynäshamn – Kiel Canal - Hull	12	05 Jul 2015
R520	**Majestic Fjordland** Hull - Ulvik - Eidfjord - Flåm - Olden - Bergen - Hull	7	17 Jul 2015
R521	**Scottish Highlands, Islands & Faroes** Hull - Kirkwall - Tórshavn - Tobermory - Liverpool	6	24 Jul 2015
R522	**Iceland & Northern Isles** Liverpool - Kollafjørður – Seydisfjordur - Akureyri - Ísafjörður - Reykjavik - Liverpool	10	30 Jul 2015
R523	**Majestic Fjordland & Scottish Isles** Liverpool - Olden - Geiranger - Flåm - Bergen - Tobermory - Liverpool	9	09 Aug 2015
R524	**British Isles Discovery** Liverpool - Cobh - St. Mary's - St. Peter Port - Le Havre - Invergordon - Stornoway - Tobermory - Liverpool	9	18 Aug 2015
R525	**Dublin Mini Cruise Break** Liverpool - Dublin - Bristol Avonmouth	2	27 Aug 2015
R526	**Treasures of British Isles** Bristol Avonmouth - Tobermory - Stornoway - Kirkwall - Invergordon - Le Havre - St. Peter Port - St. Mary's - Bristol Avonmouth	10	29 Aug 2015
R527	**Iberian Classics &** **Western Mediterranean Highlights** Bristol Avonmouth - La Coruna - Leixoes - Lisbon - Gibraltar - Malaga - Livorno	9	08 Sep 2015
R528	**Mediterranean Classics & Treasures** Livorno - Civitavecchia - Santorini - Mykonos - Kusadasi - Piraeus - Katakolon - Corfu - Korcula - Venice	11	17 Sep 2015

Magellan

Code	Cruise	Nights	Departure date
G500	**Maiden Solar Eclipse & Northern Lights** London Tilbury - Invergordon - Lerwick - Reykjavik - Tórshavn - London Tilbury	12	15 Mar 2015
G501	**Overnight Celebration Cruise** London Tilbury – Newcastle Tyne	1	27 Mar 2015
G502	**Majestic Fjordland** Newcastle Tyne- Dundee - Eidfjord - Flåm - Bergen – Newcastle Tyne	7	28 Mar 2015
G503	**Majestic Easter Fjordland** Newcastle Tyne- Dundee - Eidfjord - Flåm - Bergen – Newcastle Tyne	7	04 Apr 2015
G504	**Majestic Fjordland** Newcastle Tyne- Dundee - Flåm - Bergen - Eidfjord – Newcastle Tyne	7	11 Apr 2015
G505	**Amsterdam & Antwerp** **Summer Weekend Break** London Tilbury - Amsterdam - Antwerp - London Tilbury	3	04 Jun 2015
G506	**Summertime Fjordland** London Tilbury - Flåm - Bergen - Eidfjord - London Tilbury	6	07 Jun 2015
G507	**Summertime Fjordland** London Tilbury - Eidfjord - Bergen - Flåm - London Tilbury	6	13 Jun 2015
G508	**British Isles Discovery** London Tilbury - Invergordon - Stornoway - Tobermory - Dublin - St. Mary's - St. Peter Port - Honfleur - London Tilbury	9	19 Jun 2015
G509	**Grand British Isles Discovery** London Tilbury - Invergordon - Kirkwall - Stornoway - Belfast - Tobermory - Dublin - Ringaskiddy - St. Mary's - St. Peter Port - Honfleur - London Tilbury	12	28 Jun 2015
G510	**Scandinavian Cities & Fairy tales** London Tilbury - Amsterdam - Hamburg - Helsingborg - Copenhagen - Aalborg - London Tilbury	8	10 Jul 2015
G511	**British Isles Discovery** London Tilbury - Kirkwall - Stornoway - Tobermory - Dublin - St. Mary's - St. Peter Port - Honfleur - London Tilbury	9	18 Jul 2015

Magellan

Code	Cruise	Nights	Departure date
G512	**Iceland & Northern Isles** London Tilbury - Kirkwall - Heimaey - Reykjavik - Ísafjörður - Akureyri - Seyðisfjörður - Tórshavn - Lerwick - London Tilbury	12	27 Jul 2015
G513	**Scottish Isles, Faroes & Edinburgh Festival** London Tilbury - Kirkwall - Tórshavn - Lerwick - Edinburgh Leith - London Tilbury	8	08 Aug 2015
G514	**Baltic Cities & St. Petersburg** London Tilbury - Copenhagen - Warnemünde - Tallinn - St. Petersburg - Helsinki –Helsingborg - London Tilbury	12	16 Aug 2015
G515	**Summertime Fjordland** London Tilbury - Eidfjord - Flåm - Bergen - London Tilbury	6	28-Aug-2015
G516	**Amsterdam & Antwerp Weekend** London Tilbury - Amsterdam - Antwerp - London Tilbury	3	03 Sep 2015
G517	**Baltic Cities & St. Petersburg** London Tilbury - Copenhagen - Warnemünde - Tallinn - St. Petersburg - Helsinki - Stockholm - London Tilbury	12	06 Sep 2015
G518	**Majestic Fjordland** London Tilbury - Amsterdam - Eidfjord - Flåm - Bergen - London Tilbury	7	18 Sep 2015
G519	**Autumn Gardens & the Channel Islands** London Tilbury - Amsterdam - Zeebrugge - Cherbourg - Rouen - Honfleur - London Tilbury	6	25 Sep 2015
G520	**Scandinavian Cities & Fairytales** London Tilbury - Amsterdam - Hamburg - Helsingborg - Copenhagen - Aalborg - London Tilbury	8	01 Oct 2015
G521	**Land of the Northern Lights** London Tilbury - Amsterdam - Olden - Sortland - Alta - Honningsvåg - Tromsø - Trondheim - Åndalsnes - Bergen - London Tilbury	14	09 Oct 2015
G522	**Canary Islands & Madeira** London Tilbury - Amsterdam - Gibraltar - Arrecife - Santa Cruz de Tenerife - Las Palmas - Funchal - Lisbon - London Tilbury	15	23 Oct 2015
G523	**Treasures of the West Indies** London Tilbury - Amsterdam - Ponta Delgada - St John's - St Maarten - Basseterre - Castries - Mayreau - Kingstown - Bequia - St George's - Bridgetown - Funchal - Lisbon - London Tilbury	33	07 Nov 2015

Marco Polo

Code	Cruise	Nights	Departure date
P498	**Xmas Market Cruise** London Tilbury - Ijmuiden - Ghent - London Tilbury	3	15 Dec 2014
P499	**Xmas Market Cruise** London Tilbury - Amsterdam - Antwerp - London Tilbury	3	19 Dec 2014
P501	**Christmas & New Year Cruise** London Tilbury - Gibraltar - Arrecife - La Gomera - Santa Cruz de Tenerife - Funchal - Lisbon - London Tilbury	14	22 Dec 2014
P502	**Annual Amazon Cruise** London Tilbury - Amsterdam - Lisbon - Funchal - Mindelo - Santarém - Boca da Valeria - Manaus - Parintins - Santana - Îles du Salut - St. George's - Kingstown - Bequia - Castries - Bridgetown - Horta - Ponta Delgada - London Tilbury	42	05 Jan 2015
P503	**The Land of the Northern Lights** London Tilbury - Amsterdam - Ålesund - Tromsø - Alta - Honningsvåg - Sortland - Åndalsnes - Bergen - London Tilbury	14	16 Feb 2015
P504	**The Land of the Northern Lights** London Tilbury - Amsterdam - Ålesund - Trondheim -Tromsø - Alta – Kristiansund - Åndalsnes - Bergen - London Tilbury	14	02 Mar 2015
P500	**Solar Eclipse & Northern Lights** London Tilbury - Kirkwall - Kollafjörður - Reykjavik - Invergordon - London Tilbury	11	16 Mar 2015
P505	**Spring Gardens & Dutch Bulbfields** London Tilbury - Amsterdam - Zeebrugge - Cherbourg - Rouen - Honfleur - London Tilbury	6	27 Mar 2015
P506	**British Isles Discovery** London Tilbury - Kirkwall - Ullapool - Tobermory - Dublin - St. Mary's - St. Peter Port - Honfleur - London Tilbury	9	02 Apr 2015
P507	**Springtime Fjordland** London Tilbury - Amsterdam - Eidfjord - Flåm - Bergen - London Tilbury	7	11 Apr 2015
P508	**Springtime Fjordland** London Tilbury - Amsterdam - Eidfjord - Flåm - Bergen - London Tilbury	7	18 Apr 2015

Marco Polo

Code	Cruise	Nights	Departure date
P509	**Majestic Fjordland** London Tilbury - Amsterdam - Eidfjord - Flåm - Geiranger - Bergen - London Tilbury	8	25 Apr 2015
P510	**British Isles Discovery** London Tilbury - Kirkwall - Invergordon - Tobermory - Dublin - St. Mary's - St. Peter Port - Honfleur - London Tilbury	9	03 May 2015
P511	**Baltic Cities & St. Petersburg** London Tilbury - Aalborg - Warnemünde - Tallinn - St. Petersburg - Helsinki - Stockholm - Kiel Canal - London Tilbury	12	12 May 2015

> **"Our stand-out cruise would be *Marco Polo's* 50th Anniversary Voyage to Iceland, Greenland and the eastern seaboard of Canada. Sailing through the icebergs and iceflows around Greenland overnight was a truly memorable experience. "**
>
> Ken & Marilyn Mealand

Code	Cruise	Nights	Departure date
P512	**Whitsun Overnight Mini Cruise** London Tilbury – Newcastle Tyne	1	24 May 2015
P513	**Iceland & Northern Isles** Newcastle Tyne- Tórshavn - Eskifjörður - Akureyri - Ísafjörður - Reykjavik - Lerwick - Kirkwall - Invergordon – Newcastle Tyne	12	25 May 2015
P514	**Baltic Cities & St. Petersburg** Newcastle Tyne- Warnemünde - Tallinn - St. Petersburg - Helsinki - Stockholm - Copenhagen – Newcastle Tyne	12	06 Jun 2015
P515	**Summertime Fjordland** Newcastle Tyne- Ulvik - Eidfjord - Flåm - Bergen - Edinburgh Leith	6	18 Jun 2015
P516	**Iceland & Northern Isles** Edinburgh Leith - Lerwick - Tórshavn - Eskifjörður - Akureyri - Ísafjörður - Reykjavik - Heimaey - Kirkwall - Rosyth	11	24 Jun 2015
P517	**Scottish Isles & Faroes** Rosyth - Tórshavn - Ullapool - Stornoway - Kirkwall - Rosyth	6	05 Jul 2015

Marco Polo

Code	Cruise	Nights	Departure date
P518	**Baltic Cities & St. Petersburg** Rosyth - Copenhagen - Rostock - Helsinki - St. Petersburg - Tallinn - Nynäshamn - Kiel Canal - Rosyth	12	11 Jul 2015
P519	**Overnight Mini Cruise** Rosyth - London Tilbury	1	23 Jul 2015
P520	**Commemorative Canada & Greenland** London Tilbury - Lerwick - Tórshavn - Reykjavik - Qaqortoq - Narsarsuaq - St. John's - Sydney NS - Charlottetown - Gaspé - Québec - Montréal - Saguenay - Sept Îles - Havre St. Pierre - Cap-aux-Meules - Corner Brook - L'Anse aux Meadows - Cobh - London Tilbury	36	24 Jul 2015
P521	**British Isles Discovery** London Tilbury - Kirkwall - Stornoway - Tobermory - Dublin - St. Mary's - St. Peter Port - Honfleur - London Tilbury	9	29 Aug 2015
P570	**Autumn Commemorative Voyage to Canada** London Tilbury - Amsterdam - Cherbourg - St. John's- Halifax - Charlottetown - Gaspé - Québec - Montréal - Saguenay - Sept Îles - Havre St. Pierre - Cap-aux-Meules - Sydney NS - Corner Brook - St. Anthony - Cobh - London Tilbury	34	07 Sep 2015
P580	**Baltic Cities & St. Petersburg** London Tilbury - Amsterdam - Copenhagen - Warnemünde - Tallinn - St. Petersburg - Helsinki - Nynäshamn - Kiel Canal - London Tilbury	13	11 Oct 2015
P527	**Great European Rivers & Medieval Cities** London Tilbury - Amsterdam - Antwerp - Honfleur - Rouen - Le Havre - London Tilbury	6	24 Oct 2015

Stockholm

Montreal

Greenland

Quebec

St. Petersburg

Cruise programme summary 2010-2019

2015-2016
Azores renamed *Astoria*

Programme highlights include: -

- *Astoria* commences a summer charter to French Tour Operator **Rivages du Monde**

- The southbound voyage of *Astor* **sails via Panama for the first time** and calls at Auckland, Sydney, Adelaide and Fremantle.

- **More cruises from Bristol Avonmouth** with a choice of both *Marco Polo* and *Astoria*

Total Ports visited: **256** (66 maiden calls)

Total mileage: **292,889** nautical miles

Market Deployment/Vessels:
UK – *Marco Polo, Magellan* & *Astoria*
Australia – *Astor*
Germany – *Astor*
France – *Astoria*

Maiden Calls

Marco Polo made a 54 night South American Treasures cruise in January 2016 and introduced a number of ports on that continent to the maiden calls list which totalled 66 for the year. Port Stanley, Punta Arenas, Recife, Salvador and Ushuaia each received their first CMV call.

Title page: **Recife was the first landfall in Brazil for *Marco Polo*'s passengers on 18th January 2016.**

Astor

Code	Cruise	Nights	Departure date
A601	**Southbound Voyage to Australia** London Tilbury - Funchal - St. John's - Castries - Bridgetown - Panama Canal - Acapulco - Nuku Hiva - Papeete - Bora Bora - Auckland - Sydney - Adelaide- Penneshaw - Fremantle	53	17 Oct 2015
A604	**Southern Explorer** Fremantle - Esperance - Albany - Fremantle	5	14 Dec 2015
A605	**Christmas Day In Bali** Fremantle - Benoa - Fremantle	11	19 Dec 2015
A606	**New Year At Sea** Fremantle - Fremantle	3	30 Dec 2015
A607	**Coastal Adventure** Fremantle - Esperance - Albany - Bunbury - Geraldton - Fremantle	8	02 Jan 2016
A608	**Coastal Explorer** Fremantle - Esperance - Albany - Fremantle	5	10 Jan 2016
A609	**Party Weekend** Fremantle - Fremantle	3	15 Jan 2016
A610	**Coastal Escape** Fremantle - Esperance - Albany - Bunbury - Fremantle	6	18 Jan 2016
A611	**Australia Day At Sea** Fremantle - Fremantle	3	24 Jan 2016
A612	**Rock n Roll Cruise** Fremantle - Esperance - Albany - Fremantle	6	27 Jan 2016
A614	**Far East Treasures** Fremantle - Singapore - Kuching - Labuan - Muara - Kota Kinabalu - Hong Kong - Halong Bay - Chan May - Ho Chi Minh - Benoa - Fremantle	35	03 Feb 2016
A615	**Country & Western Music** Fremantle - Esperance - Albany - Fremantle	6	09 Mar 2016
A617	**Australia to UK Voyage** Fremantle - Port Louis - Pointe des Galets - Durban - Mossel Bay - Cape Town - Walvis Bay - Jamestown - Casablanca - Lisbon - London Tilbury	38	16 Mar 2016

Astor

Code	Cruise	Nights	Departure date
A618	**British Isles Discovery** London Tilbury - Invergordon - Stornoway - Tobermory - Dublin - St. Mary's - Honfleur - London Tilbury	8	23 Apr 2016
A673	**Season's Opening / "Welcome Europe"** London Tilbury - Bremerhaven	1	01 May 2016
A674	**From Northern to Baltic Sea & "Overland" to Port Birthday** Bremerhaven - Gothenburg - Malmo – Sassnitz - Kiel Canal - Hamburg	6	02 May 2016
A675	**Port Birthday & Homeland Wadden Sea** Hamburg - Esbjerg - List - Helgoland - Bremerhaven	5	08 May 2016
A676	**Great Britain & Ireland** Bremerhaven - Portsmouth - Falmouth - Dublin - Portree - Kirkwall - Invergordon - Rosyth - Bremerhaven	11	13 May 2016
A677	**North Cape** Bremerhaven - Vik - Flåm - Ålesund - Leknes - Honningsvåg - Tromsø - Hellesylt - Geiranger - Bergen - Kiel	12	24 May 2016
A678	**Baltic Sea** Kiel - Gdansk - Baltiysk - Klaipėda - Riga - Tallinn - St. Petersburg - Helsinki - Stockholm - Kiel Canal - Bremerhaven	12	05 Jun 2016
A679	**Iceland, Svalbard & North Cape** Bremerhaven - Kollafjörður - Reykjavik - Ísafjörður - Akureyri - Longyearbyen - Barentsburg - Honningsvåg - Tromsø - Hellesylt - Geiranger - Bergen - Bremerhaven	17	17 Jun 2016
A680	**England, Ireland, English Channel** Bremerhaven - Dover - Falmouth - Dublin - Cork - St. Peter Port - Honfleur - Bremerhaven	11	04 Jul 2016
A681	**Greenland** Bremerhaven - Seyðisfjörður - Akureyri - Ammassalik - Qeqertarsuaq - Uummannaq - Ilulissat - Sisimiut - Kangerlussuaq - Nuuk - Nanortalik - Reykjavik - Tórshavn - Bremerhaven	23	15 Jul 2016
A682	**English Channel** Bremerhaven - Ijmuiden - St. Peter Port - Honfleur - Zeebrugge - Rotterdam - Bremerhaven	6	07 Aug 2016

Cadiz

Madeira

Astor

Code	Cruise	Nights	Departure date
A683	**Edinburgh Festival, Military Tattoo** Bremerhaven – Harwich – Newcastle Tyne – Rosyth – Kiel	8	13 Aug 2016
A684	**Baltic Sea** Kiel – Tallinn – St. Petersburg – Helsinki – Stockholm – Kiel	8	21 Aug 2016
A685	**Western Europe North-to-South** Kiel – Kiel Canal – London Tilbury – La Coruna – Vigo – Lisbon – Cadiz – Malaga – Almeria – Valencia – Genoa	11	29 Aug 2016
A686	**Italian Riviera & Western Mediterranean Islands** Genoa – Livorno – Civitavecchia – Naples – Palermo – Cagliari – Olbia – Genoa	7	09 Sep 2016
A688	**Western Europe South-to-North** Genoa – Ibiza – Portimão – Leixoes – Falmouth – Bremerhaven	9	16 Sep 2016
A689	**Season's End / "Goodbye Europe"** Bremerhaven – Antwerp	1	25 Sep 2016

Astoria

Code	Cruise	Nights	Departure date
R601	**Easter Scottish Islands & Emerald Isle** Bristol Avonmouth – Belfast – Ullapool – Greenock – Dublin – Bristol Avonmouth	7	21 Mar 2016
R602	**Springtime in the Azores & Madeira** Bristol Avonmouth – Leixoes – Lisbon – Horta – Ponta Delgada – Funchal – La Coruna – Bristol Avonmouth	15	28 Mar 2016
R603	**British Isles Discovery** Bristol Avonmouth – Tobermory – Stornoway – Kirkwall – Honfleur – St. Peter Port– Falmouth – Bristol Avonmouth	9	12 Apr 2016
R604	**Scottish Islands & Faroes** Bristol Avonmouth – Portree – Lerwick – Tórshavn – Stornoway – Tobermory – Bristol Avonmouth	9	21 Apr 2016
R605	**Fjordland Splendour** Bristol Avonmouth – Eidfjord – Flåm – Geiranger – Bergen – Bristol Avonmouth	9	30 Apr 2016

Astoria

Code	Cruise	Nights	Departure date
RDMC1	**Ireland** Honfleur - St. Helier - Cobh - Galway - Belfast - Dublin - Honfleur	8	11 May 2016
RDMC2	**British Isles** Honfleur - Portsmouth - Dublin - Belfast - Greenock - Stornoway - Rosyth - London Tilbury - Dunkirk	10	19 May 2016
RDMC3	**Norwegian Fjords** Dunkirk - Bergen - Geiranger - Vik - Flåm - Stavanger - Zeebrugge	7	29 May 2016
RDMC4	**British Isles** Zeebrugge - Southampton - Dublin - Greenock - Belfast - Stornoway - Lerwick - Invergordon - Amsterdam	10	05 Jun 2016
RDMC5	**Baltic & St. Petersburg** Amsterdam - Kiel Canal - Warnemünde - Gdansk - Tallinn - St. Petersburg - Helsinki - Stockholm - Visby - Copenhagen - Zeebrugge	13	15 Jun 2016
RDMC6	**Norwegian Fjords & North Cape** Zeebrugge - Stavanger - Vik - Flåm - Hellesylt - Geiranger - Leknes - Honningsvåg - Tromsø	9	28 Jun 2016
RDMC7	**Murmansk & Spitzbergen** Tromsø - Honningsvåg - Murmansk - Longyearbyen - Tromsø	8	07 Jul 2016
RDMC8	**Spitzbergen & Norwegian Fjords** Tromsø - Longyearbyen - Ny-Ålesund - Leknes - Hellesylt - Geiranger - Bergen	10	15 Jul 2016
RDMC9	**Iceland** Bergen - Lerwick - Tórshavn - Reykjavik - Ísafjörður - Akureyri - Húsavík - Eskifjörður - Reykjavik	9	25 Jul 2016
RDMC10	**Iceland & Greenland** Reykjavik - Ísafjörður - Akureyri - Grundarfjörður - Narsaq - Nuuk - Ilulissat - Sisimiut - Kangerlussuaq	12	03 Aug 2016
RDMC11	**Greenland & Ireland** Kangerlussuaq - Ilulissat - Nuuk - Narsaq - Reykjavik - Belfast - Dublin - Le Verdon	13	15 Aug 2016
RDMC12	**Iberia & Western Mediterranean** Le Verdon - Leixoes - Lisbon - Huelva - Cadiz - Mahon - Marseille	7	28 Aug 2016

Belfast

Athens

143

Astoria

Code	Cruise	Nights	Departure date
RDMC13	**Mediterranean & Adriatic** Marseille – Genoa – Livorno – Civitavecchia – Naples – Messina – Syracuse – Brindisi – Bari – Ancona – Ravenna – Trieste – Venice	11	04 Sep 2016
RDMC14	**Adriatic** Venice – Pula – Zadar – Split – Ploče – Korcula – Dubrovnik – Kotor – Durres – Corfu	9	15 Sep 2016
RDMC15	**Greece & the Islands** Corfu – Katakolon – Gythion – Iraklion – Piraeus – Patmos – Cesme – Chios – Volos – Thessaloniki	9	24 Sep 2016
RDMC16	**Greece & the Islands** Thessaloniki – Volos – Mytilene – Cesme – Syros – Piraeus – Monemvasia – Santorini – Iraklion	9	03 Oct 2016
RDMC17	**Greece & the Islands** Iraklion – Naxos – Volos – Thessaloniki – Kavala – Cesme – Samos – Rhodes	8	12 Oct 2016
RDMC18	**Mediterranean & the Adriatic** Rhodes – Patmos – Piraeus – Corfu – Sarande – Dubrovnik – Split – Bari – Messina – Marseille	10	20 Oct 2016
RDMC19	**Western Mediterranean** Marseille – Ajaccio – Olbia – Civitavecchia – Bastia – Livorno – Marseille	6	30 Oct 2016
Charter	**Redseven Entertainment** Marseille – Palma de Mallorca – Mahon – Barcelona	5	05 Nov 2016

> **The price was a lot more affordable than I expected, as I still thought at that time that cruising was only for really rich people and as a caravanner more used to wellies and cagoules in the west of Scotland, I wasn't all that sure about cruising. But we were immediately hooked.**
>
> Roger & Linda Harkness

Magellan

Code	Cruise	Nights	Departure date
G600	**Xmas Market Cruise** London Tilbury – Amsterdam – Antwerp – London Tilbury	3	13 Dec 2015
G601	**Xmas Market Cruise** London Tilbury – Amsterdam – Antwerp – London Tilbury	3	16 Dec 2015
G602	**Xmas Market Cruise** London Tilbury – Antwerp – London Tilbury	2	20 Dec 2015
G603	**Christmas & New Year Canary Islands & Madeira** London Tilbury – Antwerp – Gibraltar – Santa Cruz de Tenerife – Las Palmas – Funchal – Lisbon – London Tilbury	14	22 Dec 2015
G604	**Amazon, West Indies & Azores** London Tilbury – Amsterdam – Lisbon – Funchal – Mindelo – Santarém – Boca da Valeria – Manaus – Parintins – Alter do Chão – Santana – Îles du Salut– St. George's – Kingstown – Bequia – Castries – Bridgetown – Horta – Ponta Delgada – London Tilbury	42	05 Jan 2016
G605	**Land of the Northern Lights** London Tilbury – Amsterdam – Ålesund – Tromsø – Alta – Honningsvåg – Sortland – Åndalsnes – Bergen – London Tilbury	14	16 Feb 2016
G607	**Iceland, the Faroes & Northern Lights** London Tilbury – Amsterdam – Kollafjørður – Reykjavik – Kirkwall – London Tilbury	11	01 Mar 2016
G608	**Springtime Canary Islands & Madeira** London Tilbury – Gibraltar – Arrecife – Las Palmas – Santa Cruz de Tenerife – Funchal – Lisbon – London Tilbury	14	12 Mar 2016
G609	**Easter Fjordland** London Tilbury – Eidfjord – Flåm – Bergen – London Tilbury	6	26 Mar 2016
G610	**Overnight Celebration Cruise** London Tilbury – Newcastle	1	01 Apr 2016
G611	**Majestic Fjordland** Newcastle Tyne – Dundee – Ulvik – Eidfjord – Flåm – Bergen – Newcastle Tyne	7	02 Apr 2016
G612	**Majestic Fjordland** Newcastle Tyne – Dundee – Flåm – Bergen – Ulvik – Eidfjord – Newcastle Tyne	7	09 Apr 2016

Magellan

Code	Cruise	Nights	Departure date
G613	**Fjordland Splendour** Newcastle Tyne - Dundee – Ulvik - Eidfjord - Flåm - Geiranger - Bergen – Newcastle Tyne	8	16 Apr 2016
G614	**Iceland, the Faroes & Northern Isles** Newcastle Tyne - Dundee - Tórshavn - Seyðisfjörður - Akureyri - Ísafjörður - Reykjavik - Lerwick - Kirkwall – Newcastle Tyne	12	24 Apr 2016
G615	**Baltic Cities & St. Petersburg** Newcastle Tyne - Dundee - Copenhagen - Warnemünde - Tallinn - St. Petersburg - Helsinki - Stockholm - Aarhus - Newcastle Tyne	14	06 May 2016
G616	**Overnight Celebration Cruise** Newcastle Tyne - London Tilbury	1	20 May 2016
G617	**Majestic Fjordland** London Tilbury - Bergen - Molde - Åndalsnes - Geiranger - Flåm - London Tilbury	7	21 May 2016
G618	**Amsterdam & Ghent** London Tilbury - Ghent - Amsterdam - London Tilbury	3	28 May 2016
G619	**Grand British Isles Discovery** London Tilbury - Invergordon - Kirkwall - Stornoway - Tobermory - Dublin - Belfast - Cobh - St. Mary's - St. Malo - Honfleur - London Tilbury	12	31 May 2016
G620	**Baltic Cities & St. Petersburg** London Tilbury - Copenhagen - Warnemünde - Tallinn - St. Petersburg - Helsinki - Nynäshamn - London Tilbury	12	12 Jun 2016
G621	**Iceland, the Faroes & Northern Isles** London Tilbury - Kirkwall - Reykjavik - Ísafjörður - Akureyri - Seyðisfjörður - Kollafjörður - Lerwick - London Tilbury	12	24 Jun 2016
G622	**British Isles Discovery** London Tilbury - Kirkwall - Stornoway - Tobermory - Dublin - St. Mary's - St. Peter Port - Honfleur - London Tilbury	9	06 Jul 2016
G623	**Baltic Cities & St. Petersburg** London Tilbury - Copenhagen - Warnemünde - Tallinn - St. Petersburg - Helsinki - Nynäshamn - London Tilbury	12	15 Jul 2016

Magellan

Code	Cruise	Nights	Departure date
G624	**Majestic Fjordland** London Tilbury - Eidfjord - Flåm - Geiranger - Bergen - London Tilbury	7	27 Jul 2016
G625	**Grand British Isles Discovery** London Tilbury - Invergordon - Kirkwall - Belfast - Liverpool - Dublin - Cobh - St. Mary's - St. Peter Port - Honfleur - London Tilbury	12	03 Aug 2016
G626	**Baltic Cities & St. Petersburg** London Tilbury - Copenhagen - Warnemünde - Tallinn - St. Petersburg - Helsinki - Nynäshamn - London Tilbury	12	15 Aug 2016
G627	**Summertime Fjordland** London Tilbury - Bergen - Molde - Åndalsnes - Geiranger - Eidfjord - London Tilbury	7	27 Aug 2016
G628	**British Isles Discovery** London Tilbury - Kirkwall - Tobermory - Liverpool - Dublin - Rouen - Honfleur - London Tilbury	9	03 Sep 2016
G629	**Baltic Cities & St. Petersburg** London Tilbury - Copenhagen - Warnemünde - Tallinn - St. Petersburg - Helsinki - Nynäshamn - London Tilbury	12	12 Sep 2016
G630	**Autumn Fjordland** London Tilbury - Amsterdam - Ulvik - Eidfjord - Flåm - Bergen - London Tilbury	7	24 Sep 2016
G631	**Baltic Cities & St. Petersburg** London Tilbury - Amsterdam - Copenhagen - Warnemünde - Tallinn - St. Petersburg - Helsinki - Aarhus - London Tilbury	13	01 Oct 2016
G632	**Canary Islands & Madeira** London Tilbury - Amsterdam - Gibraltar - Arrecife - Las Palmas - Santa Cruz de Tenerife - Funchal - Lisbon - London Tilbury	15	14 Oct 2016
G633	**The Land of the Northern Lights** London Tilbury - Amsterdam - Olden - Sortland - Alta - Honningsvåg - Tromsø - Trondheim - Åndalsnes - Bergen - London Tilbury	14	29 Oct 2016

Marco Polo

Code	Cruise	Nights	Departure date
P600	**Festive Dublin Shopping & Christmas Party Cruise** Bristol Avonmouth - Cobh - Bristol Avonmouth	2	20 Dec 2015
P601	**Christmas & New Year Canary Islands & Madeira** Bristol Avonmouth - La Coruna – Lisbon - Arrecife - Las Palmas - Santa Cruz de Tenerife - Funchal – Vigo - Southampton	14	22 Dec 2015
P602	**South American Treasures** Southampton - La Coruna - Las Palmas - Mindelo - Recife - Ilhéus - Rio de Janeiro - Buenos Aires - Montevideo - Port Stanley - Ushuaia - Puerto Madryn - Rio Grande - Santos - Salvador - Natal - Praia Santiago - Funchal - Lisbon - Bristol Avonmouth	54	05 Jan 2016

Montevideo

Code	Cruise	Nights	Departure date
P603	**Treasures of the West Indies** Bristol Avonmouth - Ponta Delgada - St. John's - Road Town - Gustavia - Philipsburg - Basseterre - Castries - Kingstown - Bequia - Mayreau - Scarborough - St. George's - Bridgetown - Funchal - Lisbon - Bristol Avonmouth	32	28 Feb 2016

Marco Polo

Code	Cruise	Nights	Departure date
P605	**Springtime Gardens** Bristol Avonmouth – Honfleur - Rouen - London Tilbury	4	31 Mar 2016
P606	**Springtime Fjordland** London Tilbury - Ulvik - Eidfjord - Flåm - Bergen - London Tilbury	6	04 Apr 2016
P607	**Springtime Fjordland** London Tilbury - Ulvik - Eidfjord - Flåm - Bergen - London Tilbury	6	10 Apr 2016
P608	**British Isles Discovery** London Tilbury - Kirkwall - Stornoway - Tobermory - Dublin - St. Mary's - St. Peter Port - Honfleur - London Tilbury	9	16 Apr 2016
P609	**Majestic Fjordland** London Tilbury - Ulvik - Eidfjord - Flåm - Geiranger - Bergen - London Tilbury	7	25 Apr 2016
P610	**Baltic Cities & St. Petersburg** London Tilbury - Aalborg - Warnemünde - Tallinn - St. Petersburg - Helsinki - Stockholm - Kiel Canal - London Tilbury	12	02 May 2016
P611	**Overnight Celebration Cruise** London Tilbury - Hull	1	14 May 2016
P612	**Fjordland Splendour** Hull - Bergen - Molde - Åndalsnes - Geiranger - Flåm - Olden - Hull	8	15 May 2016
P613	**Baltic Cities & St. Petersburg** Hull - Copenhagen - Warnemünde - Tallinn - St. Petersburg - Helsinki - Nynäshamn - Kiel Canal - Hull	12	23 May 2016
P614	**Iceland, Faroes & Northern Isles** Hull - Tórshavn - Seyðisfjörður - Akureyri - Ísafjörður – Reykjavik - Lerwick - Kirkwall - Hull	12	04 Jun 2016
P615	**Scottish Islands & Faroes** Hull - Lerwick - Kollafjørður - Kirkwall - Invergordon – Newcastle Tyne	6	16 Jun 2016
P616	**Iceland, Faroes & Northern Isles** Newcastle Tyne - Tórshavn - Seyðisfjörður - Akureyri - Ísafjörður - Reykjavik - Lerwick - Kirkwall - Invergordon – Newcastle Tyne	12	22 Jun 2016

Marco Polo

Code	Cruise	Nights	Departure date
P617	**Baltic Cities & St. Petersburg** Newcastle Tyne - Kiel Canal - Rostock - Helsinki - St. Petersburg - Tallinn - Stockholm - Copenhagen – Newcastle Tyne	12	04 Jul 2016
P618	**Overnight Celebration Cruise** Newcastle Tyne - Edinburgh Leith	1	16 Jul 2016
P619	**Baltic Cities & St. Petersburg** Edinburgh Leith - Copenhagen - Rostock - Helsinki - St. Petersburg - Tallinn - Nynäshamn - Kiel Canal - Edinburgh Leith	12	17 Jul 2016
P620	**Iceland, Faroes & Northern Isles** Edinburgh Leith - Kirkwall - Seyðisfjörður - Akureyri - Ísafjörður - Reykjavik - Kollafjørður - Lerwick - Invergordon - Edinburgh Leith	12	29 Jul 2016
P621	**Scottish Islands & Faroes** Edinburgh Leith - Tórshavn - Lerwick - Kirkwall - Stornoway - Tobermory - Greenock	7	10 Aug 2016
P622	**Fjordland Splendour** Greenock - Lerwick - Ulvik - Eidfjord - Flåm - Hellesylt - Geiranger - Kristiansund - Bergen - Greenock	9	17 Aug 2016
P623	**Weekend Mini Cruise** Greenock - Liverpool	1	26 Aug 2016
P624	**Canada in the Fall** Liverpool - Belfast - St. John's - Halifax - Charlottetown - Gaspé - Québec - Montréal - Saguenay - Sept Îles - Havre St. Pierre - Cap-aux-Meules - Corner Brook - Sydney NS - Cobh - Liverpool	28	27 Aug 2016
P625	**Autumn Fjordland** Liverpool - Lerwick - Olden - Hellesylt - Geiranger - Flåm - Bergen - Liverpool	9	24 Sep 2016
P626	**Iceland, the Faroes & Northern Lights** Liverpool - Dublin - Lerwick - Kollafjørður - Akureyri - Reykjavik - Liverpool	12	03 Oct 2016
P627	**Dublin Weekend Mini Cruise** Liverpool - Dublin - Bristol Avonmouth	2	15 Oct 2016

Marco Polo

Code	Cruise	Nights	Departure date
P628	**Canary Islands & Madeira** Bristol Avonmouth - La Coruna - Gibraltar - Arrecife - Santa Cruz de Tenerife - Las Palmas - Funchal - Lisbon - Bristol Avonmouth	14	17 Oct 2016
P 629	**Dover Flotel Charter** Bristol Avonmouth - Dover	5	31 Oct 2016

Bergen Waterfront

Tenerife

Cruise programme summary 2010-2019

2016-2017
Welcome to
Columbus

Programme highlights include: -

- *Magellan* operates CMV's **120-night Maiden Round the World Cruise** in January

- *Columbus* **joins the fleet** and sails on her maiden voyage on June 11th from London Tilbury

- **New itineraries to Cuba** in February and Greenland in July undertaken by *Marco Polo*

Total Ports visited: **245** (44 maiden calls)

Total mileage: **341,242** nautical miles

Market Deployment/Vessels:
UK – *Marco Polo, Magellan, Astoria* & *Columbus*
Australia – *Astor*
Germany – *Astor*
France – *Astoria*
(summer charter to Rivages du Monde)

Maiden Calls

The much-anticipated *Magellan* World Cruise in January 2017 pushed the total of maiden calls this year up to 44. *Astoria, Astor* and *Marco Polo* also contributed and island ports figured prominently – Male, Moorea, Ocho Rios and Tortola amongst them. Recent legislation also opened up Cuba to foreign tourists, which was an added bonus.

Astor

Code	Cruise	Nights	Departure date
A701	**Southbound Voyage to Australia** London Tilbury - Funchal - St. John's - Castries - Bridgetown - Panama Canal - Acapulco - Nuku Hiva - Papeete - Moorea Island - Auckland - Sydney - Adelaide - Penneshaw - Fremantle	55	16 Oct 2016
A702	**Coastal Voyage** Fremantle - Fremantle	2	09 Dec 2016
A703	**Coastal Escape** Fremantle - Esperance - Albany - Fremantle	5	11 Dec 2016
A704	**Christmas Weekend** Fremantle - Fremantle	3	16 Dec 2016

Havana was visited on 20th March 2017 by *Marco Polo* for the first time since the Alexandr Pushkin 'goodwill' calls in her Soviet days.

Code	Cruise	Nights	Departure date
A705	**Christmas in Bali** Fremantle - Benoa - Fremantle	11	19 Dec 2016
A706	**New Year Celebration** Fremantle - Fremantle	3	30 Dec 2016
A707	**January Escape** Fremantle - Esperance - Albany - Fremantle	5	02 Jan 2017
A708	**Southern Explorer** Fremantle - Esperance - Albany - Bunbury - Fremantle	6	07 Jan 2017

Astor

Code	Cruise	Nights	Departure date
A709	**Weekend Break** Fremantle - Fremantle	3	13 Jan 2017
A710	**Bali Escape** Fremantle - Benoa - Fremantle	10	16 Jan 2017
A711	**Australia Day Holiday** Fremantle - Fremantle	3	26 Jan 2017
A712	**Southern Escape** Fremantle - Esperance - Albany - Fremantle	5	29 Jan 2017
A713	**Summer Weekend** Fremantle - Fremantle	3	03 Feb 2017
A714	**Southern Escape** Fremantle - Esperance - Albany - Fremantle	5	06 Feb 2017
A716	**Southern Explorer** Fremantle - Esperance - Albany - Bunbury - Fremantle	6	12 Feb 2017
A718	**Bound for Southern Australia** Fremantle - Esperance - Adelaide	5	19 Feb 2017

Astor

Code	Cruise	Nights	Departure date
A719	**Weekend Escape** Adelaide - Penneshaw - Adelaide	3	24 Feb 2017
A720	**Cruise The Bight** Adelaide - Penneshaw - Port Lincoln - Adelaide	3	27 Feb 2017
A721	**Tasmania Interlude** Adelaide - Port Arthur - Hobart - Burnie - Adelaide	7	02 Mar 2017
A722	**Coastal Escape** Adelaide - Esperance - Albany - Fremantle	6	09 Mar 2017
A723	**Australia to UK Voyage** Fremantle - Port Louis - Pointe des Galets - Durban - Mossel Bay - Cape Town - Walvis Bay - Las Palmas - Casablanca - Lisbon - London Tilbury	39	15 Mar 2017
A724	**Season's Opening / "Welcome Europe"** London Tilbury - Kiel Canal - Kiel	2	23 Apr 2017

Australia with CMV

Cape Town

Astor

Code	Cruise	Nights	Departure date
A725	**Classical Baltic & Harbour Birthday** Kiel - Gdansk - Klaipėda - Riga - Tallinn - St. Petersburg - Helsinki - Stockholm - Kiel Canal - Hamburg	12	25 Apr 2017
A726	**English Channel** Hamburg - Rotterdam - Honfleur - Antwerp - Ijmuiden - Bremerhaven	6	07 May 2017
A727	**Garden Holiday** Bremerhaven - Falmouth - Foynes - Killybegs - Dublin - Cobh - Portsmouth - Bremerhaven	10	13 May 2017
A728	**Midnight Sun at the North Cape** Bremerhaven - Vik - Flåm - Ålesund - Leknes - Honningsvåg - Tromsø - Hellesylt - Geiranger - Bergen - Bremerhaven	12	23 May 2017
A729	**North Cape / SPD-Reisen Charter** Bremerhaven - Vik - Gudvangen - Molde - Svartisen - Leknes - Honningsvåg - Tromsø - Geiranger - Hellesylt - Bergen - Bremerhaven	12	04 Jun 2017
A730	**Iceland, Spitzbergen & Greenland** **/ Troll Tours Charter** Bremerhaven - Stavanger - Urke - Ålesund - Leknes - Honningsvåg - Tromsø - Djúpivogur - Akureyri - Ísafjörður - Reykjavik - Qaqortoq - Nuuk - Sisimiut - Ilulissat - Qeqertarsuaq - Heimaey - Kollafjørður - Lerwick - Invergordon - Bremerhaven	30	16 Jun 2017
A731	**Greenland** Bremerhaven - Seyðisfjörður - Akureyri - Ammassalik - Qeqertarsuaq - Ilulissat - Sisimiut - Kangerlussuaq - Nuuk - Nanortalik - Reykjavik - Kollafjørður - Bremerhaven	23	16 Jul 2017
A732	**From North Sea to Baltic Sea** Bremerhaven - Oslo - Gothenburg - Copenhagen - Kiel	5	08 Aug 2017
A733	**The Baltic Sea Islands** Kiel - Sassnitz - Heringsdorf - Rönne - Kiel Canal - Bremerhaven	5	13 Aug 2017
A734	**Iceland / SPD-Reisen Charter** Bremerhaven - Kirkwall - Heimaey - Hafnarfjörður - Ísafjörður - Akureyri - Seyðisfjörður - Klaksvik - Lerwick - Bremerhaven	12	18 Aug 2017

Astor

Code	Cruise	Nights	Departure date
A735	**The North Sea Islands** Bremerhaven - Esbjerg - List - Helgoland - Bremerhaven	4	30 Aug 2017
A736	**River Trips** Bremerhaven - London Greenwich - Rouen - Antwerp - Bremerhaven	8	03 Sep 2017
A737	**North Atlantic Heritage** Bremerhaven - Honfleur - La Pallice - La Coruna - Getxo - Bordeaux - Montoir - St. Malo - St. Peter Port - Bremerhaven	12	11 Sep 2017
A738	**Season's End / "Goodbye Europe"** Bremerhaven - Antwerp	1	23 Sep 2017

Astoria

Code	Cruise	Nights	Departure date
R700	**Amsterdam & Antwerp Weekend** London Tilbury - Amsterdam - Antwerp - London Tilbury	3	09 Mar 2017
R701	**Land of the Northern Lights** London Tilbury - Amsterdam - Bergen - Åndalsnes - Tromsø - Honningsvåg - Alta - Ålesund - Stavanger - London Tilbury	14	12 Mar 2017
R702	**Spring Gardens & River Seine Experience** London Tilbury - Amsterdam - Ghent - Rouen - Honfleur - London Tilbury	6	26 Mar 2017
R703	**Round Britain & Amsterdam** London Tilbury - Amsterdam - St. Peter Port - St. Mary's - Dublin - Tobermory - Kirkwall - London Tilbury	10	01 Apr 2017
R704	**Majestic Fjordland** London Tilbury - Ijmuiden - Eidfjord - Flåm - Bergen - London Tilbury	7	11 Apr 2017
R705	**Fjordland Splendour** London Tilbury - Rotterdam - Eidfjord - Flåm - Olden - Bergen - London Tilbury	8	18 Apr 2017
R706	**Round Britain & Amsterdam** London Tilbury - Amsterdam - Kirkwall - Portree - Tobermory - Dublin - Holyhead - St. Mary's - Portsmouth - Honfleur - London Tilbury	11	26 Apr 2017

Astoria

Code	Cruise	Nights	Departure date
N0	**Repositioning for RDM Charter** London Tilbury - Montoir	2	07 May 2017
N1	**Iberia** Montoir - Leixoes - Vigo - La Coruna - Le Havre	7	09 May 2017
N2	**Ireland** Le Havre - Cobh - Galway - Belfast - Dublin - Le Havre	8	16 May 2017
N3	**British Isles** Le Havre - St. Helier - St. Peter Port - Falmouth - Portland - Portsmouth - London Tilbury - Dunkirk	6	24 May 2017
N4	**Baltic Sea** Dunkirk - Amsterdam - Hamburg - Kiel Canal - Travemünde - Warnemünde - Szczecin - Gdansk	8	30 May 2017
N5	**Baltic Cities &. Petersburg** Gdansk - Klaipėda - Riga - Tallinn - St. Petersburg - Helsinki - Stockholm	8	07 Jun 2017
N6	**Scandinavia** Stockholm - Copenhagen - Gothenburg - Oslo - Kristiansand - Dunkirk	8	15 Jun 2017
N7	**Norwegian Fjords & the North Cape** Dunkirk - Bergen - Geiranger - Hellesylt - Vik - Flåm - Leknes - Honningsvåg - Hammerfest - Tromsø	11	23 Jun 2017
N8	**Spitzbergen and the North Cape** Tromsø – Ny-Ålesund - - Longyearbyen - Honningsvåg - Leknes - Tromsø	8	04 Jul 2017
N9	**Spitzbergen and the North Cape** Tromsø – Ny-Ålesund - Longyearbyen - Honningsvåg - Leknes - Bergen - Zeebrugge	11	12 Jul 2017
N10	**Iceland** Zeebrugge - Bergen - Lerwick - Tórshavn - Seyðisfjörður - Húsavík - Akureyri - Ísafjörður - Grundarfjörður - Reykjavik	10	23 Jul 2017

Astoria

Code	Cruise	Nights	Departure date
N11	**Iceland & Greenland** Reykjavik - Ísafjörður - Akureyri - Grundarfjörður - Narsaq - Nuuk - Ilulissat - Sisimiut - Kangerlussuaq	12	02 Aug 2017
N12	**Greenland & Northern Isles** Kangerlussuaq - Sisimiut - Ilulissat - Narsaq - Reykjavik - Tórshavn - Lerwick - Dunkirk	13	14 Aug 2017
N13	**South to the Mediterranean** Dunkirk - St. Helier - La Coruna - Vigo - Leixoes - Lisbon - Gibraltar - Malaga - Valencia - Barcelona - Marseille	10	27 Aug 2017
N14	**Amazon** Marseille - Malaga - Funchal - Mindelo - Macapá - Santarém - Boca da Valeria - Manaus - Parintins - Alter do Chão - Icoaraci - Bridgetown - Castries - Pointe-à-Pitre	27	06 Sep 2017
N15	**Azores** Pointe-à-Pitre- Horta - Ponta Delgada - Gibraltar - Marseille	13	03 Oct 2017
N16	**Italy** Marseille - Genoa - Livorno - Civitavecchia - Naples - Palermo - Syracuse - Bari - Venice	11	16 Oct 2017
N17	**Adriatic** Venice - Split - Kotor - Syracuse - Naples - Livorno - Marseille	8	27 Oct 2017

Bordeaux

"With so many exciting itineraries to choose from we think a Round Britain cruise would be a good starting point for new cruisers, with a number of different ports and plenty of on board time to enjoy the CMV hospitality."

William Honeyman
& Eileen Winsor

Columbus

Code	Cruise	Nights	Departure date
C701	**Amsterdam & Antwerp** London Tilbury - Amsterdam - Antwerp - London Tilbury	3	11 Jun 2017
C702	**Majestic Fjordland** London Tilbury - Eidfjord - Bergen - Flåm - London Tilbury	6	14 Jun 2017
C704	**British Isles Discovery** London Tilbury - Invergordon - Belfast - Dublin - St. Mary's - St. Peter Port - Honfleur - London Tilbury	9	20 Jun 2017
C705	**Iceland & Northern Isles** London Tilbury - Invergordon - Kollafjørður - Seyðisfjörður - Akureyri - Ísafjörður - Reykjavik - Kirkwall - London Tilbury	12	29 Jun 2017
C706	**Grand British Isles Discovery** London Tilbury - Antwerp - Honfleur - St. Peter Port - St. Mary's - Dublin - Belfast - Greenock - Invergordon - Kirkwall - London Tilbury	12	11 Jul 2017
C707	**Baltic Cities & St. Petersburg** London Tilbury - Copenhagen - Warnemünde - Helsinki - St. Petersburg - Tallinn - Nynäshamn - London Tilbury	12	23 Jul 2017
C708	**Majestic Fjordland** London Tilbury - Eidfjord - Flåm - Åndalsnes - Bergen - London Tilbury	7	04 Aug 2017

Columbus

Code	Cruise	Nights	Departure date
C709	**Canary Islands & Madeira** London Tilbury - Gibraltar - Arrecife - Las Palmas - Santa Cruz de Tenerife - Funchal - Lisbon - London Tilbury	14	11 Aug 2017
C710	**Amsterdam & Antwerp** London Tilbury - Amsterdam - Antwerp - London Tilbury	3	25 Aug 2017
C711	**Scottish Highlights & Faroes** London Tilbury - Kirkwall - Tórshavn - Lerwick - Invergordon - London Tilbury	7	28 Aug 2017
C712	**British Isles Discovery** London Tilbury - Honfleur - St. Peter Port - St. Mary's - Dublin - Belfast - Tobermory - Kirkwall - London Tilbury	9	04 Sep 2017
C713	**Baltic Cities & St. Petersburg** London Tilbury - Warnemünde - Tallinn - St. Petersburg - Helsinki - Nynäshamn - London Tilbury	12	13 Sep 2017
C714	**Majestic Fjordland** London Tilbury - Eidfjord - Flåm - Olden - Bergen - London Tilbury	7	25 Sep 2017
C715	**Spain, Portugal, France & Gibraltar** London Tilbury - Amsterdam - La Pallice - Getxo - Lisbon - Gibraltar - La Coruna - London Tilbury	12	02 Oct 2017
C716	**Canary Islands & Madeira** London Tilbury - Amsterdam - Le Havre - Las Palmas - Arrecife - Santa Cruz de Tenerife - Funchal - Lisbon - London Tilbury	15	14 Oct 2017
C717	**Cuba, Belize, Panama & Central Caribbean** London Tilbury - Amsterdam - Ponta Delgada - St. John's - Basseterre - Havana - Progreso - Cozumel - Belize City - Roatan - Puerto Limon - Colon - Cartagena - Oranjestad - Scarborough - St. George's - Bridgetown - Castries - Funchal - Lisbon - London Tilbury	47	29 Oct 2017

Orkney Islands

Cartagena de Indias, Colombia

Magellan

Code	Cruise	Nights	Departure date
G700	**Christmas Market & Shopping** London Tilbury - Amsterdam - Antwerp - London Tilbury	3	06 Dec 2016
G701	**Christmas Markets & Shopping** London Tilbury - Amsterdam - Hamburg - Antwerp - London Tilbury	5	11 Dec 2016
G702	**Christmas Market & Shopping** London Tilbury - Amsterdam - Antwerp - London Tilbury	3	18 Dec 2016
G703	**Christmas & New Year** London Tilbury - Amsterdam - Gibraltar - Arrecife - Las Palmas - Santa Cruz de Tenerife - Funchal - Lisbon - London Tilbury	15	21 Dec 2016
G704	**Grand Maiden Round the World Cruise** London Tilbury - Amsterdam - Ponta Delgada - Bridgetown - Willemstad - Oranjestad - Panama Canal - Acapulco - Nuku Hiva - Papeete - Bora Bora - Auckland - Wellington - Sydney - Hamilton Island - Townsville - Cairns - Darwin - Komodo Island - Benoa - Semarang - Muara - Kota Kinabalu - Manila - Hong Kong - Halong Bay - Chan May - Phu My - Singapore - Port Klang - Penang - Phuket - Chennai - Colombo - Male - Salalah - Safaga - Aqaba - Suez Canal - Ashdod - Valetta - Gibraltar - Lisbon - London Tilbury	120	05 Jan 2017
G705	**Amsterdam & Antwerp Weekend** London Tilbury – Amsterdam - Antwerp –London Tilbury	3	05 May 2017
G706	**Baltic Cities & St. Petersburg** London Tilbury - Copenhagen - Warnemünde - Tallinn - St. Petersburg - Helsinki - Nynäshamn - London Tilbury	12	08 May 2017
G707	**Fjordland Splendour** London Tilbury - Stavanger - Flåm - Geiranger - Åndalsnes - Bergen - London Tilbury	8	20 May 2017
G708	**Medieval Cities & River Seine Experience** London Tilbury - Antwerp - Rouen - Le Havre - Newport	5	28 May 2017
G709	**Charter** Newport	2	02 Jun 2017

Magellan

Code	Cruise	Nights	Departure date
G710	**Dublin Mini Cruise** Newport - Dublin - Liverpool	2	04 Jun 2017
G711	**Fjordland Splendour** Liverpool - Ulvik - Eidfjord - Flåm - Bergen - Kirkwall - Dublin - Liverpool	9	06 Jun 2017
G712	**Iceland's Land of Ice & Fire** Liverpool - Lerwick - Kollafjørður - Seyðisfjörður - Akureyri - Ísafjörður - Reykjavik - Dublin - Liverpool	12	15 Jun 2017
G713	**Spain, Portugal & France** Liverpool - La Pallice - Getxo - Lisbon - Gibraltar - La Coruna - Dublin - Liverpool	11	27 Jun 2017
G714	**Summer Gardens & River Seine Experience** Liverpool - Honfleur - Rouen - St. Peter Port - St. Mary's - Dublin - Liverpool	7	08 Jul 2017
G715	**Scottish Highlights & Faroes** Liverpool - Greenock - Tobermory - Kirkwall - Tórshavn - Lerwick - Dundee – Newcastle Tyne	7	15 Jul 2017
G716	**Iceland & Northern Isles** Newcastle Tyne - Dundee - Tórshavn - Seyðisfjörður - Akureyri - Ísafjörður - Hafnarfjörður - Lerwick - Kirkwall – Newcastle Tyne	12	22 Jul 2017
G717	**Majestic Fjordland** Newcastle Tyne - Dundee - Ulvik - Eidfjord - Flåm - Bergen – Newcastle Tyne	7	03 Aug 2017
G718	**Baltic Cities & St. Petersburg** Newcastle Tyne - Dundee - Copenhagen – Warnemünde – Tallinn - St. Petersburg – Helsinki – Stockholm – Aalborg – Newcastle Tyne	14	10 Aug 2017
G719	**Majestic Fjordland & Oslo** Newcastle Tyne - Dundee - Oslo - Kristiansand - Bergen - Eidfjord - Flåm – Newcastle Tyne	9	24 Aug 2017
G720	**Charter** Newcastle Tyne - Kirkwall - Portree - Liverpool - Dublin - Invergordon – Newcastle Tyne	7	02 Sep 2017

Magellan

Code	Cruise	Nights	Departure date
G721	**Majestic Fjordland** Newcastle Tyne - Dundee - Ulvik - Eidfjord - Flåm - Bergen – Newcastle Tyne	7	09 Sep 2017
G722	**Majestic Fjordland** Newcastle Tyne - Dundee - Ulvik - Eidfjord - Flåm - Bergen – Newcastle Tyne	7	16 Sep 2017
G722	**Overnight Party** Newcastle Tyne - London Tilbury	1	23 Sep 2017
G724	**Majestic Fjordland** London Tilbury - Eidfjord - Flåm - Alesund - Bergen - London Tilbury	7	24 Sep 2017
G725	**European Cities & Fairy Tales** London Tilbury - Amsterdam - Hamburg - Copenhagen - Aalborg - London Tilbury	9	01 Oct 2017
G726	**Land of the Northern Lights** London Tilbury - Rotterdam - Ålesund - Olden - Kristiansund - Alta - Honningsvåg -Tromsø - Åndalsnes - Bergen - London Tilbury	14	10 Oct 2017
G727	**Medieval Cities & River Seine Experience** London Tilbury - Amsterdam - Antwerp - Rouen - Honfleur - London Tilbury	6	24 Oct 2017
G728	**Land of the Northern Lights** London Tilbury - Amsterdam - Olden - Kristiansund - Alta - Honningsvåg - Tromsø - Åndalsnes - Bergen - London Tilbury	14	30 Oct 2017

Northern Lights

Marco Polo

Code	Cruise	Nights	Departure date
P700	**Festive Ireland** Bristol Avonmouth - Cobh - Dublin - Bristol Avonmouth	3	18 Dec 2016
P701	**Christmas & New Year Canaries** Bristol Avonmouth - La Coruna - Gibraltar - Arrecife - Santa Cruz de Tenerife - Las Palmas - Funchal - Lisbon - Bristol Avonmouth	14	22 Dec 2016
P702	**Amazon, West Indies & Azores** Bristol Avonmouth - Lisbon - Funchal - Mindelo - Alter do Chão - Boca da Valeria - Manaus - Parintins - Santarém - Icoaraci - Îles du Salut - St. George's - Kingstown - Bequia - Castries - Bridgetown - Ponta Delgada - Portland	39	05 Jan 2017
P706	**Land of the Northern Lights** Portland - Ålesund - Tromsø - Honningsvåg - Alta - Kristiansund - Åndalsnes - Bergen - Bristol Avonmouth	15	13 Feb 2017
P707	**Cuba, Belize, Panama & Central Caribbean** Bristol Avonmouth - Ponta Delgada - Philipsburg - Road Town - La Romana - Ocho Rios - Belize City - Cozumel - Havana - Freeport - Kings Wharf - Horta - Bristol Avonmouth	35	28 Feb 2017
P708	**Springtime Azores & Madeira** Bristol Avonmouth - La Coruna - Horta - Praia da Vitória - Ponta Delgada - Funchal - Lisbon - Leixoes - Bristol Avonmouth	15	04 Apr 2017
P709	**Scottish Highlights & Emerald Isle** Bristol Avonmouth - Belfast - Stornoway - Tobermory - Dublin - Cobh - Bristol Avonmouth	7	19 Apr 2017
P710	**Springtime Gardens & River Seine** Bristol Avonmouth - St. Mary's - St. Peter Port - Honfleur - Rouen - Bristol Avonmouth	7	26 Apr 2017
P711	**Treasures of the British Isles** Bristol Avonmouth - St. Mary's - Honfleur - Rosyth - Invergordon - Kirkwall - Stornoway - Tobermory - Belfast - Dublin - Bristol Avonmouth	11	03 May 2017

Marco Polo

Code	Cruise	Nights	Departure date
P712	**Fjordland Splendour** Bristol Avonmouth - Bergen - Olden - Geiranger - Flåm - Stavanger - Cardiff	10	14 May 2017
P713	**Spain, Portugal, France & Gibraltar** Cardiff - La Pallice - Getxo - Lisbon - Leixoes - La Coruna - Cardiff	10	24 May 2017
P715	**Summertime Gardens & River Seine** Cardiff - St. Mary's - Rouen - Dover - Hull	6	03 Jun 2017
P716	**Fjordland Splendour** Hull - Stavanger - Flåm - Olden - Åndalsnes - Bergen - Hull	8	09 Jun 2017
P717	**Iceland & Northern Isles** Hull - Tórshavn - Eskifjörður - Húsavík - Ísafjörður - Reykjavik - Lerwick - Invergordon - Hull	12	17 Jun 2017
P718	**Baltic Cities & St. Petersburg** Hull - Copenhagen - Tallinn - St. Petersburg - Helsinki - Nynäshamn – Kiel Canal – Newcastle Tyne	12	29 Jun 2017
P719	**Overnight** Newcastle Tyne - Rosyth	1	11 Jul 2017
P720	**Arctic Exploration to Greenland, Iceland & Faroes** Rosyth - Tórshavn - Seyðisfjörður - Akureyri - Julianehaab - Narsarsuaq - Qeqertarsuaq - Ilulissat - Sisimiut - Kangerlussuaq - Nuuk - Reykjavik - Rosyth	20	12 Jul 2017
P721	**North Cape, Spitzbergen & Land of Midnight Sun** Rosyth - Kristiansund - Honningsvåg - Longyearbyen - Tromsø - Geiranger - Bergen - Rosyth	14	01 Aug 2017
P722	**Scottish Islands & Faroes** Rosyth - Kirkwall - Tórshavn - Portree - Greenock	4	15 Aug 2017
P723	**Overnight** Greenock - Liverpool	1	19 Aug 2017
P724	**Grand British Isles Discovery** Liverpool - Dublin - Cobh - St. Mary's - St. Peter Port - Honfleur - Edinburgh Leith - Kirkwall - Stornoway - Tobermory - Belfast - Liverpool	12	20 Aug 2017

Marco Polo

Code	Cruise	Nights	Departure date
P725	**Canada In the Fall** Liverpool - Cobh - St. John's - Halifax - Charlottetown - Gaspé - Montréal - Québec - Saguenay - Sept Îles - Havre St. Pierre - Cap-aux-Meules - Sydney NS - Corner Brook - Belfast - Liverpool	28	01 Sep 2017
P726	**Dublin & Cobh** Liverpool - Dublin - Cobh - Bristol Avonmouth	3	29 Sep 2017
P727	**Spain, Portugal, France & Gibraltar** Bristol Avonmouth - La Pallice - Getxo - Lisbon - Leixoes - La Coruna - Bristol Avonmouth	10	02 Oct 2017
P728	**Canary Islands & Madeira** Bristol Avonmouth - Lisbon - Arrecife - Las Palmas - Santa Cruz de Tenerife - Funchal - Leixoes - Bristol Avonmouth	13	12 Oct 2017
P729	**Autumn Gardens & River Seine** Bristol Avonmouth - Honfleur - Antwerp - Rouen - Bristol Avonmouth	7	25 Oct 2017

Rouen

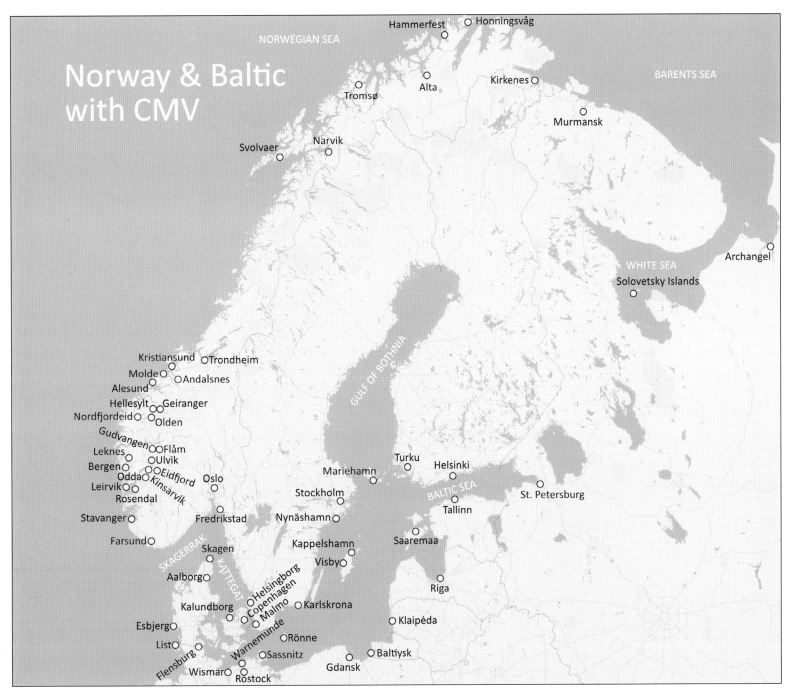

Norway & Baltic with CMV

NORWEGIAN SEA

Hammerfest
Honningsvåg

BARENTS SEA

Alta
Kirkenes

Tromsø

Murmansk

Svolvaer
Narvik

Archangel

WHITE SEA

Solovetsky Islands

Kristiansund
Trondheim

Molde
Andalsnes

Alesund

Hellesylt
Geiranger

Nordfjordeid
Olden

Gudvangen
Flåm

Leknes
Ulvik

Bergen
Eidfjord

Odda
Kinsarvik

Oslo

Turku

Helsinki

Leirvik

Mariehamn

Rosendal

Stockholm

BALTIC SEA

St. Petersburg

Stavanger

Fredrikstad

Nynäshamn

Tallinn

GULF OF BOTHNIA

Farsund

Saaremaa

Skagen
Kappelshamn

SKAGERRAK

KATTEGAT

Visby

Aalborg

Riga

Helsingborg
Copenhagen

Kalundborg

Malmo
Karlskrona

Klaipéda

Esbjerg

Warnemunde

List
Rönne

Flensburg

Sassnitz

Baltiysk

Wismar
Rostock

Gdansk

157

Cruise programme summary 2010-2019

2017-2018
Britain's leading independent cruise line

Programme highlights include: -

- *Columbus* **maiden 121-night Round World Cruise** sailed from Tilbury 5th January 2018

- **New UK regional departure ports** in Poole and Portsmouth

- **A new 15-night Mediterranean Odyssey itinerary** with *Magellan* on 22nd September

Total Ports visited: **229** (32 maiden calls)

Total mileage: **344,458** nautical miles

Market Deployment/Vessels:
UK – *Marco Polo, Magellan, Astoria* & *Columbus*
Australia – *Astor*
Germany – *Astor*
France - *Astoria* Rivages du Monde charter

Maiden Calls

2018 saw 32 more ports receive a CMV ship for the very first time with the *Columbus* World Cruise opening up new destinations in Australia, China, India, New Zealand and the United Arab Emirates amongst others. Meanwhile, *Astoria* and *Astor* explored closer to home and Cowes, Fishguard and Holy Loch made their debuts.

Title page: The Zhujiajiao Water Town was a unique experience in Shanghai for *Columbus* passengers on 15th March 2018.

Astor

Code	Cruise	Nights	Departure date
A801	**UK to Australia via Panama** London Tilbury - Le Havre - Horta - St. John's - Castries - Bridgetown - Panama Canal - Acapulco - Nuku Hiva - Papeete - Moorea Island - Auckland - Sydney - Penneshaw - Adelaide - Fremantle	56	15 Oct 2017
A802	**Christmas Party Cruise** Fremantle - Fremantle	2	08 Dec 2017
A803	**Cruise the Coast** Fremantle - Esperance - Albany - Fremantle	5	10 Dec 2017
A804	**Christmas Party Weekend** Fremantle - Fremantle	3	15 Dec 2017
A805	**Christmas at Sea** Fremantle - Benoa - Fremantle	11	18 Dec 2017
A806	**New Year Celebration** Fremantle - Busselton - Fremantle	4	29 Dec 2017
A807	**Bali Holiday** Fremantle - Benoa - Fremantle	10	02 Jan 2018
A808	**Weekend Short Break** Fremantle - Fremantle	3	12 Jan 2018
A809	**South West Escape** Fremantle - Esperance - Albany - Fremantle	5	15 Jan 2018
A811	**Coastal Adventure** Fremantle - Albany - Fremantle	4	21 Jan 2018
A812	**Australia Day Weekend** Fremantle - Busselton - Fremantle	3	25 Jan 2018
A813	**Summer Coast Escape** Fremantle - Esperance - Albany - Fremantle	5	28 Jan 2018
A814	**Weekend Celebration** Fremantle - Fremantle	3	02 Feb 2018
A815	**South West Adventure** Fremantle - Albany - Busselton - Fremantle	5	05 Feb 2018
A816	**Weekend Escape** Fremantle - Fremantle	2	10 Feb 2018
A817	**Cruise the Bight** Fremantle - Esperance - Adelaide	5	12 Feb 2018

Astor

Code	Cruise	Nights	Departure date
A818	**Tasmania Adventure** Adelaide - Melbourne - Hobart - Burnie - Adelaide	8	17 Feb 2018
A819	**Coastal Experience** Adelaide - Penneshaw - Port Lincoln - Adelaide	3	25 Feb 2018
A820	**Tasmania Explorer** Adelaide - Port Arthur - Hobart - Burnie - Adelaide	7	28 Feb 2018
A821	**Coastal Explorer** Adelaide - Albany - Fremantle	5	07 Mar 2018
A822	**Australia to UK via South Africa** Fremantle - Port Louis - Pointe des Galets - Durban - Mossel Bay - Cape Town - Walvis Bay - Jamestown - Las Palmas - Casablanca - Lisbon - London Tilbury	39	12 Mar 2018

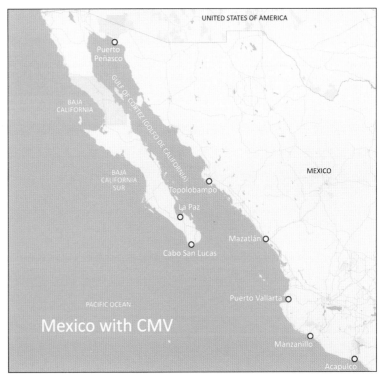

Mexico with CMV

Astor

Code	Cruise	Nights	Departure date
A823	**Welcome Europe** London Tilbury - Bremerhaven	1	20 Apr 2018
A824	**South England & Ireland** Bremerhaven - Falmouth - Glengariff - Foynes - Killybegs - Dublin - Cobh - Cowes - Bremerhaven	10	21 Apr 2018
A825	**Majestic Fjordland** Bremerhaven - Geiranger - Olden - Bergen - Eidfjord - Leirvik - Bremerhaven	13	01 May 2018
A826	**German Isles & Port Birthday Hamburg** Bremerhaven - List - Esbjerg - Helgoland - Hamburg	5	08 May 2018
A827	**Baltic Cruise** Hamburg - Kiel Canal - Gdansk - Baltiysk - Klaipėda - Riga - Tallinn - St. Petersburg - Helsinki - Stockholm - Kiel	13	13 May 2018
A828	**Baltic & Kiel Canal** Kiel - Copenhagen - Warnemünde - Kiel Canal - Bremerhaven	4	25 May 2018
aaA829	**Norway & North Cape** Bremerhaven - Vik - Flåm - Ålesund - Leknes - Honningsvåg - Tromsø - Hellesylt - Geiranger - Bergen - Bremerhaven	12	28 May 2018
A830	**Norway & North Cape (SPD Charter)** Bremerhaven - Flåm - Vik - Molde - Svartisen - Leknes - Honningsvåg - Geiranger - Hellesylt - Bergen - Bremerhaven	12	09 Jun 2018
A831	**Iceland & Greenland** Bremerhaven - Akureyri - Tasiilaq - Nuuk - Sisimiut - Uummannaq - Claushavn - Qeqertarsuaq - Qaqortoq - Ísafjörður - Reykjavík - Heimaey - Bremerhaven	23	21 Jun 2018
A832	**South England & Ireland** Bremerhaven - Falmouth - Cobh - Dublin - Fishguard - Southampton - Bremerhaven	8	14 Jul 2018
A833	**English Channel & Kiel Channel** Bremerhaven - Falmouth - St. Helier - St. Malo - Le Havre - Antwerp - Amsterdam - Kiel Canal - Kiel	9	22 Jul 2018

Astor

Code	Cruise	Nights	Departure date
A834	**Baltic Cruise (SPD Charter)** Kiel - Gdynia - Baltiysk - Klaipėda - Riga - Tallinn - St. Petersburg - Helsinki - Stockholm - Rönne - Kiel	11	31 Jul 2018
A835	**Baltic Isles (Troll Tours Charter)** Kiel - Copenhagen - Rönne - Gdynia - Visby - Sassnitz - Kiel	6	11 Aug 2018
A836	**Majestic Fjordland (Troll Tours Charter)** Kiel - Gothenburg - Farsund - Fjærland - Balestrand - Bergen - Lysefjord - Stavanger - Esbjerg - Bremerhaven	7	17 Aug 2018
A837	**British Isles & Cities** Bremerhaven - Rosyth - Kirkwall - Ullapool - Oban - Greencastle - Belfast - Dublin - Falmouth - Portland - Bremerhaven	12	24 Aug 2018
A838	**French Rivers Experience** Bremerhaven - St. Malo - Bordeaux - Getxo - Nantes - Rouen - Bremerhaven	12	05 Sep 2018
A839	**South England & Channel Islands** Bremerhaven - London Greenwich - Portland - Portsmouth - Bremerhaven	7	17 Sep 2018
A840	**Goodbye Europe** Bremerhaven - Antwerp	2	24 Sep 2018

Tallinn

Astoria

Code	Cruise	Nights	Departure date
R800	**Springtime Break & River Seine Exp** London Tilbury - Antwerp - Rouen - Honfleur - London Tilbury	5	09 Mar 2018
R801	**British Isles Discovery** London Tilbury - Invergordon - Greenock - Belfast - Dublin - Cobh - Falmouth - Portsmouth - Honfleur - London Tilbury	11	14 Mar 2018
R802	**European Rivers, Canals & Cities** London Tilbury - Amsterdam - Bremen - Hamburg – Kiel Canal - Copenhagen - Aalborg - Kristiansund - London Tilbury	9	25 Mar 2018
R803	**Grand Scottish Highlights, Islands & Faroes** London Tilbury - Kirkwall - Tórshavn - Klaksvik - Lerwick - Invergordon - Rosyth - London Tilbury	9	03 Apr 2018
R804	**Hidden Baltic Treasures & Kiel Canal** London Tilbury - Kiel Canal - Wismar - Rönne - Visby - Klaipėda - Gdansk - Kiel Canal - London Tilbury	9	12 Apr 2018
R805	**Grand Scottish Lochs, Glens, Islands & Ireland** London Tilbury - Kirkwall - Stornoway - Tobermory - Fort William - Belfast - Dublin - Holy Loch - Ullapool - Scrabster - Lerwick - Invergordon - London Tilbury	14	21 Apr 2018
RTLH	**Repositioning** London Tilbury - Le Havre	1	06 May 2018
RDM1	**British Isles** Le Havre - Ringaskiddy - Greenock - Belfast - Dublin - Le Havre	8	07 May 2018
RDM2	**Ireland** Le Havre - Glengariff - Galway - Belfast - Dublin - Dunkirk	8	15 May 2018
RDM3	**Norwegian Fjords** Dunkirk - Stavanger - Geiranger - Vik – Flåm - Bergen - Dunkirk	7	23 May 2018
RDM4	**North Cape** Dunkirk - Bergen - Vik – Flåm - Olden - Geiranger - Hellesylt - Leknes - Honningsvåg - Tromsø	9	30 May 2018
RDM5	**North Cape** Tromsø - Honningsvåg - Leknes - Hellesylt - Vik – Flåm - Bergen - Stavanger - Dunkirk	10	08 Jun 2018
RDM6	**Spitzbergen & North Cape** Dunkirk - Bergen - Leknes - Longyearbyen – Ny-Ålesund - Honningsvåg - Tromsø	11	18 Jun 2018
RDM7	**Spitzbergen & Fjords** Tromsø - Longyearbyen – Ny-Ålesund - Leknes - Svartisen - Trondheim - Hellesylt - Geiranger - Bergen - Zeebrugge	12	29 Jun 2018
RDM8	**Iceland & Greenland** Zeebrugge - Lerwick - Kollafjørður - Reykjavik - Qaqortoq - Nuuk - Ilulissat - Sisimiut - Kangerlussuaq	13	11 Jul 2018
RDM9	**Greenland & Iceland** Sisimiut - Claushavn - Nuuk - Qaqortoq - Ísafjörður - Akureyri - Grundarfjörður - Reykjavik	12	24 Jul 2018
RDM10	**Iceland & Greenland** Reykjavik - Akureyri - Grundarfjörður - Qaqortoq - Nuuk - Ilulissat - Sisimiut - Kangerlussuaq	12	05 Aug 2018
RDM11	**Greenland & British Isles** Kangerlussuaq - Ilulissat - Nuuk - Reykjavik - Belfast - Dublin - Le Havre	13	17 Aug 2018
RLHP	**Repositioning** Le Havre - Poole	1	30 Aug 2018
R806	**Rouen, Honfleur & River Seine Weekend Retreat** Poole - Honfleur - Rouen - Poole	3	31 Aug 2018
R807	**Grand British Isles Discovery** Poole - Dunkirk - Kirkwall - Stornoway - Tobermory - Fort William - Belfast - Dublin - Cobh - Glengariff - St. Mary's - Poole	12	03 Sep 2018
R808	**Special Captain's Overnight Gala Cruise** Poole - circumnavigate Isle of Wight - Portsmouth	1	15 Sep 2018
R809	**Majestic Autumn Fjordland** Portsmouth - Ijmuiden - Stavanger - Flåm - Bergen - Rotterdam - Portsmouth	9	16 Sep 2018

Astoria

Code	Cruise	Nights	Departure date
R810	**Baltic Cities & St. Petersburg** Portsmouth – Kiel Canal - Warnemünde - Tallinn - St. Petersburg - Helsinki - Nynäshamn - Kiel Canal - Rotterdam - Portsmouth	13	25 Sep 2018
R811	**European Rivers, Canals & Cities** Portsmouth - Rotterdam - Hamburg - Kiel Canal - Copenhagen - Aalborg - Kristiansund - Portsmouth	9	08 Oct 2018
R812	**Land of the Northern Lights** Portsmouth - Ijmuiden - Bergen - Tromsø - Honningsvåg - Alta - Ålesund - Stavanger - Portsmouth	14	17 Oct 2018

Columbus

Code	Cruise	Nights	Departure date
C800	**Amsterdam & German Christmas Market** London Tilbury - Amsterdam - Hamburg - London Tilbury	4	14 Dec 2017
C801	**Amsterdam & Zeebrugge** London Tilbury - Amsterdam - Zeebrugge - London Tilbury	3	18 Dec 2017
C802	**Christmas & New Year Canaries & Madeira** London Tilbury - Amsterdam - Gibraltar - Santa Cruz de Tenerife - Arrecife - Las Palmas - Funchal - Lisbon - London Tilbury	15	21 Dec 2017
C803	**Grand Round World Cruise** London Tilbury - Amsterdam - Lisbon - Funchal - Bridgetown - St. George's - Cartagena - Cristobal - Panama Canal - Nuku Hiva - Papeete - Moorea Island - Bora Bora - Auckland - Tauranga - Bay of Islands - Sydney - Yorkeys Knob - Darwin - Komodo Island - Manila - Shanghai - Hong Kong - Chan May - Phu My - Ko Samui - Laem Chabang - Singapore - Port Klang - Penang - Colombo - Cochin - Mumbai - Dubai - Muscat - Safaga - Aqaba - Suez Canal - Piraeus - Valletta - Gibraltar - London Tilbury	121	05 Jan 2018

Columbus

Code	Cruise	Nights	Departure date
C804	**British Isles Discovery** London Tilbury - Amsterdam - Kirkwall - Invergordon - Dublin - Cobh - St. Peter Port - Honfleur - London Tilbury	10	06 May 2018
C805	**Baltic Cities & St. Petersburg** London Tilbury - Amsterdam - Copenhagen - Warnemünde - Tallinn - St. Petersburg - Helsinki - Stockholm - Aalborg - London Tilbury	14	16 May 2018
C806	**Whitsun Fjordland** London Tilbury - Amsterdam - Eidfjord - Flåm - Bergen - London Tilbury	7	30 May 2018
C807	**Iceland & Northern Isles** London Tilbury - Amsterdam - Lerwick - Kollafjörður - Seyðisfjörður - Akureyri - Ísafjörður - Reykjavik - London Tilbury	12	06 Jun 2018
C808	**British Isles Discovery** London Tilbury - Amsterdam - Invergordon - Portree - Tobermory - Belfast - Dublin - Cobh - St. Mary's - St. Peter Port - Honfleur - London Tilbury	12	18 Jun 2018
C809	**Fjordland** London Tilbury - Amsterdam - Flåm - Olden - Åndalsnes - Bergen - London Tilbury	8	30 Jun 2018
C810	**British Isles Discovery** London Tilbury - Amsterdam - Invergordon - Portree - Greenock - Belfast - Dublin - Ringaskiddy - St. Mary's - St. Peter Port - Honfleur - London Tilbury	12	08 Jul 2018
C811	**Canary Islands & Madeira** London Tilbury - Amsterdam - Gibraltar - Arrecife - Las Palmas - Santa Cruz de Tenerife - Funchal - Lisbon - London Tilbury	15	20 Jul 2018
C812	**Fjordland** London Tilbury - Eidfjord - Skjolden - Olden - Bergen - London Tilbury	7	04 Aug 2018
C813	**Baltic Cities & St. Petersburg** London Tilbury - Copenhagen - Warnemünde - Helsinki - St. Petersburg - Tallinn - Stockholm - Aarhus - London Tilbury	13	11 Aug 2018

Columbus

Code	Cruise	Nights	Departure date
C814	**Fjordland** London Tilbury - Eidfjord - Geiranger - Olden - Bergen - London Tilbury	7	24 Aug 2018
C815	**British Isles Discovery** London Tilbury - Kirkwall - Invergordon - Portree - Tobermory - Belfast - Dublin - Ringaskiddy - St. Mary's - St. Peter Port - Honfleur - London Tilbury	12	31 Aug 2018
C816	**Baltic Cities & St. Petersburg** London Tilbury - Copenhagen - Rostock - Tallinn - St. Petersburg - Helsinki - Stockholm - Aarhus - London Tilbury	13	12 Sep 2018
C817	**British Isles & Cities Discovery** London Tilbury - Rotterdam - Kirkwall - Belfast - Dublin - Cobh - Honfleur - London Tilbury	10	25 Sep 2018
C818	**Fjordland** London Tilbury - Amsterdam - Eidfjord - Flåm - Bergen - London Tilbury	7	05 Oct 2018
C819	**Canary Islands & Madeira** London Tilbury - Amsterdam - Gibraltar - Arrecife - Las Palmas - Santa Cruz de Tenerife - Funchal - Leixoes - London Tilbury	15	12 Oct 2018
C820	**European Cities Break** London Tilbury - Amsterdam - Hamburg - Antwerp - London Tilbury	5	28 Oct 2018

Amsterdam

Magellan

Code	Cruise	Nights	Departure date
G800	**French Christmas Markets** London Tilbury - Rouen - Honfleur - London Tilbury	3	10 Dec 2017
G801	**Antwerp** London Tilbury - Antwerp - London Tilbury	2	13 Dec 2017
G802	**Christmas & New Year Cape Verde,** **Madeira & Canaries** London Tilbury - Amsterdam - Vigo - Lisbon - Mindelo - Praia - Santa Cruz de Tenerife - Las Palmas - Arrecife - Funchal - Leixoes - London Tilbury	21	17 Dec 2017
G803	**Amazon, West Indies & Azores** London Tilbury - Amsterdam - Vigo - Funchal - Mindelo - Santarém - Boca da Valeria - Manaus - Parintins - Alter do Chão - Icoaraci - Îles du Salut - Scarborough - St. George's - Bridgetown - Castries - St. John's - Horta - Ponta Delgada - London Tilbury	42	07 Jan 2018
G804	**Land of the Northern Lights** London Tilbury - Amsterdam - Ålesund - Tromsø - Alta - Honningsvåg - Trondheim - Åndalsnes - Bergen - London Tilbury	14	18 Feb 2018
G805	**Land of the Northern Lights** London Tilbury - Amsterdam – Torshavn - Reykjavik - Lerwick - Kirkwall - London Tilbury	12	04 Mar 2018
G806	**Canary Islands & Madeira** London Tilbury - Amsterdam - Gibraltar - Arrecife - Las Palmas - Santa Cruz de Tenerife - Funchal - Lisbon - London Tilbury	15	16 Mar 2018
G807	**Easter & River Seine** London Tilbury - Amsterdam - Rotterdam - Cherbourg - P/mouth - Honfleur - London Tilbury	7	31 Mar 2018
G808	**Grand British Isles Discovery** London Tilbury - Amsterdam - Kirkwall - Lerwick - Tobermory - Greenock - Belfast - Cobh - Rouen - Honfleur - London Tilbury	12	07 Apr 2018
G809	**Majestic Fjordland** London Tilbury - Amsterdam - Eidfjord - Flåm - Bergen - London Tilbury	7	19 Apr 2018

Magellan

Code	Cruise	Nights	Departure date
G810	**Majestic Fjordland** London Tilbury - Amsterdam - Eidfjord - Flåm - Olden - Bergen - London Tilbury	8	26 Apr 2018
G811	**Overnight positioning** London Tilbury – Newcastle Tyne	1	04 May 2018
G812	**Majestic Fjordland** Newcastle Tyne - Dundee - Ulvik - Eidfjord - Skjolden - Bergen – Newcastle Tyne	7	05 May 2018
G813	**Majestic Fjordland** Newcastle Tyne - Dundee - Ulvik - Eidfjord - Olden - Bergen – Newcastle Tyne	7	12 May 2018
G814	**Baltic Cities & St. Petersburg** Newcastle Tyne - Dundee - Copenhagen - Warnemünde - Nynäshamn - Helsinki - St. Petersburg - Tallinn - Aalborg - Newcastle Tyne	14	19 May 2018
G815	**Grand British Isles Discovery** Newcastle Tyne - Dundee - Kirkwall - Tobermory - Dublin - Ringaskiddy - St. Mary's - St. Peter Port – Newcastle Tyne	10	02 Jun 2018
G816	**Iceland & Northern Isles** Newcastle Tyne - Dundee - Kollafjørður - Akureyri - Ísafjörður - Reykjavik - Lerwick - Kirkwall – Newcastle Tyne	12	12 Jun 2018
G817	**Scottish Islands & Faroes** Newcastle Tyne - Dundee - Lerwick - Klaksvik - Tórshavn - Kirkwall - Tobermory - Liverpool	7	24 Jun 2018
G818	**Iceland & Northern Isles** Liverpool - Dublin - Kirkwall - Kollafjørður - Seyðisfjörður - Akureyri - Ísafjörður Reykjavik Liverpool	12	01 Jul 2018
G819	**Fjordland** Liverpool - Dublin - Kirkwall - Bergen - Olden - Eidfjord - Liverpool	9	13 Jul 2018
G820	**River Seine Experience** Liverpool - Dublin - St. Mary's - St. Peter Port - Rouen - Honfleur- Liverpool	7	22 Jul 2018
G821	**Spain, Portugal & Gibraltar** Liverpool - Dublin - La Coruna - Cadiz - Gibraltar - Lisbon - Leixoes - La Pallice - Liverpool	12	29 Jul 2018

Magellan

Code	Cruise	Nights	Departure date
G822	**Canary Islands & Madeira** Liverpool - Dublin - La Coruna - Gibraltar - Arrecife - Las Palmas - Santa Cruz de Tenerife - Funchal - Lisbon - Liverpool	15	10 Aug 2018
G823	**Weekend Dublin** Liverpool - Dublin - Bristol Portbury	2	25 Aug 2018
G824	**British Isles Discovery** Bristol Portbury - Portree - Kirkwall - Honfleur - St. Peter Port - St. Mary's - Dublin - Bristol Portbury	10	27 Aug 2018
G825	**Baltic Cities & St. Petersburg** Bristol Portbury - Rotterdam - Copenhagen - Warnemünde - Tallinn - St. Petersburg - Helsinki - Aarhus - Cobh - Bristol Portbury	16	06 Sep 2018
G826	**Mediterranean** Bristol Portbury - Lisbon - Barcelona - Cannes - Civitavecchia - Gibraltar - Cobh - Bristol Portbury	15	22 Sep 2018
G827	**Canary Islands & Madeira** Bristol Portbury - La Coruna - Gibraltar - Arrecife - Las Palmas - Santa Cruz de Tenerife - Funchal - Lisbon - Cobh - Bristol Portbury	15	07 Oct 2018
G828	**European Cities & Rivers** Bristol Portbury - Rouen - Antwerp - Amsterdam - London Tilbury	6	22 Oct 2018
G829	**Land of the Northern Lights (Norway)** London Tilbury - Rotterdam - Olden - Kristiansund - Alta - Honningsvåg - Tromsø - Trondheim - Åndalsnes - Bergen - London Tilbury	14	28 Oct 2018

La Coruña – Santiago de Compostela   **Barcelona**

Marco Polo

Code	Cruise	Nights	Departure date
P800	**Easter Spring Gardens & River Seine** Bristol Avonmouth - Portsmouth - Honfleur - Rouen - Bristol Avonmouth	7	31 Mar 2018
P801	**Scottish Highlights & Emerald Isle** Bristol Avonmouth - Belfast - Stornoway - Tobermory - Dublin - Cobh - Bristol Avonmouth	7	07 Apr 2018
P802	**Portugal, Gibraltar & Seville Fiesta** Bristol Avonmouth - Lisbon - Tangier - Gibraltar - Cadiz - Leixoes - La Coruna - Bristol Avonmouth	12	14 Apr 2018
P803	**Treasures of the British Isles** Bristol Avonmouth - Tobermory - Ullapool - Kirkwall - Rosyth - Honfleur - St. Helier - St. Mary's - Bristol Avonmouth	10	26 Apr 2018
P804	**Majestic Fjordland** Bristol Avonmouth - Bergen - Olden - Geiranger - Flåm - Stavanger - Cardiff	10	06 May 2018
P805	**Iceland** Cardiff - Kollafjörður - Seyðisfjörður - Húsavík - Reykjavik - Ringaskiddy - Cardiff	11	16 May 2018
P806	**Emerald Isle & Isles of Scilly** Cardiff - Dublin - Cobh - Glengariff - St. Mary's - Cardiff	5	27 May 2018
P807	**Weekend Cruise to Honfleur** Cardiff - Honfleur - Harwich	3	01 Jun 2018
P808	**Baltic Cities & St. Petersburg** Harwich - Copenhagen - Warnemünde - Tallinn - St. Petersburg - Helsinki - Visby - Harwich	12	04 Jun 2018
P809	**Overnight positioning** Harwich - Hull	1	16 Jun 2018
P810	**British Isles Discovery** Hull - Invergordon - Kirkwall - Stornoway - Tobermory - Dublin - Cobh - St. Mary's - St. Peter Port - Honfleur - Hull	12	17 Jun 2018
P811	**Fjordland** Hull - Eidfjord - Flåm - Olden - Åndalsnes - Bergen - Hull	8	29 Jun 2018
P812	**Baltic Cities & St. Petersburg** Hull - Warnemünde - Tallinn - St. Petersburg - Helsinki - Stockholm - Kiel Canal - Hull	12	07 Jul 2018
P813	**Scottish Islands & Faroes** Hull - Lerwick - Klaksvik - Tórshavn - Kirkwall - Invergordon - Hull	8	19 Jul 2018
P814	**Overnight positioning** Hull - Harwich	1	27 Jul 2018
P815	**Arctic & Greenland Expedition Voyage** Harwich - Kirkwall - Tórshavn - Eskifjörður - Akureyri - Tasiilaq - Narsarquaq - Sisimiut - Kangerlussuaq - Nuuk - Qaqortoq - Reykjavik - Harwich	21	28 Jul 2018
P816	**Overnight positioning** Harwich - London Tilbury	1	18 Aug 2018
P817	**North Cape, White Sea & Murmansk** London Tilbury - Kirkwall - Trondheim - Tromsø - Honningsvåg - Archangel - Murmansk - Sortland - Bergen - London Tilbury	17	19 Aug 2018
P818	**Canada in the Fall** London Tilbury - Glengariff - St. John's - Halifax - Charlottetown - Montréal - Québec - Saguenay - Baie-Comeau - Havre St. Pierre - Corner Brook - Sydney NS - Cobh - London Tilbury	30	05 Sep 2018
P819	**Scottish Highlights, Edinburgh & Faroes** London Tilbury - Edinburgh Leith - Klaksvik - Tórshavn - Kirkwall - Invergordon - London Tilbury	9	05 Oct 2018
P820	**Hidden Baltic Treasures & Kiel Canal** London Tilbury - Kiel Canal - Wismar - Rönne - Visby - Klaipėda - Gdansk - Kiel Canal - London Tilbury	9	14 Oct 2018
P821	**Land of the Northern Lights** London Tilbury - Kristiansund - Alta - Honningsvåg - Tromsø - Trondheim - Åndalsnes - Bergen - London Tilbury	13	23 Oct 2018
P822	**West Indies & Azores** London Tilbury - Amsterdam - Ponta Delgada - Horta - St. John's - Philipsburg - Basseterre - Castries - Mayreau - Kingstown - Bequia - St. George's - Bridgetown - Lisbon - London Tilbury	30	05 Nov 2018

Cruise programme summary 2010-2019

2018-2019
CMV's 10th operational year and anniversary season

Programme highlights include: -

- Magellan's voyages to/from Mexico and **inaugural Mexican cruises**

- Marco Polo's **'Circle South America Voyage'** and **'75th D-Day Anniversary Cruise'**

- **Introducing Vasco da Gama**. Her Maiden Voyage from Singapore to Tilbury sailed 24 April 2019

Total Ports visited: **277** (50 maiden calls)

Total mileage: **390,183** nautical miles

Market Deployment/Vessels:
UK – *Columbus, Magellan, Marco Polo* & *Astoria*
Australia – *Astor* & *Vasco da Gama*
Germany – *Astor* & *Vasco da Gama*
Mexico – *Magellan*
France – *Astoria* (charter to Rivages du Monde)

Maiden Calls

The last year of the first decade produced 50 maiden calls with *Marco Polo*'s circumnavigation of South America. Japan figured highly due to The Columbus World Cruise, whilst in Scandinavia and the Baltic, Fredrikstad, Loen, Saaremaa and Skagen registered their inaugural calls.

Title page: The ancient wonder that is Machu Picchu was visited from Callao, Peru by *Marco Polo* guests on 21st February 2019.

Astor

Code	Cruise	Nights	Departure date
A901	**Southbound Voyage Fremantle** London Tilbury - Amsterdam - Lisbon - Funchal - Bridgetown - St. George's - Cartagena - Colon - Panama Canal - Nuku Hiva - Papeete - Bora Bora - Auckland - Sydney - Adelaide - Fremantle	54	15 Oct 2018
A902	**Christmas Party Weekend** Fremantle - Fremantle	2	08 Dec 2018
A903	**Festive South West Escape** Fremantle - Esperance - Albany - Fremantle	5	10 Dec 2018
A904	**Christmas Party Weekend** Fremantle - Fremantle	2	15 Dec 2018
A905	**Christmas Cruise to Bali** Fremantle - Bali - Fremantle	11	17 Dec 2018
A907	**New Year Celebration** Fremantle – Busselton - Fremantle	4	29 Dec 2018
A908	**Coastal Adventure** Fremantle - Esperance - Fremantle	4	02 Jan 2019
A909	**South West Escape** Fremantle - Esperance - Albany - Fremantle	5	06 Jan 2019
A910	**Weekend Party Cruise** Fremantle - Busselton - Fremantle	3	11 Jan 2019
A911	**Bali Holiday Cruise** Fremantle - Bali - Fremantle	11	14 Jan 2019
A912	**Australia Day Weekend** Fremantle - Busselton - Fremantle	4	25 Jan 2019
A913	**South West Escape** Fremantle - Esperance - Albany - Fremantle	5	29 Jan 2019
A914	**Cruise the Bight** Fremantle - Esperance - Adelaide	5	03 Feb 2019
A915	**Weekend Coastal Experience** Adelaide - Kangaroo Island - Port Lincoln - Adelaide	3	08 Feb 2019
A916	**Tasmanian Explorer** Adelaide - Hobart - Burnie - Adelaide	7	11 Feb 2019
A917	**Coastal Experience** Adelaide - Kangaroo Island - Port Lincoln - Adelaide	3	18 Feb 2019
A918	**Tasmanian Explorer** Adelaide - Hobart - Burnie - Adelaide	7	21 Feb 2019

Hobart

Port Lincoln

Esperance

Table Mountain

Astor

Code	Cruise	Nights	Departure date
A919	**Weekend Coastal Experience** Adelaide - Kangaroo Island - Port Lincoln - Adelaide	4	28 Feb 2019
A920	**Cruise the Bight** Adelaide - Esperance - Albany - Fremantle	6	04 Mar 2019
A921	**Fremantle to UK Voyage** Fremantle - Port Louis - Pointe des Galets - Maputo - Richards Bay - Durban - Mossel Bay - Cape Town - Walvis Bay - Praia - Mindelo - Casablanca - Lisbon - Leixoes - London Tilbury	43	10 Mar 2019
A922	**Welcome Europe** London Tilbury - Kiel Canal - Kiel	2	22 Apr 2019
A923	**Baltic Cities** Kiel - Stockholm - Helsinki - St. Petersburg - Tallinn - Riga - Klaipėda - Gdansk - Wismar	12	24 Apr 2019
A924	**Baltic Sea to North Sea** Wismar - Malmo - Gothenburg - Fredrikstad - Kristiansand - Hamburg	7	05 May 2019
A925	**German Ocean Islands** Hamburg - Esbjerg - List- Helgoland - Bremerhaven	6	11 May 2019
A926	**Ireland & Southern England** Bremerhaven - Torquay - Bantry - Galway - Killybegs - Belfast - Dublin - St. Mary's - Bremerhaven	11	16 May 2019
A927	**Norway** Bremerhaven - Vik - Flåm - Honningsvåg - Tromsø - Ålesund - Geiranger - Bergen - Stavanger - Bremerhaven	13	26 May 2019
A928	**SPD Charter** Bremerhaven - Rosyth - Invergordon - Portree - Belfast - Dublin - Ringaskiddy - Falmouth - St. Peter Port - London Tilbury - Ijmuiden - Bremerhaven	13	07 Jun 2019
A929	**Iceland** Bremerhaven - Lerwick - Djúpivogur - Akureyri - Grundarfjörður - Reykjavík - Heimaey - Bremerhaven	13	19 Jun 2019

Astor

Code	Cruise	Nights	Departure date
A930	**Greenland & Iceland** Bremerhaven - Eskifjörður - Akureyri - Tasiilaq - Nuuk - Sisimiut - Uummannaq - Ilulissat-Qeqertarsuaq - Qaqortoq - Ísafjörður - Reykjavik - Heimaey - Bremerhaven	24	01 Jul 2019
A931	**Baltic Cities** Bremerhaven - Kiel Canal - Szczecin - Baltiysk - Riga - Tallinn - St. Petersburg - Helsinki - Mariehamn - Stockholm - Kiel	13	24 Jul 2019
A932	**SPD Charter** Kiel - Kiel Canal - Kirkwall - Heimaey - Hafnarfjörður - Patreksfjörður - Akureyri - Seyðisfjörður - Tórshavn - Lerwick - Bremerhaven	16	05 Aug 2019
A933	**England, Scotland & Ireland** Bremerhaven - Rosyth - Invergordon - Larne - Liverpool - Dublin - Portsmouth - Bremerhaven	13	17 Aug 2019
A934	**French River Passages** Bremerhaven - St. Malo - Bordeaux - Getxo - Nantes - Saint Nazaire	13	29 Aug 2019
A935	**Canaries** Saint Nazaire - Leixoes - Funchal - Sta Cruz de la Palma - San Sebastián de La Gomera - Sta Cruz de la Palma - Casablanca - Portimão - Lisbon - Brest - Cherbourg - Bremerhaven	19	10 Sep 2019
A937	**Baltic Cities** Bremerhaven - Kiel Canal - Gdansk - Riga - Tallinn - St. Petersburg - Helsinki - Stockholm - Kiel	11	28 Sep 2019
A938	**Northern Lights** Kiel - Ålesund - Kristiansund - Alta - Honningsvåg - Tromsø - Åndalsnes - Bergen - Hamburg	13	08 Oct 2019
A939	**Azores** Hamburg - Torquay - Leixoes - Praia da Vitória - Horta - Ponta Delgada - Funchal - Porto Santo - Lisbon - Le Havre - Hamburg	20	20 Oct 2019
A940	**Northern Lights** Hamburg - Olden - Kristiansund - Alta - Honningsvåg - Tromsø - Åndalsnes - Bergen - Hamburg	13	08 Nov 2019
A941	**Goodbye** Hamburg - Antwerp	2	20 Nov 2019

Saksun, Faroe Islands

Isafjörður

Astoria

Code	Cruise	Nights	Departure date
R900	**Springtime Break & River Seine Experience** Poole - Honfleur - Rouen - Poole	3	07 Mar 2019
R901	**Iceland & Northern Lights** Poole - Belfast - Reykjavik - Tórshavn - Lerwick - Kirkwall - Poole	13	10 Mar 2019
R902	**British Isles Discovery** Poole - Dunkirk - Invergordon - Lerwick - Kirkwall - Stornoway - Oban - Dublin - Cobh - Poole	11	23 Mar 2019
R903	**Scottish Highlands, Islands & Lochs** Poole - Belfast - Stornoway - Tobermory - Oban - Greenock - Dublin - St. Mary's - Poole	10	03 Apr 2019
R904	**Fjordland Splendour** Poole - Dunkirk - Rosendal - Flåm - Olden - Bergen - Poole	9	13 Apr 2019
R905	**Hidden Baltic Treasures & Kiel Canal** Poole - Kiel Canal - Wismar - Rönne - Visby - Klaipėda - Gdansk - Kiel Canal - Poole	11	22 Apr 2019
C1	**British Isles** Le Havre - Dublin - Ayr - Oban - Stornoway - Invergordon - Rosyth - Dunkirk	9	04 May 2019
C2	**Norwegian Fjords** Dunkirk - Bergen - Geiranger - Vik - Flåm - Stavanger - Dunkirk	7	13 May 2019
C3	**Norwegian Fjords** Dunkirk - Bergen - Geiranger - Vik - Flåm - Stavanger - Dunkirk - Zeebrugge	7	20 May 2019
C4	**British Isles** Zeebrugge - Portsmouth - Dublin - Belfast - Greenock - Stornoway - Lerwick - Peterhead - Rosyth - Zeebrugge	12	28 May 2019
C5	**Norwegian Fjords and the North Cape** Zeebrugge - Stavanger - Vik - Flåm - Geiranger - Hellesylt - Leknes - Honningsvåg - Tromsø - Bergen - Zeebrugge	13	09 Jun 2019

Astoria

Code	Cruise	Nights	Departure date
C6	**Norwegian Fjords and the North Cape** Zeebrugge - Bergen - Flåm - Vik - Olden - Geiranger - Hellesylt - Leknes - Honningsvåg - Tromsø	10	22 Jun 2019
C7	**Spitzbergen** Tromsø - Longyearbyen – Ny-Ålesund - Leknes - Olden - Bergen - Dunkirk	12	02 Jul 2019
C8	**Iceland** Dunkirk - Kirkwall - Tórshavn - Eskifjörður - Akureyri - Ísafjörður - Grundarfjörður - Reykjavik	10	14 Jul 2019
C9	**Iceland** Reykjavik - Grundarfjörður - Ísafjörður - Akureyri - Eskifjörður - Reykjavik	8	24 Jul 2019
C10	**Iceland & Greenland** Reykjavik - Ísafjörður - Akureyri - Grundarfjörður - Qaqortoq - Nuuk - Ilulissat – Eqi Glacier - Kangerlussuaq	13	01 Aug 2019
C11	**Greenland & Iceland** Kangerlussuaq - Ilulissat - Nuuk - Qaqortoq - Reykjavik - Belfast - Dublin - Dunkirk	12	14 Aug 2019
R906	**Rouen & River Seine Experience** Portsmouth - Rouen - Portsmouth	2	28 Aug 2019
R907	**Weekend Summer mini cruise** Portsmouth - Hull	2	30 Aug 2019
R908	**British Isles Discovery** Hull - Kirkwall - Tobermory - Belfast - Dublin - St. Mary's - St. Peter Port - Portsmouth - Hull	11	01 Sep 2019
R909	**Fjordland Splendour** Hull - Eidfjord - Flåm - Geiranger - Bergen - Hull	8	12 Sep 2019
R910	**Baltic Cities & St. Petersburg** Hull - Tallinn - St. Petersburg - Helsinki - Nynäshamn - Copenhagen - Hull	14	20 Sep 2019
R911	**Autumn Fjordland** Hull - Stavanger - Flåm - Olden - Åndalsnes - Bergen - Hull	8	04 Oct 2019
R912	**Norway & Land of the Northern Lights** Hull - Bergen - Åndalsnes - Tromsø - Honningsvåg - Alta - Ålesund - Stavanger - Hull	13	12 Oct 2019
R913	**Iceland & Land of the Northern Lights** Hull - Kollafjörður - Reykjavik - Akureyri - Kirkwall - Hull	11	25 Oct 2019

Geiranger

St Petersburg

171

Yokohama, MountFuji, Japan

Columbus

Code	Cruise	Nights	Departure date
C900	**German Christmas Markets, Amsterdam & Antwerp** London Tilbury - Amsterdam - Hamburg - Antwerp - London Tilbury	5	06 Dec 2018
C901	**Festive Getaway to Amsterdam** London Tilbury - Amsterdam - London Tilbury	2	11 Dec 2018
C902	**German Christmas Markets & Amsterdam** London Tilbury - Amsterdam - Hamburg - London Tilbury	4	13 Dec 2018
C903	**Christmas Market & Festive Getaway** London Tilbury - Antwerp - Amsterdam	3	17 Dec 2018
C904	**Christmas & New Year Canaries & Madeira** Dover - Amsterdam - Santa Cruz de Tenerife - Arrecife - Las Palmas - Funchal - Lisbon - London Tilbury	15	21 Dec 2018
C905	**Grand Round the World Cruise** London Tilbury - Amsterdam - Ponta Delgada - Bridgetown - Oranjestad - transit Panama Canal - Puerto Quetzal - Acapulco - Papeete - Bora Bora - Bay of Islands - Auckland - Tauranga - Akaroa - Picton - Sydney - Yorkey's Knob - Rabaul - Yokohama - Kagoshima - Tianjin - Shanghai - Hong Kong - Ha Long - Phu My - Ko Samui - Laem Chabang - Singapore - Port Klang - Penang - Patong - Cochin - Mumbai - Salalah - Safaga - Aqaba - transit Suez Canal - Ashdod - Valletta - Gibraltar - Lisbon - London Tilbury	120	05 Jan 2019
C906	**British Isles Discovery** London Tilbury - Amsterdam - Kirkwall - Portree - Tobermory - Dublin - St. Mary's - St. Peter Port - Honfleur - London Tilbury	10	05 May 2019
C907	**Grand Baltic Cities & St. Petersburg** London Tilbury - Amsterdam - Copenhagen - Warnemünde - Tallinn - St. Petersburg - Helsinki - Stockholm - Aarhus - London Tilbury	14	15 May 2019
C908	**Majestic Fjordland** London Tilbury - Amsterdam – Ijmuiden	7	29 May 2019

Columbus

Code	Cruise	Nights	Departure date
C912	**British Isles Discovery** London Tilbury - Rotterdam - Invergordon - Portree - Tobermory - Dublin - Cobh - St. Peter Port - Honfleur - London Tilbury	11	11 Jul 2019
C913	**Majestic Fjordland** London Tilbury - Eidfjord - Flåm - Bergen - London Tilbury	6	22 Jul 2019
C914	**Grand Baltic Cities & St. Petersburg** London Tilbury - Rotterdam - Copenhagen - Warnemünde - Tallinn - St. Petersburg - Helsinki - Stockholm - Aarhus - London Tilbury	14	28 Jul 2019
C915	**Canary Islands & Madeira** London Tilbury - Rotterdam - Gibraltar - Arrecife - Las Palmas - Santa Cruz de Tenerife - Funchal - Lisbon - London Tilbury	15	11 Aug 2019
C916	**Majestic Fjordland** London Tilbury - Rotterdam - Flåm - Olden - Geiranger - Bergen - London Tilbury	8	26 Aug 2019
C917	**Grand British Isles Discovery** London Tilbury - Rotterdam - Kirkwall - Portree - Tobermory - Belfast - Dublin - Cobh - St. Mary's - St. Peter Port - Honfleur - London Tilbury	12	03 Sep 2019
C918	**Grand Baltic Cities & St. Petersburg** London Tilbury - Rotterdam - Aarhus - Rostock - Tallinn - St. Petersburg - Helsinki - Nynäshamn - Copenhagen - London Tilbury	14	15 Sep 2019
C919	**Majestic Fjordland** London Tilbury - Rotterdam - Eidfjord - Flåm - Bergen - London Tilbury	7	29 Sep 2019
C920	**British Isles & Cities Discovery** London Tilbury - Rotterdam - Kirkwall - Tobermory - Belfast - Dublin - St. Mary's - St. Peter Port - Honfleur - London Tilbury	10	06 Oct 2019
C921	**Canary Islands & Madeira** London Tilbury - Rotterdam - Gibraltar - Arrecife - Las Palmas - Santa Cruz de Tenerife - Funchal - Lisbon - London Tilbury	15	16 Oct 2019
C922	**Weekend Cruise to Amsterdam & Antwerp** London Tilbury - Amsterdam - Antwerp - London Tilbury	3	31 Oct 2019

Panama Canal

Magellan

Code	Cruise	Nights	Departure date
G900	**Rouen & Honfleur Christmas Markets** London Tilbury - Rouen - Honfleur - London Tilbury	3	09 Dec 2018
G901	**Antwerp Christmas Market** London Tilbury - Antwerp - London Tilbury	2	12 Dec 2018
G902	**Christmas & New Year Mexico & Caribbean** London Tilbury - Amsterdam - Lisbon - Funchal - Las Palmas - Mindelo - Bridgetown - Mayreau - St. John's - Road Town - La Romana - Ocho Rios - Cozumel	25	16 Dec 2018
G903	**Trans Panama** Cozumel - Roatan - Puerto Limon - Cartagena - Colon - Panama Canal - Puntarenas - Puerto Caldera	11	10 Jan 2019
G904	**Panama Charter** Puerto Caldera - Golfito - Saboga - Taboga - Balboa- Puerto Caldera	10	21 Jan 2019
G905	**Mexican Riviera** Acapulco - Cabo San Lucas - Mazatlán - Puerto Vallarta - Manzanillo - Acapulco	7	03 Feb 2019
G906	**Mexican Riviera** Acapulco - Cabo San Lucas - Mazatlán - Puerto Vallarta - Manzanillo - Acapulco	7	10 Feb 2019
G907	**Mexican Riviera** Acapulco - Cabo San Lucas - Mazatlán - Puerto Vallarta - Manzanillo - Acapulco	7	17 Feb 2019
G970	**Mexican Riviera** Acapulco - Cabo San Lucas - La Paz - Mazatlán - Puerto Vallarta	5	24 Feb 2019
G971	**Trans-Panama** Puerto Vallarta - Acapulco - Puntarenas - Panama Canal - Puerto Limon - Roatan Island - Belize - Cozumel - Montego Bay	14	01 Mar 2019
G972	**Caribbean & Azores Experience** Montego Bay - La Romana - Road Town - Philipsburg - St. John's - Bridgetown - Horta - Ponta Delgada - London Tilbury	19	15 Mar 2019
G973	**British Isles Discovery & River Seine Experience** London Tilbury - Amsterdam - Kirkwall - Oban - Belfast - Cobh - Rouen - Honfleur - London Tilbury	10	03 Apr 2019

Acapulco

Magellan

Code	Cruise	Nights	Departure date
G974	**Majestic Fjordland** London Tilbury - Eidfjord - Flåm - Geiranger - Bergen - London Tilbury	7	13 Apr 2019
G975	**Hidden Baltic Treasures** London Tilbury - Kalundborg - Warnemünde - Visby - Nynäshamn - Klaipėda - Gdansk - Skagen - London Tilbury	12	20 Apr 2019
G916	**Amsterdam Spring Break** London Tilbury - Amsterdam – Newcastle Tyne	2	02 May 2019
G917	**Baltic Cities & St. Petersburg** Newcastle Tyne - Dundee - Copenhagen - Warnemünde - Tallinn - St. Petersburg - Helsinki - Stockholm - Aalborg – Newcastle Tyne	14	04 May 2019
G918	**Majestic Fjordland** Newcastle Tyne - Dundee - Bergen - Geiranger - Flåm – Newcastle Tyne	7	18 May 2019
G919	**Baltic Cities & St. Petersburg** Newcastle Tyne - Dundee - Aarhus - Warnemünde - Tallinn - St. Petersburg - Helsinki - Stockholm - Copenhagen – Newcastle Tyne	14	25 May 2019
G920	**Iceland, Faroes & Northern Isles** Newcastle Tyne - Dundee - Tórshavn - Eskifjörður - Akureyri - Ísafjörður - Reykjavik - Lerwick - Invergordon – Newcastle Tyne	13	08 Jun 2019
G921	**Round Britain & River Seine Experience** Newcastle Tyne - Dundee - Kirkwall - Tobermory - Dublin - Cobh - St. Peter Port - Rouen – Newcastle Tyne	11	21 Jun 2019
G923	**Scottish Isles & Faroes Experience** Newcastle Tyne - Dundee - Lerwick - Kollafjørður - Kirkwall - Portree - Belfast - Liverpool	7	02 Jul 2019
G924	**Iceland & Faroes** Liverpool - Dublin - Reykjavik - Ísafjörður - Akureyri - Klaksvik - Tórshavn - Liverpool	11	09 Jul 2019
G925	**Summer Gardens & River Seine Experience** Liverpool - Dublin - St. Mary's - St. Peter Port - Rouen - Honfleur - Liverpool	7	20 Jul 2019

Rio de Janeiro, Brazil

Jerusalem

Magellan

Code	Cruise	Nights	Departure date
G926	**Grand Fjordland Splendour** Liverpool - Dublin - Lerwick - Bergen - Olden - Geiranger - Flåm - Eidfjord - Stavanger - Kirkwall - Liverpool	12	27 Jul 2019
G927	**Spain, Portugal & Gibraltar** Liverpool - Dublin - La Coruna - Cadiz - Gibraltar - Lisbon - Liverpool	10	08 Aug 2019
G928	**Summertime Fjordland** Liverpool - Dublin - Lerwick - Bergen - Olden - Geiranger - Flåm - Eidfjord - Stavanger - Liverpool	11	18 Aug 2019
G929	**Dublin & Isles of Scilly** Liverpool - Dublin - Ringaskiddy - Bristol Portbury	3	29 Aug 2019
G930	**British Isles Discovery** Bristol Portbury - Honfleur - Invergordon - Lerwick - Kirkwall - Tobermory - Belfast - Ringaskiddy - Bristol Portbury	11	01 Sep 2019
G931	**Iceland's Land of Ice & Fire** Bristol Portbury - Reykjavik - Ísafjörður - Akureyri - Seyðisfjörður - Cobh - Bristol Portbury	12	12 Sep 2019
G932	**Baltic Cities & St. Petersburg** Bristol Portbury - Rotterdam - Copenhagen - Warnemünde - Tallinn - St. Petersburg - Helsinki - Visby - Cobh - Bristol Portbury	16	24 Sep 2019
G933	**Dublin Mini Cruise** Bristol Portbury – Dublin - Liverpool	3	10 Oct 2019
G934	**Faroes & Iceland, Land of the Northern Lights** Liverpool - Tórshavn - Akureyri - Reykjavik - Belfast - Dublin - Liverpool	13	13 Oct 2019
G935	**River Seine Experience** Liverpool - Rouen - Honfleur - Dublin - Liverpool	6	27 Oct 2019

Marco Polo

Code	Cruise	Nights	Departure date
P900	**Rotterdam, Rouen & Honfleur Christmas Market** London Tilbury - Rotterdam - Rouen - Honfleur - Bristol Avonmouth	5	09 Dec 2018
P901	**Festive Dublin & Party Cruise** Bristol Avonmouth - Dublin - Bristol Avonmouth	3	16 Dec 2018
P902	**Festive Ireland & Party Cruise** Bristol Avonmouth - Cobh - Bristol Avonmouth	3	19 Dec 2018
P903	**Christmas & New Year Canaries & Madeira Cruise** Bristol Avonmouth - Gibraltar - Santa Cruz de Tenerife - Arrecife - Las Palmas - Funchal - Lisbon - Bristol Avonmouth	15	22 Dec 2018
P904	**Grand Circle South America** Bristol Avonmouth - Lisbon - Funchal - Las Palmas - Mindelo - Praia - Natal - Recife - Rio de Janeiro - Buenos Aires - Montevideo - Port Stanley - Carcass Island - Punta Arenas - Ushuaia - Puerto Williams - Puerto Montt - Valparaiso - Arica - Callao - Guayaquil - Manta - Panama Canal - Cartagena - Kingstown - St. George's - Bridgetown - Ponta Delgada - Bristol Avonmouth	70	06 Jan 2019
P905	**Land of the Northern Lights (Norway)** Bristol Avonmouth - Ålesund - Tromsø - Honningsvåg - Alta - Kristiansund - Åndalsnes - Bergen - Bristol Avonmouth	15	17 Mar 2019
P906	**Grand British Isles Discovery** Bristol Avonmouth - Plymouth - Honfleur - Newcastle Tyne - Invergordon - Kirkwall - Ullapool - Tobermory - Belfast - Peel - Bristol Avonmouth	11	01 Apr 2019
P907	**Spring Gardens & River Seine** Bristol Avonmouth - Honfleur - Rouen - St. Peter Port - Bristol Avonmouth	7	12 Apr 2019
P908	**Easter Break to Ireland & Isles of Scilly** Bristol Avonmouth - Ringaskiddy - St. Mary's - Cardiff	3	19 Apr 2019

Iceland

Petra, Jordan

Marco Polo

Code	Cruise	Nights	Departure date
P909	**British Isles Discovery** Cardiff - St. Mary's - Le Havre - Invergordon - Kirkwall - Lerwick - Tobermory - Belfast - Cobh - Cardiff	11	22 Apr 2019
P910	**Iceland Circumnavigation & Northern Isles** Cardiff - Belfast - Tórshavn - Seyðisfjörður - Akureyri - Ísafjörður - Reykjavik - Cardiff	12	03 May 2019
P911	**Isles of Scilly & Honfleur Weekend** Cardiff - St. Mary's - St. Peter Port - Honfleur - Portsmouth	4	15 May 2019
P912	**Grand British Isles Discovery** Portsmouth - Newcastle Tyne - Kirkwall - Lerwick - Greenock - Belfast - Douglas - Dublin - Ringaskiddy - St. Mary's - Portsmouth	13	19 May 2019
P913	**Special 75th D-Day Anniversary Cruise** Portsmouth - Antwerp - Honfleur – cruise Normandy Beaches - Rouen - Portsmouth	6	02 Jun 2019
P914	**Rouen Armada & River Seine Experience** Portsmouth - St. Mary's - Dublin - Ringaskiddy - Rouen - Le Havre - Portsmouth	8	09 Jun 2019
P915	**Iceland Circumnavigation & Northern Isles** Portsmouth - Kollafjørður - Seyðisfjörður - Akureyri - Reykjavik - Ringaskiddy - Portsmouth	12	17 Jun 2019
P916	**Weekend Mini Cruise** Portsmouth - London Tilbury	1	29 Jun 2019
P917	**Arctic & Greenland Expedition Voyage** London Tilbury - Kirkwall - Tórshavn - Eskifjörður - Akureyri - Tasiilaq - Maniitsoq - Sisimiut - Kangerlussuaq - Nuuk - Qaqortoq - Reykjavik - London Tilbury	21	30 Jun 2019
P918	**Arctic & Greenland Expedition Voyage 2** London Tilbury - Reykjavik - Qaqortoq - Narsarsuaq - Sisimiut - Ilulissat - Qeqertarsuaq - Nanortalik - Lerwick - London Tilbury	22	21 Jul 2019
P919	**Rotterdam Mini Cruise** London Tilbury - Rotterdam - Newcastle Tyne	2	12 Aug 2019
P920	**Overnight Mini Cruise** Newcastle Tyne - Rosyth	1	14 Aug 2019

Marco Polo

Code	Cruise	Nights	Departure date
P921	**Charter** Rosyth - Lerwick - Kirkwall - Rosyth	3	15 Aug 2019
P922	**Faroes & Northern Isles** Rosyth - Kirkwall - Lerwick - Tórshavn - Rosyth	5	18 Aug 2019
P923	**Summertime Fjordland** Rosyth - Flåm - Geiranger - Olden - Bergen - Rosyth	7	23 Aug 2019
P925	**Mini Cruise** Rosyth - Newcastle Tyne	1	30 Aug 2019
P926	**Mini Cruise** Newcastle Tyne - London Tilbury	1	31 Aug 2019
P924	**Canada in the Fall** London Tilbury - Bantry - Halifax - Charlottetown - Montréal - Québec - Saguenay - Baie-Comeau - Havre St. Pierre - Corner Brook - Cap-aux-Meules - Sydney NS - Ringaskiddy - London Tilbury	30	01 Sep 2019
P927	**Hidden Baltic Treasures** London Tilbury - Kiel Canal - Wismar - Rönne - Visby - Riga - Klaipėda - Gdansk - Kiel Canal - London Tilbury	11	01 Oct 2019
P928	**Iceland & Land of the Northern Lights** London Tilbury - Kollafjørður - Akureyri - Reykjavik - Kirkwall - London Tilbury	12	12 Oct 2019
P929	**Norway & Land of the Northern Lights** London Tilbury - Olden - Kristiansund - Alta - Honningsvåg - London Tilbury	13	24 Oct 2019

Ålesund

Jersey

Vasco da Gama

Code	Cruise	Nights	Departure date
V900	**Maiden Voyage** Singapore – Penang – Phuket – Langkawi – Cochin – Mormugao – Mumbai – Salalah – Safaga - Aqaba - Suez Canal – Ashdod – Santorini – Mykonos – Piraeus – Valletta – Messina – Naples – Civitavecchia – Barcelona – Gibraltar – Casablanca – Lisbon – London Tilbury	48	23 Apr 2019
V901	**Repositioning** London Tilbury - Bremerhaven	2	07 Jun 2019
V902	**Southern Norwegian Fjordland** Bremerhaven - Ålesund - Geiranger - Olden - Vik - Flåm - Bergen - Eidfjord - Leirvik - Stavanger - Bremerhaven	9	10 Jun 2019
V903	**Norway & North Cape** Bremerhaven - Vik - Flåm - Åndalsnes - Leknes - Honningsvåg - Olden - Bergen - Bremerhaven	12	19 Jun 2019
V904	**Iceland & Spitzbergen** Bremerhaven - Reykjavik - Ísafjörður - Akureyri - Longyearbyen - Barentsburg - Honningsvåg - Leknes - Ålesund - Geiranger - Rosendal - Kiel	18	01 Jul 2019
V905	**Kattegat & Great Belt** Kiel - Gothenburg - Copenhagen - Kiel	3	19 Jul 2019
V906	**Vegan Charter - Baltic** Kiel - Sassnitz- Gdynia - Riga - Tallinn - St. Petersburg - Helsinki - Stockholm - Kiel	10	22 Jul 2019
V907	**Baltic Cities** Kiel - Sassnitz - Gdansk - Klaipėda - Riga - Saaremaa - Tallinn - St. Petersburg - Helsinki - Stockholm - Kiel	12	01 Aug 2019
V908	**TH Charter** Kiel - Copenhagen - Gothenburg - Kiel	4	13 Aug 2019
V909	**Southern Norwegian Fjordland** Kiel - Bergen - Geiranger - Hellesylt - Loen - Vik - Flåm - Eidfjord - Leirvik - Bremerhaven	8	17 Aug 2019
V910	**English Channel** Bremerhaven - Southampton - St. Helier - St. Peter Port - Le Havre - Amsterdam - Bremerhaven	8	25 Aug 2019
V925	**British Isles Discovery** Bremerhaven - London Tilbury - Kirkwall - Tobermory - Belfast - Dublin - Cobh - St. Mary's - St. Peter Port - Honfleur - London Tilbury - Bremerhaven	14	01 Sep 2019
V926	**Goodbye to Europe** Bremerhaven - Antwerp	1	15 Sep 2019

Dublin

Gibraltar

Gdynia

Chapter Eleven

A decade of highlights

1996

June: Chris Coates and Richard Bastow set up Cruise & Maritime Services (CMS) in serviced office premises in Dartford, Kent. CMS appointed UK General Sales Agents for the Arcalia Shipping Company Lisbon, then operators of a two-ship fleet comprising *Funchal* and *Princess Danae*.

October: Appointed by Transocean Tours Bremen to look after their interests in the UK and Ireland. Transocean operated *Astor, Calypso* and *Gripsholm.*

1997

January: Charters are brokered with various UK and overseas tour operators for cruises or events with tonnage primarily from their two principals.

May: The first CMS negotiated charter, which also had the first ever CMS cruise and entertainment team on board, sailed from Harwich aboard *Funchal* for the tour operator Travelsphere.

1998

June: New office premises are obtained, a converted Baptist church in Sutton-at-Hone, Kent. The staffing level is five people.

2002

July: CMS enter into an agreement with South Quay Travel & Leisure (SQT) to operate a cruise programme of Arcalia Shipping, now under their brand name of Classic International Cruises, on the UK market for the 2003 season.

2003

May: A dedicated brochure is launched to the UK travel trade featuring a series of 13 Classic International Cruises sailings mainly from London Tilbury with their latest acquisition, the 330 passenger *Arion*. Successfully marketed and sold by CMS through SQT and a total of 3,300 passengers are carried.

2004

June: A special charter was arranged with the Norwegian authorities for a commemorative visit of *Arion* to Caen, Normandy to celebrate the little-known Norwegian military involvement in the D-Day invasion of Europe on the 60th Anniversary.

2005

April: To celebrate the 200th anniversary of the Battle of Trafalgar and the death of Nelson, CMS programmed a special voyage with *Arion* from Portsmouth to a number of Mediterranean ports with a Nelson connection. A special Trafalgar Dinner was held on board in Gibraltar.

June: A series of cruises with *Athena*, a further Classic International Cruises acquisition, is marketed and sold by CMS. This ship, formerly sailing with the defunct Festival Cruises, is later to become better known as CMV's *Azores* and then *Astoria*.

2006

May: Louis Cruise Lines, having appointed CMS as General Sales Agents to market their cruises in the UK, launch a seasonal programme of ex-UK cruises from London Tilbury with the 500-passenger *Calypso*.

June: Louis Cruise Lines announce a charter of their vessel *Aquamarine* to Transocean Tours in Germany. She is renamed *Arielle* and was well known on the British market as *Carousel* of Airtours/My Travel.

2007

January: With pressure on space at its existing office, CMS completed the purchase of the adjoining property which enabled the company to have a shop front and reception area for visitors and the general public.

May: CMS, having reached agreement to sub-charter *Arielle* from TransOcean Tours, operate six cruises in the spring and the autumn sailing from London Tilbury exclusively for the British market. With a capacity of 1,100 passengers, *Arielle* represented a considerable expansion of the CMS operation. The staffing levels in Sutton-at-Hone increased to 18 and *Arielle* carried over 6,000 UK passengers.

2008

April: In what was to be a significant development, CMS sub-chartered *Marco Polo* from Transocean Tours for an initial summer season of 14 cruises. *Marco Polo* was chartered to Transocean by a unit of the Global Maritime Group, which had recently acquired the ship from Orient Lines/NCL.

2009

September: Transocean Tours go into administration and CMS agree to take over *Marco Polo* charter commitment with Global Cruise Lines. *Ocean Countess* also chartered in order to present a regional cruise programme sailing from London Tilbury, Hull, Liverpool and Glasgow Greenock. A rebranding to consolidate the closer links with the Global Maritime Group, was undertaken with a new name, Cruise & Maritime Voyages, and a stylish logo being introduced in time for the launch of 2010 cruising season.

December: With a total programme of 46 cruises, offering 36,000 berths on the UK market, the enlarged Cruise & Maritime operation and its 24 staff relocated to a newly leased office building by the River Thames in Dartford. Kent.

2010

January: Marco Polo set sail for the first time under the Cruise & Maritime Voyages flag from London Tilbury on 2nd January 2010 with an inaugural 30-night West Indies cruise.

2011

June: In order to create a sound commercial base from which to expand, there was a significant corporate restructure of investors. A new travel and leisure group, CMV Holdings London Ltd was formed by the Global Maritime Group with the CMV and South Quay Travel directors as well as private investors taking positions. The new group comprised the cruise line, a tour operator, coach wholesaler, and travel agency.

August: A sales office was established in Ft Lauderdale, USA to generate additional business from North America.

2012

April: Britain's Maritime Heritage Cruise with *Marco Polo* commemorated the loss of RMS *Titanic* with a special itinerary visiting Cherbourg, Cobh (Queenstown), Belfast and Liverpool.

May: *Ocean Countess* sets sail from Liverpool Pier Head, amid great celebration, being the first vessel to do so from the new city centre cruise terminal facility.

June: To mark the Diamond Jubilee, *Marco Polo* visited all four capital cities of Her Majesty's United Kingdom on a special 9-night cruise from Leith.

October: Agreement is not reached to extend the *Ocean Countess* charter. Farewell sailing from Liverpool departs on 9th October, terminating in Barcelona on 22nd October.

December: Once again, the CMV operation, now with 42 shoreside staff,

is on the move: this time across the River Thames into new office premises in Purfleet, Essex. Gateway House has extensive accommodation which will hopefully preclude further removals in the foreseeable future!

2013

February: *Astor* chartered to operate a winter (Austral summer) season of cruises sailing from Fremantle (Perth), Australia. A sales office in Sydney was opened primarily to promote the new *Astor* season of cruises.

March: Joint Venture with All Leisure Group commences to market their cruise ship *Discovery* which replaces *Ocean Countess* in CMV's regional cruise programme. A ship management office is opened in Munich, Germany.

June: Harwich is added as a departure port and a notable *Discovery* cruise sails to the White Sea with maiden calls for CMV in Arkhangelsk, the Solovetsky Islands and Murmansk.

2014

January: The German tour operation Transocean Kreuzfahrten is acquired by the group with *Astor* operating summer cruises from Kiel, Bremerhaven and Hamburg on the German domestic market. In addition, there is a four-ship river-cruise fleet operating on many of Europe's mighty waterways.

March: Further expansion into the German market with the acquisition of the commercial sales and marketing management of Passat Kreuzfahrten. Consequently, the existing German ship management operation is moved to the Offenbach office inherited from Passat.

May: CMV inaugurates its 'Signature' River Cruise programme, which offers 7- and 14-night cruising holidays on the Rhine and Danube rivers. The premium-rated *Vienna 1* sailed from Nuremberg to Amsterdam on 19th May with the first contingent of CMV river-cruise passengers.

June: Two special D-Day 70th Anniversary sailings are operated to offer the opportunity to veterans and their families to cruise off the Normandy beaches on the 6th June. *Discovery* sailed from Bristol Avonmouth on 1st June whilst *Marco Polo* departed London Tilbury on 2nd June.

September: The All Leisure Group announce that the joint venture arrangement with *Discovery* is to terminate two cruises early in October and CMV move swiftly to secure a short-term charter of Portuscale Cruises' *Funchal* in an endeavour to complete the published programme.

An early morning aerial view of a busy Damen Shipyard in Amsterdam where *Astor* (foreground), *Marco Polo* (next to her) and *Magellan* (in the drydock) are receiving the new livery. *(CMV Library)*

November: Negotiations with the Carnival Corporation are concluded satisfactorily and its 1,250 passenger *Grand Holiday*, operated by Ibero Cruceros, a Carnival subsidiary, is duly acquired by the Global Maritime Group and is to be renamed *Magellan*.

December: Completing an eventful year, Global Maritime Group finalise the outright purchase of *Astor* from Premicon AG.

2015

January: The 550-passenger *Azores* of Portuscale Cruises joins the fleet, having been secured on a long-term charter basis. Her inaugural sailing departed from Plymouth on the 26th January.

March: *Magellan,* CMV's largest vessel yet, both in terms of gross tonnage and passenger capacity, enters service with a christening ceremony performed by Gloria Hunniford OBE and an evening event at the London International Cruise Terminal on 12th March. The long awaited 2015 Solar Eclipse was best witnessed from a specific location

between the Faroe Islands and Iceland and, having sailed on her maiden voyage from London Tilbury on 15th March, it was planned that *Magellan* should rendezvous with her fleet-mates, *Marco Polo* and *Azores,* at position 64°25A 56A N; 6°38A 32A W. A unique occasion.

July: Saw a special 36-night cruise to Canada to celebrate *Marco Polo*'s 50th anniversary of entering service as the transatlantic liner *Alexandr Pushkin* with the Baltic Shipping Company of Leningrad in August 1965.

December: *Magellan* hosted the annual Cruise Lines International Association (CLIA) dinner alongside at the London International Cruise Terminal in Tilbury. This prestigious event was attended by 1,250 cruise and travel industry guests.

2016

March: A fifth ship to join the CMV fleet was announced. P&O's *Pacific Pearl* based in Australia will operate a final season there before proceeding to a shipyard in Singapore from where she will emerge as *Columbus.*

March: *Magellan* sails for the first time from London Tilbury to Iceland as an alternative to Norway, in search of the Northern Lights.

May: *Azores*, now renamed *Astoria,* commences her charter with the French tour operator Rivages du Monde. Her first sailing is from Honfleur on 11th May with an 8-night cruise around Ireland.

2017

January: *Magellan* inaugurates CMV's maiden Round World Cruise, which departed from London Tilbury on 5th January. A 120-night itinerary calling at 40 ports saw a westbound route via the Panama Canal visiting New Zealand, Australia, Hong Kong, Vietnam and India before heading back via Suez.

May: On 14th May, *Marco Polo* begins a series of three cruises from Cardiff followed by two *Magellan* cruises from Newport extending regional departures to 12 UK and Ireland ports.

June: *Columbus* joins the fleet as the new flagship arriving into London Tilbury on 6th June. She first positioned from Singapore and then had a short dry-docking in Rotterdam. A renaming event took place at the London International Cruise Terminal on 8th June, with the ceremony performed by Angela Rippon CBE, prior to Columbus commencing service under the CMV flag.

December: The CMV Australia operation under new Managing Director, Dean Brazier, relocates from Sydney, New South Wales to Adelaide, South Australia. It was announced that a CMV Mexico sales office was being set up with a series of cruises on the Mexican domestic market to be operated by *Magellan*.

2018

March: The news of a further vessel for the fleet is released. P&O Australia's *Pacific Eden* is to be renamed for CMV operation from the spring of 2019.

August: The port of Poole makes its debut as a CMV turnaround port with *Astoria* operating three cruises from this popular Dorset town.

October: Awarded 'Best Cruise Line' at the Group Leisure & Travel Awards made a hat-trick of accolades in 2018 alongside 'Best Specialist Cruise Line' at the cruise industry Wave Awards, and 'Best Ocean Cruise Line Operator for Groups' at the Group Travel Awards.

2019

February: *Magellan* sails on the 3rd February from Acapulco on the first of her short series of Mexican Riviera cruises for the local market.

April: An innovative series of 11-night 'Treasures of the Sea of Cortez' cruises to be performed by *Astoria* in early 2020 is announced as an enhancement to the Mexican programme.

April: Delivery of the sixth ship for the CMV fleet: *Vasco da Gama* is the new name and she is handed over in Singapore on the 8th April. Following some essential works and rebranding, she departs on a 43-night maiden voyage, arriving in Tilbury on 6th June.

June: *Vasco da Gama* is renamed by Annett Louisan, the popular contemporary German singer, at an event in Bremerhaven on 9th June.

The 75th anniversary of D-Day was suitably marked by the company with a special Anniversary Dinner aboard *Marco Polo* in Portsmouth on 1st June followed by a 6-night cruise which culminated in cruising off the Normandy beaches on 6th June.

November: Press launches in Paris and in Marseille signal the establishment of a CMV France operation as the latest step in the group's international development. A new sales office opened in Marseille in January 2020 and sailings commence in May 2021. Further acquisitions from P&O Australia are announced: *Pacific Aria*, a sister to *Vasco da Gama,* and her fleet-mate *Pacific Dawn* will join the CMV fleet in 2021 to serve the German and UK markets respectively. In line with this significant expansion, it was decided that there will be a standardisation of the fleet's livery. During their annual docking periods, *Marco Polo* and *Magellan* become the first to sport the new CMV blue hull with a double white stripe. The other vessels will follow suit as their docking periods fall due.

A special Gala Event for Diamond and Platinum Tier Columbus Club members is held aboard Columbus in Tilbury on the 9th/10th November

December: In the space of 10 years, CMV has grown from carrying 37,000 passengers to approaching 150,000 passengers internationally. The brand has developed from being unknown to award-winning and recognised as one of the world's few truly independent cruise lines.

CMV Senior Management Team

The success of CMV has been driven by its dedicated senior managers, each with their individual areas of responsibility, who work together to create a truly strong and dynamic international team. On 1st January 2020, in recognition of their long standing commitment and dedication to the growth of the business, all UK Heads of Department were promoted to become non-executive directors.

Dave Eastwood, Head of Passenger Sales (2010 to date). Having gained a wealth of experience in the travel industry, Dave Eastwood joined Cruise & Maritime Voyages nearly 10 years ago to manage the Call Centre and, with the help of a loyal and knowledgeable team, has developed it to become a vital part of the business. The Call Centre is the first point of contact for most customers and travel agents and prides itself on delivering an excellent standard of service. As Head of Passenger Sales, Dave also manages the cabin availability and yield to ensure passengers always have a good choice of cruises to sail on at affordable prices.

Mike Hall, Head of Marketing (2007 to date). He joined Cruise & Maritime Services in 2007 and since CMV's launch in 2010, Mike has been responsible for the marketing and Public Relations

of the CMV brand, which has grown from zero to become the UK's leading independent cruise line. He has a wealth of travel industry experience in sales, marketing and training, plus travel writing and magazine publication. Mike is well known throughout the UK travel industry, particularly in the cruise sector, and is often called upon for his views and comment.

Gary Hides, Head of Technology (2016 to date). He first became involved with CMV in late 2011, whilst working for Castus Ltd and providing website solutions and direction for the introduction of a new online booking system. As Head of Technology, Gary is responsible for the continuous improvement of CMV's web-based technology solutions and reporting systems to cope with the ever-increasing capacity, as well as enabling CMV to expand rapidly in to new parts of the world through the use of technology. Gary's team, whilst based in the UK, supports all of the international offices.

Miranda Hill, Head of HR & Office Management (2010 to date). Her passion for cruising started very early on: at nine months old to be exact, when she took her first cruise aboard *Astor* on an Indian Ocean itinerary. Her love for

travel has continued ever since, joining CMV in 2010 after working in the fashion industry in London. As Head of HR, she is the company's UK Employment Law specialist, CIPD qualified, working closely with the Senior Management team ensuring the smooth running of the UK office and all 140 members of staff. She oversees the company's payroll and has supported the development of the business, implementing many of the employee systems, policies and procedures.

Lisa Jacobs, Head of Trade Sales & Groups (2010 to date). Lisa Jacobs is certainly no stranger to the travel and cruise community, having spent more than 30 magnificent years in the industry, and has been privileged to hold several senior sales positions. Lisa joined Cruise & Maritime Voyages in April 2010 from Norwegian Cruise Lines and has built a team of 12 enthusiastic and talented sales professionals, who are collectively responsible for developing business via the UK travel agent network and the groups market.

Michelle Lupino, Head of Shore Excursions & Itinerary Planning (2010 to date). She is proud to be a direct descendant of one of the most celebrated theatrical families. Despite her roots, travel has been her passion and she has spent more than 25 years in the industry. Michelle joined Cruise & Maritime Voyages in 2010, having worked previously for Saga and P&O Cruises. As Head of Shore Excursions & Itinerary Planning, she works closely with directors, developing and coordinating CMV vessel itineraries and is responsible for a dedicated team, operating a diverse range of excursions that feature on our worldwide voyages.

Robert McGowan, Head of Customer Services (2013 to date). Bob McGowan joined Cruise & Maritime Voyages in 2010 initially working on board *Marco Polo* and *Ocean Countess* as

Cruise Director and also Passenger Services Director. Following this, he joined the team at Head Office in the role of Head of Customer Services and is responsible for all cruise customer services and shoreside operations. As well as being a key member of the product development committee he is involved in delivery of all charter cruises.

Dean Medley, Information Security & Data Protection Officer (2013 to date). Dean first joined Cruise & Maritime Services in 2001 as a Sound and Light Engineer serving aboard *Funchal* and *Princess Danae*, and he continued to work at sea in several positions, including that of Cruise Director, until 2007. Since coming ashore, he has worked with CMV in two spells and managed both the IT and e-commerce departments, more recently taking charge of information security and data protection. Dean has a wealth of industry experience and a passion for promoting privacy and security in the travel industry.

Mo Parvez, Head of Finance (2017 to date). Mo is a qualified accountant and has been working

in finance within the Travel Industry for over 27 years. His experience includes holding senior finance positions in businesses, such as travel agency, flight consolidation, tour operation, bed bank, business travel and cruise operation. He has worked with Longwood Holidays, DNATA, where he was involved in the set-up of the UK operation Funway Holidays and Travel Leaders UK, the largest business travel company in the world. Mo was also involved in a management buyout in 2007, and then successfully ran his own tour operation for a number of years before selling it.

Dean Brazier, Managing Director Australia (2017 to date). After more than 30 years' experience in the travel industry in the UK and Australia, Dean took the helm of Cruise & Maritime Voyages in 2017. His background covered sales, tour operating and technology and he was ideally qualified to manage the relocation of the CMV business from Sydney to Adelaide in 2017. He has successfully established, what is effectively, a new operation in South Australia and manages the office of 18 staff. He feels that the company is now ideally positioned to further develop and grow the CMV Australian cruise market.

John Dennis, Vice President Sales – CMV USA & Mexico (2012 to date). He began his travel industry career with Norwegian Cruise Line whilst attending college in Miami in the early 90s. His passion for ships and the cruise experience overall developed and he has had the opportunity to be a part of unique cruise operations with Premier Cruise Lines and American Classic Voyages, operators of American Hawaii Cruises and the Delta Queen Steamboat Company. Ultimately, he spent over 12 years with Norwegian Cruise Line over two stints. He also spent time with ClubMed prior to taking the helm at the expanding Cruise & Maritime Voyages operation in the US and opening Latin America with a Mexico City office.

Klaus Ebner, Head of Marketing & Sales TransOcean Kreuzfahrten (2014 to date). Born on Lake Constance, Klaus Ebner grew up with water. After studying at the Swiss School of Tourism in Zurich, he initially worked for the Robinson Club abroad. His next career move took him to Costa Crociere and since that time, for over 25 years, the cruise industry has been in his blood. He moved to Passat Cruises in Offenbach in December 2011 as Head of Sales & Marketing, and since March 2014 Klaus has been responsible for the CMV operation in Germany. He has a passion for smaller ships which has been well served during the time that he has worked with *Astor* and, from 2019, *Vasco da Gama*.

Clément Mousset, Directeur Général, Croisières et Maritime Voyages (2019 to date). Clément has spent 21 years in the cruise industry in France, and is very pleased to now have the opportunity to manage the French subsidiary of CMV. His experience in large industry corporations, as well as with perhaps lesser-known specialist tour operators, has given him a wealth of experience. He has put together a team of enthusiasts in Marseille ready to give the 'French-style' cruise its rightful place. CMV France will operate *Jules Verne*, the former *Astor*, from 2021 as a most delightful ambassador of that style.

Ten Years of Loyal Service

CMV's 10th Anniversary also marks a decade of service for a number of the company's staff and it is appropriate that such loyalty is duly acknowledged and recorded here.

Name	Job Title	Department	Start Date
Sarah Partridge	Passenger Sales Manager	Reservations	February 2004
Gemma Bassy	Customer Services Manager	Customer Service	March 2006
Victoria Aldridge	Office Administrator	Reception	February 2008
Katie O'Doherty	Shoreside Operations Asst	Shoreside Ops	April 2008
Priscilla Roud	Reservations Supervisor	Reservations	September 2008
Peter Varandas	Tour Operator Administrator	Reservations	November 2009
Hannah Haran	Passenger Sales Team Leader	Reservations	November 2009
Sharon Brown	Shoreside Operations Asst Manager	Shoreside Ops	January 2010
Gary Heather	Customer Services Team Leader	Customer Service	January 2010
Lucinda Fountain	Customer Relations Manager	Customer Relations	January 2010
Darren Yarrow	Database Systems Manager	IT	February 2010

Global Maritime Group Management Team

The Global Management Team is based just outside Athens, Greece and is responsible for all facets of Ship Management. This hugely talented and experienced team work together to deliver a unique product, high standards of service and marine compliance.

Emmanuel Michelakakis, Director of Operations & General Counsel hails from both Greece and Scotland and joined Global Cruise Lines in 2014. Emmanuel studied at the University of St Andrews before starting his career in the legal department in the midst of the company's growth from a one-vessel niche operator to the six-vessel, multi-market operation. As Director of Operations, he acts as a co-ordinator between all operational departments in Global Cruise Lines and as a focal point between Global Cruise Lines and CMV while as General Counsel he is responsible for overseeing all aspects of the Group's legal strategy.

Alexios Tsokos, Director of Finance & Reporting joined Global Maritime Group in 2009 as a trainee in the marine operations department straight out of the University of Birmingham. Since then Alexios has helped set up the international offices in Germany, Australia and especially the US where he lived for 5 years. Since 2016, Alexios has overseen the finance and reporting of GMG, and is responsible for all financial matters in relation to the operation and management of the CMV/GMG fleet of vessels.

Captain Pino Sumbula, Director of Marine Operations was trained as a naval officer at the Hellenic Naval Academy in Athens, and following his graduation he joined the Greek Navy as Sub-lieutenant. After a career in the navy he followed his passion for travel and pursued a career in the cruise industry rising to the rank of Staff Captain. Captain Pino studied at Cass Business School before joining Global Cruise Lines in 2008 as Marine Operations Director, and is responsible for overseeing all aspects of navigational audits, planning and safety management onboard the CMV fleet.

Roxanne Onufriyenko, Director of Port Operations joined Global Cruise Lines in 2011, following over a decade in chartering and operating cargo vessels. She currently manages the port operations

of 6 cruise ships trading worldwide for the brands under the Cruise & Maritime Voyages umbrella. Her Port Operations Team works closely with CMV in developing and executing vessel's cruise itineraries and deals among other with port bookings, port costs, liaising with Ports & Port Agents and attending to vessels' day-to-day operations.

Christos Papatheodorou, DPA/CSO joined Global Cruise Lines in 2016 and assumed the role of the DPA/CSO and Compliance Manager in 2017. Having always been fascinated by the sea and the ships, he holds a degree in Naval Architecture and Marine Engineering and a working experience in excess of

30 years in various positions in the maritime industry. His responsibility is to ensure all of CMV's vessels operate in compliance with company policies and all applicable rules, regulations and best practices.

Elian Clauss, Director of Hotel Operations was born and raised on board his parents' cargo river ship. After studies in hotel management, Elian joined a river cruise line and started his career in the hotel department and before long had taken over his first vessel as hotel manager. Elian is passionate about the complexity of hotel operations on board cruise vessels and developed his experience within a major cruise line before joining the Global Maritime Group as Director of Hotel Operations.

Markos Angelakis, Director Deck & Engine Procurement joined Global Maritime Group in 2019 and is responsible for all Deck & Engine procurement. Markos brings with him a wealth of experience in technical, logistics and financial planning in

relation to ship management having worked for some of the largest ship management companies in Greece.

Fotini Lymperopoulou, Financial Controller has been part of the GMG group of companies and its predecessor companies since 1981. Fotini has served as financial controller and head of accounts for many years. Currently Fotini is responsible for office administration and shoreside human resources and brings a tremendous amount of dedication, loyalty and cohesiveness to the company with all her years of dedication.

Costas Morfovasilis, Technical Director joined Global Maritime Group in 2007 and is responsible for the Technical and safety operation of the vessels. Costas is a naval architect by training and has 20 years of experience in shipyards, working on new builds. major conversions and repairs for cruise ships and mega yachts. Costas leads a team of qualified superintendent engineers who together are responsible for the first and foremost safe sail-

ing of the vessels, maintenance of critical systems and the smooth operation of all hotel engineering systems ensuring comfortable travel for CMV guests.

Ieva Priedite, Entertainment Manager joined Global Maritime Group in 2010 in the entertainment department. A classical musician by training with further studies in classical antiquity, Ieva is ideally primed to head the entertainment department responsible for show production and enrichment of the onboard product through guest lecturers and voyage specific entertainment.

Vaios Venios, Shoreside IT Manager has been working in the Global Maritime Group since 2001 and is responsible for overseeing all of the company's shoreside IT infrastructure and systems. Solutions-focused with hands-on experience across a wide array of systems and hardware, Vaios oversees the email infrastructure and communication platforms across the entire group.

George Kalatzopoulos, Fleet IT Manager studied at Oxford Brooks and trained at a number of positions which included a stint as a quality control expert working on the Mini Cooper line in BMW's UK factory and working as IT manager onboard the Marco Polo. George joined Global Cruise Lines in 2007 and has since been responsible for shipboard IT systems and communication channels onboard.

Daniel Reiter, Director of Hotel Procurement was born into a hotelier family and grew up in the Austrian Alps. After a rewarding career in luxury hotel management – which included ten years as the manager of his own hotel – Daniel pursued a career in the cruise industry. He joined the Global Maritime Group in 2008 serving as Hotel Director onboard the Marco Polo and has served onboard most of CMV's vessels before joining Global Cruise Lines as Director of Hotel Procurement.

Elena Vetsera, Shipboard Human Resources Director joined Global Cruise Lines in 2002. Her previous economic studies, ships experience, passion and dedication to her job helped her to grow fast and become HR Manager of GCL since 2008.Since then she successfully runs the company's HR Department and looks after all GCL fleet crew recruiting, deployment and rotation in-house. With her HR team and in cooperation with the company's 4 sub offices and 10 manning agencies, she rotates around 4,000 crew of approximately 50 nationalities and ensure their compliance with all the existing International requirements for seafarers.

Ten Years of Loyal Service

The Global Maritime Group in Greece also has a number of long serving staff members and all those shown here work directly with the ships of the CMV fleet.

Name	Job Title	Department	Start Date
Stavroula Banana	Accountant	Finance	2001
Halyna Oleksiv	Textile Clerk	Entertainment	2004
Christina Papadimitriou	Assistant Manager	Human Resources	2006
Voula Karnezi	Technical Ops Manager	Technical Operations	2007
Theano Tapeinak	Accountant	Finance	2007
Andreas Ioannides	Legal Representative	Finance	2008
Christina Katermayer	Crew Operations	Crewing	2008
Christina Beksakou	Marine Disbursements	Marine	2009
Fani Boukouvala	Administrator	Administration	2009
Pinelopi Paradeisi	Accountant	Finance	2010
Panagiotis Trigkas	Hotel Services Manager	Hotel Services	2010

Further Reading

Baptista, C & Baptista, C. (2013). *Funchal Ser Do Mar/Being of the Sea*. [Funchal]: Pearl Cruises-Maritime Transport.

Clammer, R. (2014). *Marco Polo: Celebrating Fifty Golden Years Of Ocean Travel*. Ramsey, Isle of Man: Lily Publications.

Cudahy, B.J. (2001). *The Cruise Ship Phenomenon in North America*. Centreville, Maryland: Cornell Maritime Press.

Dawson, P. (2000). *Cruise Ships: An Evolution in Design*. London: Conway Maritime.

Eliseo, M. (1998). *The Sitmar Liners and the V Ships 1928–1998*. London: Carmania Press.

Kludas, A. (1977). *Great Passenger Ships of the World Volume 5 1951–1976*. Cambridge: Stephens.

Mayes, W. (2011). *Cruise Ships: A Guide to the World's Passenger Ships*. 4th ed. Windsor: Overview Press

Maxtone-Graham, J. (1992). *Crossing & Cruising: From the Golden Era of Ocean Liners to the Luxury Cruise Ships of Today*. New York: Scribner

Peter, B. (2017). *Cruise Ships. A Design Voyage*. Ramsey, Isle of Man: Lily Publications.

Saunders, A. (2013). *Giants of the Seas: The Ships that Transformed Modern Cruising*. Barnsley: Seaforth Publishing.

Acknowledgements

The authors are grateful for the wide range of assistance freely given to help bring this book to fruition. It is testament to the family spirit that CMV has created in its first decade that so many have given their time so ably and willingly to record the story with accuracy. The following have contributed significantly to this book: Bethany Barker, Sharon Bastow, John Bryant, Chris Coates, Andrew Cooke, Paul Foster, Mike Hall, Ryan Jackson, Rebecca Jones, Meriel Lowe, Michelle Lupino, Kevin Mitchell, and Carlo Todisco.

Miles Cowsill and Andrew Lowe have applied their usual wizardry to convert the authors' scribblings into a book worthy of the name. Sara Donaldson helped convert these ramblings into a coherent text.

Any errors are the sole responsibility of the authors.